SNAPSHOTS ALONG THE UMPQUA

A History of Winston, Oregon and the Greater Winston Area

Eric Wilson

WINSTON, OREGON USA

ISBN-13: 978-1480193000
ISBN-10: 1480193003

Copyright © 2012 by Eric Wilson

All rights reserved. No part of this book may be reproduced or utilized in any form or by any means whether mechanical or electronic without written permission from the author. For general information contact: E-mail: wilsonfedor@charter.net - Telephone: (541) 679-4245, (541) 671-0107

DEDICATION: To my three grandchildren – Bohdan Kenneth Wilson, Zane Anthony Moore, and Shiloh Eric Wilson.

Tomorrow's scholastic catalyst.

Printed in the United States of America

Snapshots Along the Umpqua

Contents

Acknowledgements	vi
Preamble	vii

Chapter 1
    Douglas County — 12
    School District #116 — 14
    Douglas High School and Alumni — 19
    School District #116 Statistics — 32

Chapter 2
    Chamber of Commerce — 33
    Lookingglass 1849 – 1971 — 39
    Remember When — 44
    Night Clubs — 44
    Benetta Theater — 45
    Winston's Woman Mayors — 47
    The Brockway Store — 49
    Civil Bend Pioneer Cemetery — 50

Chapter 3
    Winston-Dillard Water District — 52
    Winston-Dillard Fire District — 61
    District Statistics — 73
    Green Sanitary District Controversy — 74

Chapter 4
    From Coos Junction to Winston — 89
    Winston City Mayors — 100
    Winston City Councilors — 101
    Winston City Administrators — 110
    Winston City Staff — 111
    Winston Newspapers — 112

Chapter 5
Biographies: 27   113

Chapter 6
    Historical Tidbits 1820 – 1966   199
    Historical Tidbits 1967 – 2012   224

Chapter 7
    History Stories:
        Champagne Riot of 1866   249
        Who Killed Alexander McNabb?   254
        Train Wreck in Dillard 1907   262
        Housewives for Highway 42   265
        The Tragedy of the Runaway
        Stage Coach in 1907   273
        Plane Crash in Dillard 1953   276

Chapter 8
    Historical Snapshots:
        Winston Green Bridge/1964 Flood   280
        Winston Green Bridge 2012   280
        Winston City Council /Mayor 1985 281
        Aerial View of Winston 1993   282
        Tenmile Methodist Church   282
        Tenmile Post Office   283
        Winston Christian Church   283
        Riverbend Park Theater   284
        Winston Community Center   285
        Winston Area Community
        Partnership   285
        Melon Festival   286
        Wildlife Safari   288

Bibliography   291

About the Author   294

ACKNOWLEDGEMENTS

I want to express my heartfelt gratitude to all those who contributed to the research and publication of this book. Since there was no budget in the project to hire a professional editor, I wish to thank my wife Vickie and the following friends who spent countless hours editing the pages of this book: Erica Rubin, Dorothy Hoskins, Edie Young, Norm Oswald, Bill Mull, Bobette Hern, Kathy Holcomb, Frankie Fedor, Karen Moen, Bruce Kelly and Bernice McClellan.

The staffs of the Douglas County library system and the Winston Branch Library deserve ample credit for their assistance in simplifying my research. Special thanks go out to Karen Bratton, research librarian of the Douglas County Museum of History and Natural History. Her enthusiasm and help in researching the records is highly appreciated. The courtesy and help given to me at Winston City Hall, Winston-Dillard Water District, Winston-Dillard Rural Fire District and Winston-Dillard School District are overwhelmingly appreciated.

I also thankfully acknowledge the hard work and time devoted to the design of the cover of the book. I genuinely wish to thank Steve Dighton for the preliminary design of the cover, the formatting and the final editing of the book. To my daughter-in-law, Yvette Wilson, I extend my sincere gratitude for the professional touch to the final design of the cover. Many thanks to Sina Vadaei and Alicia Adams for their assistance in helping me develop the necessary computer skills.

Gary Leif of Leif Photography graciously allowed me to use his photographs of the Winston citizens and students. For that generous gesture I am deeply grateful. Also, to all those who contributed photographs to be used in the book, thank you. Finally, thanks to all those of you in the Umpqua Basin area who expressed a keen interest in seeing the completion of the book.

PREAMBLE

In 1971 my wife Vickie and I left San Francisco, California to go to Belize, Central America, to teach the Baha'i Faith. We brought along with us some favorite quotations from the writings of Bahá'u'lláh, the Prophet Founder of the Bahá'í Faith. One especially that resonated with the Belizean people is: "The world is but one country and all mankind its citizens." While in Belize, I worked as an engineer, building a section of the new capital, Belmopan, and Vickie taught business at the Belmopan Compressive High School. After 15 years of working and assimilating into the Belizean culture, we returned to the United States in 1986 for the purpose of educating our children.

In April of 1987 I was offered the job of Superintendent of Public Works in the City of Winston, Oregon. In the fall of 1987 we went to enroll our daughter Ruha at Douglas High School. As we entered the breezeway to the main office, we noticed a ceramic tile mural on the wall which captured our attention. The mural exhibits a quotation from Thomas Payne with the words amazingly similar to those of Bahá'u'lláh: "The world is my country, all mankind are my brethren." Even more captivating about the mural are the numerous symbols and the way they are displayed. At the top are five religious ones: from left to right are the symbols for Christianity, Islam, Buddhism, Judaism, and Confucianism. Under the Christian cross is the symbol of a sun smiling as it rises. In the center of the mural is a tree bearing fruits, as well as seven white doves in flight – three to the left and four to the right. At the base of the tree are four human figures representing the fundamental races of mankind: Negroid, Mongoloid, Caucasoid, and an American Indian pointing to the majesty of the tree. (That is my interpretation.) This image reminded us of another quotation in the Baha'í Writings which says that: "We are all leaves of one tree and fruits of one branch." That day Vickie and I looked at each other with a feeling of satisfaction and said, "We want our children to come to this school."

A few days later, we saw another ceramic tile mural sharing the same wall but on the opposite side facing the west. It is majestic and thought-provoking. At the center of that mural is the symbol of the world and across the world is a white hand shaking a hand of many colors. Curiously, it is two left hands shaking. To the right of the world are words of Thomas Jefferson: "Reason and free inquiry are the only effective agents against error." To the left are ten symbols: the number 3, the wheel, the quill, the key, the scale, the symbol (caduceus) of medicine, the square, the eye, the letter "a", and a symbol that looks like an F or an E.

In the spring of 2005 I decided to research the meaning of all these ten symbols. Using Google and askjeeves.com, I found satisfactory explanations for nine of them but not for the one that looks like an F or an E. I took a picture of the mural and showed it to my Baha'i friend, Dr. Clyde Keys of Roseburg. He looked at the symbol and, without even studying it, he said with confidence: "That is PEACE written in Morse code." He went on the internet and printed a copy of Morse code, including the alphabet. I quickly decided that Dr. Keys was correct in his analysis of that final puzzling symbol.

At that very moment I began the quest to discover who did the murals and how they were done. The mural on the west face of the wall has the inscription – "Foster and Kimbrell - 1953." I questioned most of the teachers of the high school, the administration office staff and many alumni of Douglas High School. No one I asked knew anything about the murals, the meaning of the symbols or the two names. Then one evening, I was speaking to my friend, Neal Hadley at the "YMCA" in Roseburg. I told him about the two murals at Douglas High School and elaborated on the one that has the word PEACE written in Morse code. Neal chuckled as he played with his beard and said, "If the word PEACE was written in Morse code in 1953, it may have been a statement against McCarthyism." I had no knowledge of the McCarthy era, so I delved into Wikipedia and the book *The McCarthy Era in Perspective—Nightmare in Red* " by Richard M.

Fried. I became convinced that McCarthyism was a period of political persecution which affected the whole country and that at least one of the murals was speaking out against it. I then became obsessed in my search for the artists of the murals.

George Brosi, a member of the first graduating class of 1956 of Douglas High School (now deceased), told me to "speak to Vince McGovern, he may know." I immediately found Vince's telephone number and called him. He invited me to his home in Roseburg. As I began to talk to him about the murals, he looked at me with a magnetic pull of my eyes into his and said: "son, they were two long-haired hippies from the University of Oregon who did the murals. They were very secretive and did not want anyone hanging around them while they were working. No one, including us teachers, understood the symbols in the murals." Vince McGovern was in a good position to know what he was talking about because he had worked for the school district for 35 years.

Vickie attended the University of Oregon for four years and was quite familiar with the campus layout. We went first to the library to do research there, but we were referred immediately to the Alumni Office. There we looked at a copy of the university year book for 1953. In it we found "Foster" listed several times, but we were fortunate that the name "Leonard Kimbrell" appeared only once. From this book we obtained Kimbrell's telephone number in Portland. When we returned to Winston, I called Mr. Kimbrell. He was not home, but I left my name, telephone number, and a message on his answering machine requesting information about the two murals at Douglas High School. That same evening Vickie received a call from Howard Glazer, the original architect of Douglas High School. He invited us to meet him and Dr. Leonard Kimbrell in Portland the following week. He also informed her of the tragic death of Professor David Foster. He told her that Foster had been hit and killed by a vehicle in Springfield, Oregon in 2002. In June of 2005, we drove to Portland to meet with Howard Glazer and Leonard Kimbrell.

Our meeting took place at the home of Dr. Leonard Kimbrell in the Washington Heights district of Portland. Howard Glazer, then retired, lived in the same neighborhood. As Dr. Kimbrell greeted me at the door, I immediately noticed that he was far from being a long-haired hippie. He was dressed in a long-sleeved white shirt with a tie, his hair neatly combed and his face clean-shaven. I was casually dressed and thought I was at the wrong address. Then, Howard Glazer showed up wearing casual attire. I had a litany of questions for them. However, before I began to read from my prepared list, Howard informed me that there are actually three murals, the third one being located on the wall of the cafeteria. He then echoed a loud laugh and said, "After 52 years we are caught." Before I could ask any of my questions, he explained how the

murals were done. Since the entire school structure was designed where the walls were built on the ground and then tilted up into place, the tiles were laid out on paper in the frame before the steel and concrete were placed. He said that both he and school board chairman, Paul B. Hult, of Dillard (now deceased) wanted to pay tribute to the board by decorating the school with these murals that expressed the country's civilized beliefs at a time when the country was experiencing the wrath of McCarthyism. Howard answered most of my questions, but I had one specifically for Dr. Kimbrell. I then addressed him saying, "Dr. Kimbrell, what is the significance of a left-hand shake?" He put his coffee down on the table, looked at me and said, "David and I screwed up!"

When we returned to Winston, I went to the high school to look for the third mural. There it was, hidden behind a plum tree and climbing ivy vines. I then understood why it was placed in a more secluded location since it evokes a statement against the war in Korea. (The Korean War occurred between 1950 and 1953). About a week before the school celebrated its 50th anniversary of the first graduating class, I asked the maintenance man if we could clean up the area. We did so, and thus exposed the hidden mural.

In October of 2005, Douglas High School asked me to be one of the guest speakers at the 50th anniversary of the first graduating class. I declined but asked the school to extend that honor to Howard Glazer, the architect of the high school. The school agreed and Howard Glazer accepted. The event took place on October 28, 2005.

Subsequently, Howard and his wife Jane and my family became very good friends. Sadly, Howard Glazer passed away on September 20, 2010, at the age of 87.

My whole adventure with the murals at Douglas High School, especially the revelations which I was able to uncover, opened up for me a new and fascinating awareness: HISTORY! Since very little had been written at the time about Winston and the neighboring communities, I decided to research and write their history myself.

CHAPTER ONE

DOUGLAS COUNTY

This body of 5,071 square miles of fertile land stretches between the Cascade Mountains and the Pacific Ocean. Within its vastness there are 100 valleys and two major rivers, the North Umpqua and the South Umpqua, which join together to form the Umpqua River which flows into the Pacific Ocean. This land is called Douglas County. It is the fifth largest county in the State of Oregon. Before the advent of the pioneers' trek to Douglas County in the late 1840s, the area was inhabited by Umpqua Indians. However, at the end of the Rogue River Indian War of 1855-1856, the Indians were defeated and taken to an Indian Reservation at Grand Ronde. As a point of historical interest, seven families of the Umpqua tribe managed to escape the wrath of the war and hid in the hills for several years. This tribe, "The Cow Creek Band of Umpqua Tribe of Indians," is one of nine federally recognized Indian Tribal Governments in the State of Oregon.

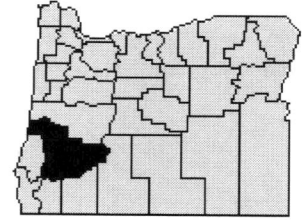

This area was first called Umpqua County, but on January 7, 1852, a portion was partitioned from that county to form Douglas County. In 1857 Camas Valley was annexed to Douglas County from Coos County. Later, in 1862, another portion was added to the county when Umpqua County ceased to exist. It was not until 1915, with debates and boundary lines adjustments with Jackson and Lane Counties that Douglas was legally established. Oregon Territorial Legislator named the county Douglas in honor of Senator Stephen Arnold Douglas of Illinois (March 4, 1847 – June 3, 1861). He was a strong advocate for Oregon's statehood. The passage of the Donation Land Claim Act of 1843 by the Oregon Provisional Government encouraged an influx of settlers to come to this area and many parts of Oregon. Settlers came to Oregon by way of the Oregon Trail and by ship to Scottsburg. However, by 1846 the Applegate Trail became the preferred route of travel.

Since Winchester had the largest settlement in the area, it became the defacto seat of the county. However, Aaron Rose of

Snapshots Along the Umpqua   13

Deer Creek (which later became Roseburg) contested the seat and called on the legislature to establish a permanent seat. In 1854 the communities voted, and Deer Creek, now Roseburg, became the permanent seat. Originally, Douglas County operated under the county's court judge and two commissioners, but by 1965 that system was changed to three commissioners sharing equal status.

Photo: 2001 County Commissioners
Douglas County Planning Department

Between 1872 and 1953 twelve communities became incorporated. They are: Roseburg in 1872, Oakland 1878, Drain 1888, Glendale 1893, Canyonville 1901, Yoncalla 1901, Myrtle Creek 1903, Sutherlin 1911, Reedsport 1919, Elkton 1948, Riddle 1949 and Winston 1953. In 2009 Douglas County had a population of 105,395.

References:
Land of the Umpqua by Stephen Dow Beckham, *A Place Called Douglas County*: Douglas County Planning Department, From Tricia's Desk: *"The Novice years"* by Tricia Dias.

SCHOOL DISTRICT No. 116

The history of the South Umpqua basin shows that many of the pioneers who settled Douglas County between the middle of the 1800s and the early 1900s were educated, adventuresome, self-reliant and ambitious. In spite of the hardships they incurred, their pursuits of education are noteworthy.

Brockway Elementary School dedicated 2003

Lookingglass was one of the first school districts to be formed in Douglas County. It was established as District No. 13 in 1850. In 1875 the school moved from its log building on Lookingglass Creek to a new building on the Coos Bay Wagon Road. In the fall of 1919, the district added high school to the curriculum. In 1930 Flournoy Valley School District No. 56, which had been formed in 1860, discontinued classes and consolidated with Lookingglass. By 1943 Lookingglass was struggling to maintain its high school facility and sent its students to Roseburg. However, in 1951, due to overcrowding at Roseburg High School, the Roseburg District Board decided it would accept pupils from outlying districts only on a tuition basis for the 1952-1953 school year. The decree also gave those districts the option to consolidate with Roseburg District No. 4 or to form their own high school districts.

The South Umpqua River had been a severe obstacle to travel for the early pioneers who lived in such localities as Dillard, Willis Creek, Rice Creek and Brockway. In 1854 Willis Creek established School District No. 14. Students from the neighboring communities attended the one-room schoolhouse there. However, the building was destroyed by fire during the Indian War of 1855 to 1856. After the war ended, the school was rebuilt, and the district continued until 1941 when it joined with Dillard.

Tenmile School District No. 7 was one of seven school districts in Douglas County when it was established in 1854. In 1945 it was joined by Olalla School District No. 49 when the placer mines at Olalla closed their mining operations. Then, in 1950, Reston

Snapshots Along the Umpqua

School District No. 42, which had been formed in 1860, added its students when the Roseburg-Coos Bay Stage Coach Companies stopped transportation service on the Coos Bay Wagon Road. Similarly, Upper Olalla School District No. 107 also consolidated with Tenmile in 1950.

The story of education in Dillard is another one which began in the mid 1800s. Actually, the children from the community of Dillard attended Brockway School District No. 16 for 42 years. However, by 1897 Dillard had become the hub for many of the surrounding communities and, hence, decided to form its own school district. By 1900 access to and from Dillard across the South Umpqua River had been made easier via a foot bridge, and in 1913 a vehicular bridge was constructed. As a result, between 1901 and 1948, six independent school districts consolidated with Dillard School District No. 116. They were: Kent Creek District No. 59, Mountain Bolsinger District No. 134, Winston District No. 48, Willis Creek District No. 14, Rice Creek District No. 100, and Brockway District No. 16.

Brockway School built 1855 burnt 2001

By January of 1948 enrollment at Dillard Elementary School was very high for the size of the building. The board of directors called for a new and bigger school in order to handle the load. On October 25, 1948, the residents of District No. 116 voted in favor of a bond issue of $125,000 to build a new school. In August of 1949, Dillard took possession of the first modern school in the county.

On December 14, 1951, the school districts of Dillard, Tenmile, Lookingglass, and Green voted against consolidating with Roseburg School District No. 4. Dillard then invited Tenmile, Lookingglass, Camas Valley and Green to form a new high school district. Camas Valley and Green rejected the proposal. However, after much preliminary preparation, on October 22, 1952, the residents within Dillard School District No. 116 and those of Lookingglass and Tenmile voted by an overwhelming majority to consolidate. Soon after the consolidation, the three-man Dillard School Board, which had been composed of L. R. Andrus, Fred Albertus and Paul B. Hult, added James William of Lookingglass and Virgil Vance of Tenmile to the board. One month later the newly consolidated district again voted overwhelmingly to establish a first-class high school and to incur a budget deficit of $3,000.00 to hire a district superintendent. William R. Bromley, who was principal of Dillard Elementary at the time, was given the position. It came as no surprise when Dillard, Tenmile and Lookingglass voted in favor of a bond issue of $586,000 to build the new high school. On the other hand, voters in both Green and the Roseburg area voted to consolidate with Roseburg District No. 4.

Prior to the formation of its high school district No. 116 in November of 1952, the Dillard School Board had already purchased a 32.88-acre site on Highway 42 in Brockway from the Nichols family. They hired the architecture firm of Dugan and Heims of Portland, Oregon, along with Howard Glazer of Eugene, Oregon, to design and build the proposed school.

In February of 1952, before the contract was actually awarded to build the high school at Brockway, an essay contest was presented to the students of all the elementary schools in the newly consolidated district to select a name for the new school. That gesture was well received by all the communities. The judging of the contest was done by the combined school boards. Margaret Sherman, an eighth-grade student of Tenmile, wrote the winning essay. She submitted the name "Douglas" after naturalist David Douglas, a well-known figure in Oregon's history for whom the Douglas fir was named. In March of 1953, before the school board had approved the plans for construction of the high school, they formed a citizens' committee composed of members of each of the elementary districts to work with them and the architect, Howard Glazer.

In April of 1953 the school board offered the contract to build Douglas High School to the contracting firm of Browning, Randolph and Newman of Salem, Oregon. Unfortunately, the gymnasium had to be dropped from the original contract since the bids had come in much higher than anticipated. However, the voters passed another bond issue of $188,000 in August of 1953 to finance the gymnasium and two additional classrooms. It should be noted that on August 14, 1953, during the construction of the high school's sewer system, 56-year-old Paul Caskey of Roseburg and his co-worker, Don Addis, were laying a sewer line when the walls of the trench collapsed. Mr. Caskey was crushed to death, but Don Addis narrowly escaped the tragedy.

Disappointingly, the new high school building was not ready for use by students for the fall of 1953. Therefore, classes for grades seven through ten were held at Lookingglass Elementary School, while the Lookingglass elementary students were transferred by bus to and from Dillard Elementary School. The students in grades eleven and twelve continued to go to Roseburg High, where they eventually graduated with the classes of 1954 and 1955. Parts of Douglas High School were finished and ready for use in January of 1954. However, there were not enough classrooms completed, so seventh grade was transferred to Dillard, where classes for them were held in the play shed until March of 1954. Finally, in December of 1954, District No. 116 took delivery of the 67,613 square-foot campus, including the gymnasium, at a cost of $702,856. Douglas High School was officially dedicated on January 14, 1955, before a crowd of 350.

Douglas County experienced a huge influx of migrant workers seeking employment in the timber industry between the mid 1940s and the mid 1950s. Increasing student enrollment impacted almost every school in District No. 116. As a result, the school board called for more and larger school structures. In August of 1959 Civil Bend Elementary (renamed McGovern in 1986) was built off Cary Avenue at a cost of $312,466. In September of 1963 Douglas High School was expanded with four more classrooms. With the steady rise in enrollment within District 116, the school board approved the construction of a junior high school on Thompson Avenue in Winston. That facility was dedicated in September of 1967.

For the next 34 years the school board made countless attempts to persuade the district voters to upgrade various facilities, but to no avail. However, in the spring of 2000, the voters passed a bond levy of $9.5 million by 59.5 percent to build a new elementary school on Brockway Road in Winston and to finance necessary expansions and repairs to several other school buildings in the district. Joyfully, on January 8, 2003, the Winston-Dillard School Board cut the ribbon to celebrate the completion of Brockway Elementary School that now houses K-3. In the words of Mike Bottaro, an elementary school teacher, "This is the best building in Douglas County for as long as I can remember. It's state-of-the-art, promising wonderful things." This 57,000 square-foot majestic elementary school was designed by Paul R. Bentley, Architect, of Roseburg and built by Harmon Construction Company of Coos Bay for about $7 million.

However, by fall term of 2003, many parents of the district were not pleased with the board's decision to switch to a four-day school week. That was one of the many decisions the board had to make in order to solve the budget deficit of $1.65 million for fiscal year 2003 to 2004.

References:
The *News Review*: 1948–2012, District #116 Office Records, Douglas County Schools – *A History Outline* by Larry Moulton, *The History of Dillard* by Sherley Clayton, Douglas County Elections and Boundaries records, Douglas County Museum Records, Douglas County Library – The Vertical Files. Photos: one by a friend of the author and the other by author.

DOUGLAS HIGH SCHOOL AND ITS ALUMNI

Douglas High School: 1953-2012

From the very beginning Douglas High School clearly exhibited signs of difference and innovation. It was the first high school in Oregon to be designed with a campus setting with individual special-function buildings. All its concrete walls were built on the ground and then tilted up into position, a first of its kind in school construction. Three large ceramic tile murals not only enhance the face of the facility but greet its students with the mantra of humanitarian virtues. The 32.88-acre school site is located on a knoll dotted with oak trees off Highway 42 overlooking the South Umpqua River to the south and the landmark Brockway Store to the west. It shares the northern fence with Davlin Cemetery. Between 1953 and 2011 student enrollment at Douglas has ranged from a high of 640 students to a low of 417. According to the Oregon classification of high schools, Douglas was ranked as a 4A school in 2011.

Photo: Howard Glazer-Family

Douglas High School was built between 1953 and 1954 by the architectural firm of Dougan and Heims of Portland, Oregon with Howard Glazer and Associates of Eugene as the designer. The general contractor was Browning, Randolph, and Newman of Salem, Oregon. The school was named Douglas by an eighth grade student named Margaret Sherman and the "Trojans" was selected as the mascot. Douglas is part of

District No. 116 which is governed by a board of directors. The first five-man board consisted of: L. R. Andrus, Paul B. Hult, Fred Albertus, Virgil Vance and James William. The school's first faculty included: William R. Bromley, Superintendent, David Potter, Principal and Howard E. Parks, Vice-Principal. On January 14, 1955, Douglas High School was dedicated with more than 350 people attending the ceremony. That same month high school students began attending classes on the campus.

In February of 1956 Douglas Musical Department received state recognition for the production of the play *Oklahoma*, the famed Rodgers and Hammerstein musical comedy. The play was directed by two Douglas High School Teachers: Mrs. Irene McLaughlin and Miss Laura Grubs. The production was staged for five nights before a packed audience. Mayor Frank True of Winston proclaimed February 23, 1956, which was the first day of production of the play, "Oklahoma Day". He called on the city merchants to decorate their businesses and wear western clothes that expressed that era. In November of 1992 Douglas Drama Class again put on the play *Oklahoma* at Wildlife Safari's Theatre. The show ran for three nights and was a smashing success. In April of 1956 the Douglas High School band and choir won their division in the Southern Oregon District Music Contest at Southern Oregon College in Ashland.

At the commencement of the first graduating class of 1956, District Superintendent William Bromley and Douglas Principal Dave Potter were proud to announce and display some of the school's achievements. At the top of their list were Keith Ryder's scholastic achievements: Keith graduated at the top of his class of 49 graduates and was editor of the school's newspaper the *Troy Times*. He was one of twelve students in Southwestern Oregon to pass the National Merit Scholarship Exam. Keith took the examination along with 60,000 high school seniors selected from the top five percent of their classes. He also received a letter of congratulation from U. S. Rep. Harris Ellsworth and a copy of the Congressional Record magazine in which Keith's name is mentioned. In May of 1956 the school's ceramic tile murals were accorded national recognition. The design of Douglas High School was one of 147 newly designed schools to enter the nationwide contest sponsored by the magazine, *The School Executive*. Those school designs were submitted by 118 architectural firms throughout the country. Douglas was the only school from Oregon to be honored.

In 1958 the wood shop building was constructed and served as temporary classrooms due to an increase in enrollment. In October of 1958 Grant Ledgerwood, a senior at Douglas High School, was one of five students from Douglas County to achieve a semi-finalist position in the National Merit Scholarship Exam competition. Out of 479,000 students nationwide who took the qualifying examination, Grant was one of the 10, 000 students who qualified. In September 1963 five more classrooms were added to the campus. Douglas's diversified educational program was applauded when their agricultural program, administered by John Baird, was recognized as the best in the State of Oregon for 1990 and 1991 and continued to be one of the top programs for the next five years. The Special Education Program, training handicapped students, administered by Ted Martch, also received both state and national recognition.

Douglas has had and still continues to have a very competitive athletic program. In the summer of 1971, Mike Palmer brought international recognition to Douglas High School. Mike went to the International Games in Japan with the Oregon Cultural Exchange Wrestling Team. Mike won nine and tied one of the ten wrestling matches. The City of Winston, together with Winston-Dillard Chamber of Commerce, named July 27, 1971, the "Mike Palmer Day." They entertained their champion with a dinner at the Dillard Steakhouse.

In 1975 the Douglas boys' track and field team ran away with the State AA championship trophy. The team scored 82 points which was the highest ever scored in a State AA Championship game. The team outscored its nearest competitor by 26 points. Douglas recorded its first state victory in the 22 years of school history. In 1976 the boys' track and field team again won the State AA Championship games outscoring its opponents by 55 points. The highlight of the Douglas victory was the mile relay team who set a new State AA record of 3:26.34

Under the coaching guidance of Mike Anderson in 1980 and 1981 and coach Steve Fisher in 1982, the Douglas boys' tennis team smashed their opponents by winning three consecutive State

AA Tennis Championship Meets. In 1980 the team won with ease with Jim Owre winning the State AA singles title. In 1981 the boys won both their District and the State AA championship titles. By 1982 the team was well prepared and brought home the State AA title with John Miller winning the State AA singles tournament.

Under the leadership of baseball coach Dan Withers and his assistant Rod Trask, Douglas High School baseball team, the Trojans, took second place in the Class 3A State championship game in 1989. They competed against St. Helens Lions who tore them apart by a score of 10 – 1 for the trophy. However, the 1989 baseball season was the Trojans' best season ever in baseball. They entered the state playoffs as the number two team from the Far West League and a season record of 25-4. In 1990 the Trojans tied with Reedsport for first place in the conference, but they were defeated by Pleasant Hill in the state playoff. Focused and prepared, the Trojans came into the 1991 season with confidence. They finished the season with a 14-0 in the league to win the Far West Conference. With that kind of record the Trojans were ranked first in the state for most of the season. Unfortunately, they were eliminated from the state playoff by Henley in a close game of 7-6. The 1992 baseball season started with the Trojans crushing Glide 13-3. From that game, the team saw championship in its cross-hairs for the rest of the season. With Rod Trask as the head coach and Dave Fricke as the assistant, the team shot its way to a 27-1 record for the season. The Trojans lost one of its games 6-3 to the Roseburg Indians. But, at the state playoff games, Douglas blind-sided Scappoose in a 6-0 victory and went on to embarrass Newport in Newport with a score of 9-3. That win gave the Trojans the home field advantage for the state semifinals game against Dallas. The Dallas Dragons were no match for the Trojans and were soon eliminated by a score of 3-0. Douglas fans thronged the field in celebration chanting: "one more game." Saturday, June 6, 1992, at Civic Stadium in Portland, will always be remembered as an emotional and jubilant moment when 16 Douglas baseball players mobbed each other in celebration when they defeated the St. Helens Lions 6-2 to become the Class 3A state champions.

In December of 2010, the Douglas Trojans football team played for the OSAA Class 4A Championship for the first time in the school history. They lost the trophy to the Baker Bulldogs by a score of 34-20 on Saturday, December 3, 2010, at Hillsboro Stadium. However, the Douglas victory over Estacada was recorded in the history books Saturday, November 23, 2010. They defeated the Estacada Rangers by a score of 8-0 in the state semifinals giving them the right to play for the OSAA Class 4A championship trophy. It was a sweet revenge since Estacada had knocked out Douglas in the state playoffs in 1992 and in 2008. Facebook was littered with congratulations from Douglas alumni who played in that memorable muddy 1992 game.

Dennis Boyd was the first Douglas High School graduate to give the school national exposure for many years. He came to Douglas from Washington, DC in 1968 and graduated in the top five percent of his class in 1973. Upon his graduation, Oregon State University offered him a football scholarship. He played defensive end for the Beavers, and became the nemesis of the opposing running backs, linemen and quarterbacks. In 1977 Dennis Boyd was drafted by the Seattle Seahawks in the third round to play for the National Football League. He was defensive lineman No. 68. He was 6'-6" and weighed 255 pounds. He played for the Seahawks from 1977 to 1982. Douglas High School and the Winston-Dillard Community were proud of Dennis's accomplishments not only for his athletic ability but his scholastic achievements as well. During his off season he went back to school and earned both a Bachelors and a Masters Degree in Chemical Engineering from Washington State University. Dennis and his wife Linda live in Washington. They have two children, Danni and Alex.

Dennis Boyd

Josh Bidwell's book, *When it's Fourth and Long,* can be found in book stores across the United States and Canada. He became a role model for young athletes and a mountain of strength for anyone diagnosed with a serious illness. He grew up in Tenmile, Oregon and graduated from Douglas High School in 1994. He played football, basketball and baseball and was exceptionally talented in football and baseball. In high school he was the kicker, the punter and the quarterback for the Douglas Trojans. He was given a scholarship to play football for the University of Oregon Ducks. He was both the kicker and punter for the team. In 1998 he was named first team All-Pac 10 and graduated with a Bachelor's Degree in English. Josh was drafted by the Green Bay Packers in 1999 in the fourth round to play in the National Football League.

Photo: Courtesy of Leif Photography

Unfortunately, in September 1999, at the beginning of the football season, Josh was diagnosed with testicular cancer and was given a leave of absence to be medically treated for the disease. Both medically and courageously he overcame the disease. In 2000 he returned to the Green Bay's roster with a power punt which won him the starting position. He was the starting punter in every game between the years 2000 and 2003.

In March of 2004 Josh signed a three-year contract to play for the Tampa Bay Buccaneers. He was selected to play in the 2006 Pro Bowl in Hawaii. The people of Douglas County, Oregon were extremely proud to have two of its players, Josh and Troy Polamalu of the Pittsburgh Steelers on the 2006 Pro bowl roster. It was the first time in NFL history for two players from the same 3A high school to play in the same pro bowl game. Josh played with the Tampa Bay Buccaneers until March of 2010. That same month he signed a contract to play for the Washington Redskins. He was released from the team in July of 2011 due to a hip injury and no longer plays professional football.

Josh met and married his soul mate Bethany Smith in June of 2000. She was his pillar of strength when he was diagnosed and recovering from cancer in 1999. The couple has three children and lives in Eugene, Oregon. In 2006 Josh started the "Josh Bidwell Foundation" whose motto is "Giving back to improve, inspire and strengthen our community and its future." The main recipients of his foundation are: The Community Cancer Center of Roseburg, Douglas County Sports Programs and Youth Service Organization. Every year he sponsors the "Josh Bidwell Celebrity Golf Classic" at the Country Club in Roseburg to raise funds for cancer patients.

Snapshots Along the Umpqua 25

Photo: Courtesy Leif Photography

Max Montano and his sister, Carmen, grew up in the Rice Creek area and were home-schooled from K through eighth grade. He attended Douglas High School as a freshman and graduated in the top ten per cent of his class in 1996. He enrolled at Pacific University in Salem, Oregon and graduated magna cum laude with a Bachelor's Degree in Chemistry in 2000. He was awarded the distinguished honor of Outstanding Senior in the Natural Sciences. Max spent much of his summers doing research at the University of Wyoming and Pacific University. He worked for Intel Electronic Company in Hillsboro, Oregon before attending graduate school at the University of California Berkeley in 2002. In June of 2006, Max was awarded a Ph.D. in Chemistry.

Troy Polamalu's athleticism was very noticeable as early as middle school. He played football, basketball and baseball and was exceptionally good in all three sports. He grew up in Tenmile, Oregon and graduated from Douglas High School in the top ten per cent of his class in 1999. In February of 1999, he was awarded with the honor of Student First Citizen for 1998 by the Winston-Dillard Area Chamber of Commerce.

Photo: Courtesy of Leif Photography

In his senior year he received state and league honors in all three above mentioned sports. His football record at Douglas was impressive: scoring 54 touchdowns and rushing for over 3100 yards. He accepted a scholarship to play football for the University of Southern California, USC. He began the 1999 season as a backup player for both offence and defense. But within two years he became the strong safety for the USC Trojans. Once the Trojans' defense took the field, most spectators' eyes were on player No. 43, Troy Polamalu. He anticipated the opponent's plays, and with his speed and toughness he disrupted their game plan. Many opponents' coaches had to re-design their plays when they saw No. 43 on the field. At the end of his college football career, Troy was decorated with several honors: He was a two-time All-Pac 10 teamer. He was honored with First Team All-American from ESPN and the Associated Press. But, most of all, he was awarded the Most Important Player Award by his teammates. His coach Pete Carroll, who now coaches the Seattle Seahawks, applauded his talents by saying, "He is as good a safety as I have coached."

Troy Polamalu was drafted by the Pittsburgh Steelers in the first round of the NFL Draft of 2003 and is currently playing for the team. He has brought a quality of finesse, charisma, and versatility to the game that is nationally admired. He was featured on the cover of *Sports Illustrated* dated November 15, 2005, as "Steelers' Hard-hitting Safety Troy Polamalu." Nunyo Demasio, the author of the article on Troy, began by saying, "He is soft-spoken and self-effacing off the field, but when the safety Troy Polamalu hits the gridiron, his hair comes down and the rampage begins."

For the eight years he has been in the NFL, he has built up an impeccable record: He has been selected to play in the Pro-Bowl six times. He was All-Pro selection four times. He played in three Super Bowls and was champion in two. He was awarded the Joe Greene Great Performance Award of 2003. He was awarded the Steelers Most Valuable Player Award in 2010 and was named 2010 AP NFL Defensive Player of the Year. On July 23, 2007, the Pittsburgh Steelers offered Troy the largest contract in the franchise history. The contract was worth $30.19 million for four years to end in 2011. The contract made Troy the highest paid player on the roster and one of the highest paid defensive backs in the NFL. When the news of the contract hit the media, Steelers defensive coordinator, Dick LeBeau, acknowledged the contract by saying, "Troy Polamalu is a very special football player who has been a key ingredient to our success over the past few seasons." Art Rooney II, who is the president of the Steeler team, said, "We are excited to know he will be a Steeler for many seasons to come."

Troy Polamalu's life off the football field is serene and yet humanitarian. He is married to Theodora Holmes, the younger sister to Alex Holmes, former NFL player. Troy and Alex were teammates and good friends at USC. The couple has two sons, Paisios and Ephraim. In 2007 Troy and Theodora converted to Greek Orthodox Christianity and made a pilgrimage to Greece and Turkey. He and his wife started the Troy and Theodora Polamalu Foundation which supports several charitable programs. Recipients of that foundation are: humanitarian aid to the people of American Samoa affected by the tsunami of 2009, The Pittsburg Children's Hospital and sports programs in American Samoa. They also created the Harry Panos Fund for Veterans, a fund of the Pittsburgh Foundation. Harry Panos, who served in World War II, was Theodora's grandfather. In March of 2007 Troy received a congratulatory handshake from President George Bush at the White House. In May of 2007 the YMCA of Downtown Pittsburgh named Troy Polamalu their Person for the Year 2007. The Award Committee selected Troy for his "strength in spirit, mind and body and for his support for the YMCA's core values which include caring, honesty, respect and responsibility." During the NFL lockout in 2011 Troy went back to the University of Southern California, USC, to finish his education. In May of 2011 he graduated with a Bachelor's Degree in History.

In the 58 years of Douglas High School history, there have been several untimely deaths for some students, and therefore the author chooses to memorialize them. May 26, 1954, was a very sad day for the sophomore class of Douglas High School. Avery Morgan of Lookingglass and Frank Collins of Dillard lost their lives at Sunset Bay, 20 miles south of Coos Bay, Oregon. Both boys, 16 years of age, were swept off a rock by a "sneaker wave" and drowned. They were members of a biology science class on a field trip collecting marine samples. Avery's body was found 20 days later by a fishing boat, five miles off Cape Arago. About one month after the tragedy, Frank's body was found one-half mile off Cape Arago.

In September 1973 Douglas High School mourned the loss of 16-year-old Henry Dale Thompson, a sophomore student who was struck and killed by a car while crossing Highway 42 in front of the school during his lunch break. Dale, who lived in Winston, died at Sacred Heart Hospital in Eugene, Oregon.

Snapshots Along the Umpqua 28

A bronze plaque sits on the lawn in front of Douglas High School in memory of Anna-Marie Powell of Tenmile, Oregon. The plaque reads: "Roses planted in memory of Anna-Marie Powell for the class of 1993." Monday, May 3, 1993, Douglas High School sent the students and faculty home due to a loss of electric power on the campus. Anna-Marie was returning to Tenmile when the pickup truck she was driving collided with Schwan's delivery truck on the "Schattenkerk Curve" on Highway 42. She sustained injuries to the head, spine and left leg. Anna-Marie Powel, age 17, died at Portland Oregon Health Science University May 3, 1993.

Photo: Courtesy of Leif Photography

The Community of Tenmile and Douglas High School were in shock and disbelief when they learned of the vehicle accident that killed Bobbie-Jo Dwight on August 4, 1997, on Highway 42. She was a graduate of the class of 1996 and the younger sister of Anna-Marie Powell who lost her life in a vehicle accident in May of 1993. Bobbie-Jo, 19, was driving a 1989 Subaru sedan with three other teenagers: Brandy Duke 14, Terry Creach 19, and Carrie Ross 16, westbound on Highway 42 when she lost control of the vehicle and slammed into a tree. Her three passengers were treated for minor injuries at Douglas Community Hospital in Roseburg but Bobbie-Jo never recovered from the severe head injury sustained and later died at Douglas Community Hospital.

Photo: Courtesy of Leif Photography

He enjoyed the outdoor life - hiking, camping, snowboarding, and rock-climbing to name a few - with all its pleasures, beauty and risk. He was a TAG student in math. At the Hershey's Invitational Track and Field Games held at Eugene, Oregon in August of 1995, his relay track team took second place in the 400 meter relay. He had a passion for playing the guitar and was good at it. He graduated from Douglas High School with the class of 1999. Kevin Ray Parker, age 19, and his best friend Ryan K. Beauchamp, 17, who also attended Douglas High School, lost their lives to Mother Nature on April 28, 2000 at Sunset Bay 20 miles south of Coos Bay, Oregon. Kevin and Ryan with three other Douglas High School Graduates - Josh Sherman, 23, Mike Pool, 20, and Jeremy Henderson, 20, all of Winston - went on a four-day hiking trip to the Oregon Coast. They set up camp at Sunset Bay State Park near Charleston. On the evening of the second day of their hiking expedition, just before sunset, they were drawn by the beauty and majesty of the rocks along the beach line. Since the tide was low and the tallest rock was accessible, they decided to climb that rock. According to Coast Guard Cadet, Blake Kilbourne, that same rock is 100 yards from the beach and 30 feet in height. Kevin and his friends were already climbing the rock when suddenly a 20-foot sneaker wave crashed onto the rock striking all five climbers. Kevin and Ryan were thrown off the rock into the frigid water while the other three luckily grabbed a hold on the rock. While struggling to keep his buoyancy, Kevin managed to remove the backpack he was carrying. He then began to swim frantically back to the shore. But the strong under-current and the frigid salt water impeded his progress. After a half-hour of exertion, he was pulled out to sea and drowned. He was thrown from the rock at about 6:30 PM on Friday, April 28, 2000, and his body was recovered on May 13, 2000 at 8:30 PM. Jeremy Henderson and Mike Pool ran to get the Coast Guard while Josh Sherman remained to keep his eyes on his distressed friends. He told the Coast Guard cadet, Blake Kilbourne: "Ryan was washed back in, hit a rock and was washed back out again. He disappeared right away." Ryan K. Beauchamp's body was never found.

Photo: Courtesy of Leif Photography

STUDENT FIRST CITIZENS

DATE	MALE	FEMALE
1988	Ardel Wicks	Amber Albertson
1989	J. C. Fisher	Tembi Buckingham
1990	Jason Dickover	April Ellenwood
1991	Brent Black	Amy Dake
1992	Brent Redenius	Debbie Phelps
1993	Kevin Tommasini	Ambyr Dow
1994	Darren Polamalu	Bonnie Langworthy
1995	Steve Cleveland	Autumn Taylor
1996	Russell Hobson	Katrina Randol
1997	Trevor Joers	Leslie Manchester
1998	Aaron Ziebart	Faith Tommasini
1999	Troy Polamalu	Amy Manchester
2000	Jonathan Haeber	Emily Blum
2001	Joel Young	Megan Hermes
2002	David Adams	Sarah Tommasini
2003	Michael Murphy	Erin Bone
2004	Caleb Tommasini	Krystal Frost
2005	Christopher Zuver	Megan Polamalu
2006	Brad Guyer	Elizabeth Smith
2007	Jacob Quanbeck	Kati Quimby
2008	Barra Brown	Meredith Jones
2009	David Yecha	Alaina Findlay
2010	Matt Williams	Megan Smith
2011	Mathew Cugley	Deanna Boyd
2012	Tyler Foster	Nichole Spurlin

A MOMENT TO REMEMBER

Troy Polamalu and Josh Bidwell 2006 Pro-Bowl Game in Hawaii
The first time in Oregon's history where two players form the same 3A
High School played in the same Pro-Bowl Game.

References:

The News Review 1952 – 2012, Douglas High School: Dedication Program January -1954, Douglas High School Year Book 1970-1999, Interviews with Douglas High School Architect, Howard Glazer – 2005, *Sports Illustrated* – September 2005. Internet/Wikipedia Encyclopedia, *The Coos Bay World. When It's Fourth and Long* by Josh Bidwell. Photos of the Students: Courtesy of Leif Photography, Photo of Troy and Josh: Courtesy of Polamalu's family. The other: by the author.

WINSTON-DILLARD SCHOOL DISTRICT 116 STATISTICS

SCHOOL DISTRICT N0. 116 SUPERINTENDENTS

William R. Bromley	1953 – 1957
John Cox	1957 – 1958
George Corwin	1958 – 1970
Dr. Henry Hunt	1970 – 1984
Ray Hajduk	1984 – 1988
John Rogers	1988 – 1989
Dr. Ralph Reed	1989 – 1991
Tom Huebner	1991 – 1992
Dr. Jim Burton	1992 – 2000
Art Johns	2000 – 2002
David Hanson	2002 – 2004
Joe Harris	2004 – 2005
Duane Yecha	2005 - 2008
Kevin Miller	2008 - Present

DOUGLAS HIGH SCHOOL PRINCIPAL

David C. Potter	1953 - 1956
Marvin Cox	1956 - 1957
Clyde Foster	1957 - 1958
Ray Talbert	1958 - 1963
Norman Bergstrom	1964 - 1968
Dale Petersen	1969 - 1988
Don Fisher	1988 - 1998
Jim O'Conner	1999 - 2000
Kevin McDaniel	2001 – 2008
Graden Blue	2008 – 2010
Brian Gardner	2010 – 2011
Robert Boyé	2011 – Present

References:
The News Review, Winston-Dillard School District Office.

CHAPTER TWO

WINSTON-DILLARD AREA CHAMBER OF COMMERCE

Russell "Russ" Turner is the "de facto" cornerstone of the Winston-Dillard Area Chamber of Commerce. Very little is known of him, except for his active service in Winston. He came to Coos Junction (name changed to Winston in 1953) around 1948 from Portland and opened an electric motor shop. He became the mouthpiece for Coos Junction for its development and prosperity. His favorite phrase was: "let us boost and better the community." He organized a male "booster club" made up of business and professional men of the community. The first meeting was held at the Benetta Theater on Main St. He was appointed temporary chairman of the organization. The mission of the club was to "boost and better the community." The club, which was growing very quickly, renamed the organization Winston Chamber of Commerce. That organization got its birth in a meeting held in the home of Russell R. Turner on June 13, 1950. A fair number of business and professional people were present at the meeting. Al Dotson was appointed temporary secretary. The focus of the discussion at the meeting was the critical problems facing the rapidly growing Coos Junction community.

"Russ" Turner rearranged his garage so the Chamber could hold its meetings there. Even the newly incorporated City of Winston's Council held its November 16, 1953, meeting in his garage. The Chamber conducted most of its meetings there until March 1954 when they changed the venue to the Winston-Dillard Fire Department meeting hall. At their July 1950 meeting they elected Russell Turner as President and Al Dotson as Secretary. They discussed constructing shelters on Highway 99 (later called Main Street) and on Highway 42 (later called Douglas Boulevard.) for school kids waiting for the school bus to protect them from the harsh weather during the winter months.

As the community began to grow, so too did the cost of fire insurance, especially for businesses. By 1951 the Winston Chamber of Commerce got fired up designing plans to form a fire district. With the help of the Winston Community Club they conducted a house-to-house survey in Winston, Dillard and nearby areas with regard to supporting a rural fire district. They sought advice from Roseburg Fire Chief W. E. Mills and the State Fire Marshal A. J. Butch. They held public meetings at the Winston Community Center and Dillard Elementary School, and on March 25, 1952, a petition carrying 207 names was filed in Douglas County Court. On June 6, 1952, the Winston Chamber of Commerce celebrated the birth of the Winston-Dillard Rural Fire Protection District.

By 1952 the poor living conditions in Coos Junction were spiraling out of control. The state sanitary inspector had already approached the community about leaking septic tanks and outhouses. The roads were so bad with potholes school buses refused to go into certain areas to pick up kids. There were no traffic signs or street lights. With no law enforcement in the area, barroom fights were regular. Since there were no garbage disposal sites, household waste was indiscriminately thrown out. The Winston Community Club approached the Winston Chamber of Commerce with the idea of incorporating Coos Junction into a city. Coincidentally, the Chamber already had the project of incorporation as the next item on their agenda. They immediately embarked on a house-to-house campaign to inform people of the idea. On November 20, 1952, both groups sponsored a public meeting at the Community Center and invited Attorney Dudley Walton of Roseburg to speak on the advantages of incorporating Coos Junction into a city. A crowd of over 100 persons filled the center in order to hear Mr. Walton speak. He began his talk by supporting the incorporation campaign, saying: "It would cost more in the long run for the Winston community to form its own sanitary, fire, water and road district than to incorporate." The question and answer period regarding the advantages and disadvantages of incorporation enlivened the meeting. On several occasions the consultation drifted onto the terrible conditions of the roads, especially those in the Suksdorf Addition. The meeting was cordial, and at the end the majority of the people present were in favor of incorporation. The Chamber hired civil engineer James Daugherty to draw up the boundaries for the incorporation. Both the Chamber and the Community Club co-sponsored several meetings at the Water District office to appraise the residents on the progress of incorporation. They hired attorney Harrison Winston to prepare and file the necessary papers for incorporation in the Douglas County Court. On June 21, 1953, both the Winston Chamber of Commerce and the Winston Community Club celebrated the birth of a new city; Coos Junction became the City of Winston. Unfortunately, at the City Council's first meeting in September in 1953, Russell Turner, who represented the Chamber of Commerce, was the only member of the public present at the meeting.

Between 1953 and 1955 the newly formed City Council depended on the Winston Chamber of Commerce for physical assistance with making and placing street signs around the city. When the City Council was in session, the Chamber would place a lighted lantern on a post in front of the address where said meeting was taking place. That action informed the public as to where the meeting was being held. Before the city hired any public employees, that body would fill potholes on streets and roadways with gravel where necessary and clear ditches that impeded drainage flow, especially during the winter months. In 1957 the Chamber was involved with other social and church groups in the development of the picnic area at the Community Park. Again, in 1961, they were involved with the building of the tennis court and the horseshoe pits at the Community Park. At a special meeting held at the Fire Department the Chamber called on the State Highway Department to repair the dangerous east-west Highway 42, and at the same meeting they endorsed the cause "Housewives for Highway 42". They placed directional signs at the intersection of Highway 99 and Highway 42.

During the flooding disasters of 1950, 1953 and 1955, the Chamber of Commerce was the "Community Savior" for many sections of Winston, Dillard and surrounding areas. The Chamber called upon the Red Cross and the Civil Defense Unit for assistance in evacuating stranded families, especially in the Dillard basin. The Chamber's rescue team was highly commended by the Red Cross for their togetherness and expediency.

In 1964, since the Chamber wanted to broaden its scope in the area, it changed its name to "Winston-Dillard Area Chamber of Commerce" and began holding its meetings at Winston City Hall. It began to advertise Winston by installing signs along Highway 99 between Roseburg and Winston. In the 1960s, the Chamber embarked on a program to attract businesses and tourists to Winston and was quite successful. The City of Winston received a wave of businesses during the 1960 decade.

In the 1970s the Chamber was well established in the community with a large membership base. On October 24, 1972, the Winston-Dillard Area Chamber of Commerce adopted a set of by-laws for the organization. That charter has been amended 17 times between 1972 and 2007. They agreed to honor an outstanding citizen each year. In January 1978, at a banquet held at the Winston Middle School, before a group of 100 guests, they selected and honored Mrs. Burnette Wilson with the First Citizen Award. Mrs. Wilson, who lived in Winston, was an outstanding civic leader in both Winston and Roseburg. She was the only citizen from the area to receive that award that year. That night they also honored Katherine Cory with the Humanitarian Award for her outstanding youth activity leadership. Winston-Dillard Senior Citizens Club was honored with the Best Organization Award. For the past 34 years the Chamber has been honoring both men and women with the First Citizen Award and has used the Winston Middle School as the venue until February 2008 when the new Community Center was used. 67 portraits of these honored citizens are on display at the Community Center.

In the early 1980s the City of Winston, the Winston School District, and the Winston Area Chamber of Commerce had an artist from Wildlife Safari design their respective logos. The final product, which satisfied all three entities, was a tree representing the timber industries and a running cheetah representing tourism. In December of 2010 the City of Winston made a small change to its logo.

In 1983 the Chamber began producing a newsletter. Marge Brady was the editor until 1984 when Jim McClellan took over the position. He resigned as editor in December 2010, and Paula Riggs from Wildwood Nursery was appointed editor.

At one of the Chamber's meetings in 1983 they consulted and agreed that the property taxes in Winston were too high. They convinced the Winston-Dillard School Board to freeze the salaries of the teachers and district employees. However, they were unsuccessful in getting the City of Winston and the Winston-Dillard Fire District to do the same. The freezing of the salaries of the teachers and employees of the School District not only backfired on the Chamber of Commerce but it put a wedge between the employees and the Chamber for several years. The district employees boycotted the local merchants.

During the 1990s the Chamber sponsored the Winston Safari Run. Runners began at the intersection of Main Street and Douglas Boulevard. They ran around the east side of Winston and returned to the intersection. The following year the Chamber enhanced the program by inviting basketball star Jerome Kersey of the Portland Trailblazers to the event. In addition, the Chamber had Wildlife Safari bring Khayam the cheetah to the event. Winston was packed with spectators for the occasion. About 1995 the Chamber sponsored an art show at the Winston Community Park. For the first two years the show was called "Art in the Park." The name was later changed to "A Gathering of Artists." Bob Trnka, who was a member of the Chamber, spearheaded the art show. The Chamber advertised the event by hanging banners throughout the city.

While the city of Winston was concentrating on getting homeowners to beautify their yards, it overlooked the dilapidated condition of the triangle at the intersection of Main St. and Douglas Blvd. The entire area was overgrown with tall weeds creating a sight problem for traffic. Among the weeds were broken concrete blocks and garbage. It was definitely an eyesore in the center of town! In addition to cleaning up the triangle, the Chamber wanted to beautify it. In 1986 they formed a "Triangle Beautification Committee." Within a few months they decided to construct a statue looking like Khayam, the cheetah at Wildlife Safari, one of the dominant attractions at the park. (Wildlife Safari is Winston's and the State of Oregon's famous drive-through animal park.) The Committee was busy finding an artist, raising funds and convincing Oregon Department of Transportation, ODOT, to relax its rules regarding the structure at the intersection of Highway 99 and Highway 42. Meanwhile, the City paved the triangle with a layer of asphalt. In May 1987, the Committee achieved its goal. They found an artist who constructed a bronze statue 126 inches long and 56 inches high. They raised the $30,000 estimated cost by a grant from the Oregon Arts Commission, donations and selling names inscribed on the base tiles of the statue.

The Chamber has been and still is involved in a multiplicity of community events. It gives unquestionable support to such events like the Melon Festival, Riverbend Live, Trader Days and the 4th of July. As soon as visitors enter the City of Winston, the Chamber is the first to greet them. It has welcome signs at the north, south and west entrances to the city. For the past 47 years the Chamber has been catering to needs of visitors and operates a year-round Visitors Center. After 62 years of operating under the motto of "We Help Our Community Grow," history observes the Winston-Dillard Area Chamber of Commerce as the most cohesive organization in the community.

Chamber of Commerce Visitors Center

References:
The News Review 1949 – 2012, Winston City Council Minutes, Information from Chamber of Commerce Visitor's Center. Photos by the author.

LOOKINGGLASS 1849-1971

Even today Lookingglass still commands the vista and beauty of the Umpqua valley. No matter the time of the year, the valley exudes magnificence and charm and forces the visitor to fall in love with it. No wonder then that when Hoy Flournoy, with an exploration party in 1846, came to the top of Whitetail Mountain in the coastal range and looked down into the basin of shimmering green grass, he said: "It looks like a looking glass." Hence, Lookingglass became the name of the valley. Prior to the settlement of the white man in 1849, the Umpqua Indians lived in that area for thousands of years. However, the Indians met their demise in what became known as the "Lookingglass Massacre" in October of 1855 during the Indian War of 1855 to 1856. (See *Land of the Umpqua* by Stephen Dow Beckham.)

History remembers Reverend Abbot L. J. Todd, a pioneer of Lookingglass, for his compassion and love for humankind demonstarted when he attempted to protect 20 Indians - men, women, and children - who lived in the area. Upon learning that a group called the White Volunteers proposed extermination of the Indians in Douglas County, he and his friend J. M. Arrington gathered up the Indians in an attempt to protect them. In order to convince the White Volunteers that the Indians wanted peace he encouraged the Indians to give up their arms, which they did, and he became their guardian. He put them in a camp, and he and his friend guarded the camp each night. On the morning of October 25, 1855, at 3:30 AM, Rev. Todd and his friend Arrington went to their respective homes. Under the cover of darkness, while the Indians were asleep, the White Volunteers attacked the camp, killing or wounding all the Indians. That day is remembered as a dark period in the history of Lookingglass.

Reverend Todd gave up his trade as a potter and candle maker and concentrated on preaching the gospel. He was responsible for spreading the Christian Church in 14 communities across Douglas County. He started the first church in Lookingglass in 1856 and from there he started churches as far north as Elkton and as far south as Glendale. In the early 1870s he and his family began mining for mercury at Elkhead Mine.

The Lookingglass Valley is located 6 miles northwest of Winston and 8 miles west of Roseburg. This rural community is approximately two miles long and one and a half miles wide, with a current estimated population of 280 people. The area was first settled in 1849, and by 1859 just about all the fertile lands were taken. In the 1860 census taken in Douglas County, Lookingglass had a population of 279 residents, the fifth highest in the county at the time. In the beginning the area was planted in wheat and pastures for stock, but later on many farmers concentrated on planting fruit orchards. Hence, by the beginning of the 1900s, many wheat fields had given way to orchards of apples, peaches, pears and prunes.

Octagonal Barn 1892

Like many of the pioneers who settled Douglas County, residents of Lookingglass placed the education of children high on their list of priorities. Lookingglass had one of the first school districts to be formed in the county. School District No. 13 was formed in 1850 with Reverend Abbot L. J. Todd as the first teacher, serving without salary. Classes were held in a one-room log cabin on his settlement near Lookingglass Creek with 60 students of different grades. (That land was later acquired by Elijah Ollivant.)

In 1875 the school was moved from Reverend Todd's settlement to a new two-story building on the Coos Bay Wagon Road. The lower level was used for the school, and the upper floor was used as a community dance hall and for other social functions.

By 1890 more than 100 students attended classes at the school. (Douglas County Judge Carl Hill is remembered as a teacher in Lookingglass in the early 1900s.) In 1908 the old two-story building was torn down and a single story two-room structure was built in its place which now forms a part of the present school complex. In the fall of 1919 a high school was added to District No. 13. Classes were held on the upper floor of the Methodist Church. In 1930 the two-room school building was expanded to accommodate the students from Flournoy Valley. However, by 1943 School District No. 13 was having trouble maintaining its 70-student high school and therefore agreed to send them to Roseburg High School. In 1952 Lookingglass School District No. 13 consolidated with Dillard School District No. 116. In 1954 District 116 built its own high school which is presently in operation. In 1951 Lookingglass Valley Extension Unit opened a library for the public's use at the grade school building.

Lookingglass Store 1852

In January of 1871, when postal services were established at the Lookingglass Store, the area became the terminus for the Oakland-Lookingglass mail route. It was also one of the main stations on the Roseburg-Coos Bay Stage Line completed in 1872. The valley became a gathering point for area residents, and pioneers came from different parts of the county to trade and socialize with friends. Peter William's racetrack drew large crowds to watch and bet on the horse racing meets. Since horse racing and betting were legal, just about every settler in Lookingglass was involved with breeding, rearing, or training horses for the races. By then Lookingglass had two hotels, two general merchandise stores (present-day Lookingglass Store being one of them built in 1852), two blacksmith shops, two barber shops, two saloons, a dance hall, a metal shop, two livery stables, a grist mill and the Odd Fellows Lodge. Mail service expanded to free home delivery during the Great Depression but soon ended when the Post Office discontinued mail service to Lookingglass in 1942. The community now gets its mail from Roseburg.

Lookingglass was the second community in Douglas County to open a Grange Hall (Camas Valley being the first in 1901) and continues to maintain operation to this very day. In 1867 Oliver H. Kelley founded the organization Patrons of Husbandry, better known as the Grange. The organization was organized to meet the needs of the nation's agricultural community. It took a while for communities nationwide to understand the organization's objectives, value and power. But, by 1872, Grange organizations took off like wild fires across the nation. Their social net-workings were extremely beneficial, especially during the Great Depression. The first Grange Hall in Lookingglass was built in 1910 on Lookingglass Road near the Lookingglass Store and was replaced with the present building in June of 1959. Lookingglass Grange was called the Rescue Grange until 1949 when it changed its name to the Grange after reorganization.

On July 17, 1971, de facto mayor of Lookingglass and owner of the Lookingglass Store, Norman Nibblett, attended the dedication of a new public telephone booth. In his address to the small gathering he expressed a desire for a manhole cover to give the 40-resident community a more civic appearance. A parking meter had already been installed and dedicated. The Mayor of Cedar Rapids, Iowa called "Mayor" Nibblett and offered him two manhole covers. He told Mr. Nibblett that he heard his request on the local radio station. With respect to local government, the Mayor of Cedar Rapids said, "We all have many problems, maybe not of the same magnitude. So I thought I would help this one out a little." He thought "Mayor" Nibblett had a "tremendous sense of humor." The Cedar Rapids Television Station filmed both the loading at Cedar Rapids Airport and the offloading at Roseburg Airport. Curious visitors from as far east as New York and Florida came to Lookingglass following the national publicity.

Two months later the community was more than surprised when Charles Kuralt, the famous CBS Television commentator and reporter, paid a visit to Lookingglass Valley. His "on-the-road" features were often watched on Walter Cronkite's CBS evening news. He and his three-man television crew were there to make a movie about the famed parking meter, telephone pay booth and the manhole covers all installed at the intersection of Coos Bay Wagon Road and Lookingglass Road in front of the Lookingglass Store. He too was intrigued by the publicity. Coincidentally, and uniquely so, the community had just experienced the birth of triplet Holstein calves – a phenomenon which occurs once in every 100,000 births. Kuralt also included the calves in his movie. The publicity of the "town" of Lookingglass caught the attention of Congressman John Dellenback. When he heard the news, he thought the town needed a flag, not just any flag, but one that had flown over the nation's capitol in Washington D. C. On Saturday, October 9, 1971, the Congressman visited Lookingglass and presented "Mayor" Norman Nibblett with a flag from the capitol. Douglas Electric Co-operative donated a 45-foot pole for the flag.

Development was slow in coming to Lookingglass Valley. Prior to the advent of the 20th Century, the community got its water from wells and springs and lighted its houses with candles and kerosene lanterns. Wood stoves were used to heat homes. It was not until the late 1960s that treated water came to the valley via Umpqua Basin Water Association. The venture was made possible with a grant of $80,000 and a loan of $108,000 from FHA of the U.S. Department of Agriculture. The community, through the Lookingglass Water Association, contributed $10,000 to complete the project. In June of 1964 the community started a Volunteer Fire Department. It acquired its fire equipment from Douglas County Forest Protection Association. In 1965 the volunteers built a fire building to house the equipment and hold meetings.

References:
The News Review, Douglas County Museum, *Land of the Umpqua:* by Stephen Dow Beckham, *Lookingglass: Emma's Little Patch of Ground* by Lucia Rogers Smith and Margaret Rogers Maier. Photos by the author.

REMEMBER WHEN

Night Clubs

Between the early 1940s and the middle of the 1960s nightclubs were quite popular in Douglas County. And, yes, the Winston-Dillard area had its share too. From Camas Valley to Green and Lookingglass to Dillard there were Saturday night dances all across the valley. A few of those night clubs deserve mentioning. Night spots like: "Tenmile Hall" featuring "Smoky & The Cascade Mountaineers", Winston Community Hall under the banjo strings of "Lou Franco & The Happy Valley Cowboys", Dillard's neighbor Coon Hollow came alive at the "Playmor Gardens" with Bob Weaver and his Dixieland Band". It was the only place in the County where the dancing took place on a dance floor without walls or roof. It was located two miles south of Dillard on Highway 99 where the River RV Park now sits. The 1964 flood washed away the dance floor and the adjoining snack bar. The community of Olalla, which was quite large, then, held their dances at the Olalla Community Hall. On many occasions they kicked up their heels to the music of "Tom Edwards and his Timberjacks." The famous Coos Junction Café and Tavern (name changed to Willee's in 1992) had developed a reputation for its rowdiness and fights. In spite of its reputation, it was one of the most popular night clubs outside of Roseburg. However, the Melody Inn was the premier of nightclubs in the area.

A Winston "old-timer" figuratively described the Melody Inn as a nightclub that was picked up from the City of Las Vegas and placed in Coos Junction. That first class night club opened its doors to the public on October 31, 1949, with R. J. "Rick" Simmons as the owner. It was located at the top of the hill on Highway 99 north of Sherry Street. For several years it was considered to be a landmark for Coos Junction. The chain-saw shop at 28 N.W. Main Street

Melody Inn 1949-1956

once occupied the site. The building was designed with a dining room, a banquet room and a lounge known as the "Oregon Lounge Room." It was capable of accommodating over a hundred guests at a time. It opened for business six days of the week from 5 PM to 2 AM and carried live entertainment all night. Reservations were strongly encouraged, and all guests were expected to dress formally. Over the span of its seven years' existence, the nightclub ownership passed through many hands. In 1955 Tony Cocciolo, then owner of the Bamboo Grove in Roseburg, owned the club and hired Berchie Holmes to operate the business. After several months Berchie leased the business from Mr. Cocciolo. That landmark and exotic nightclub went up in flames on February 13, 1956, at 3:45 AM. The estimated cost of damage was $32,000.

Even though the Community Granges were not night clubs they used their halls to hold dances and other festivities. Those organizations were the social backbone of the communities, especially during the Great Depression. The Evergreen Grange in Green and the Lookingglass Grange held dances every Saturday night, especially during the above mentioned depression. The officers of the grange policed the dances in order to avert any drinking of alcohol and to curb any rowdiness or fights.

Benetta Theater

The Benetta Theater was "it" to many who lived in Coos Junction and the surrounding communities. It was a place to hang out, take someone on a date, relax from a hard day's work at the mill and meet friends. From Camas Valley to Green and Lookingglass to Dillard, people in the valley were excited to have their own movie theater. It was a common site to see long lines of moviegoers along Highway 99 waiting to buy their tickets. The admission price was 50 cents for adults and 20 cents for children. People were hungry for entertainment, and stars such as Robert Mitchum, Barbara Stanwyck, Mario Lanza and Shelley Winters satisfied their appetites.

In 1946 Paul and Loretta Bender moved from Oswego, Kansas, to Roseburg. While there, they operated the Shamrock Motel but sold it after three years and moved to Coos Junction (renamed

Winston). It was 1949, and Coos Junction was growing by leaps and bounds with no recreational outlet for the young or the old. The Benders built a movie theater on Highway 99 and called it Benetta, a combo of Bender and Loretta. In June 1950 the Benetta Theater opened its doors to the public. It was a Quonset-style structure. It had a seating capacity of 450 persons. The auditorium was colorful, had comfortable cushion seats and was fully air-conditioned. The picture was projected on an 18-foot screen, and the sound came from three state-of-the-art loud speakers. The facility even had a cry room for mothers with babies. It was possible for a mother to watch and listen to the movie from a sound-proof room while taking care of her baby. The lobby was quite attractive with its woodwork, its doors and cabinets finished in mahogany.

Benetta Theater

The Benetta Theater was quite successful, and, as a result, the Benders became famous and well respected in the community. It was no surprise when Paul Bender got the highest vote in the general election to win a seat on the first city council in Winston in 1953. The family got into the real estate business and leased the theater to Art McGuire. However, with the advent of drive-in theaters, coupled with poor management from the theater's new owners, the Benetta closed its doors in the early 1960s. The Benders sold the structure to Suiter's Hardware, but to the people of Winston the "Benetta Theater" still remained an object of illusion. The structure was modified, and in 1998 K & L Furniture Store was operating from that building.

A northwesterly wind blew into Winston on the night of November 28, 1998 and dropped the ambient temperature considerably for that time of the year. The Winston-Dillard Fire Department responded to a 911 call from the neighborhood of 90 S.E. Main Street. The voice on 911 shouted: "The K & L Furniture Store is on fire!" By the time the Fire Department arrived at the scene, the entire structure was engulfed in flames. When the fire was extinguished, the building and its contents were completely destroyed at an estimated damage of $250,000. In spite of the cold, Main Street was jammed with spectators. Some of the friends were curious while others had tears in their eyes mourning the loss of a piece of Winston's history. That building that fell to ashes had once housed their beloved Benetta Theater.

Winston's Woman Mayors

In November of 1980 a political twister blew across the country rooting out many political incumbents from office. Ronald Reagan destroyed incumbent Jimmy Carter in a landslide victory for the President of the United States. The Republican Party gained control of the Senate for the first time in 26 years. Doug Robertson ousted incumbent Commissioner Paul Makinson and still holds that position. Dr. John Kitzhaber of Roseburg butchered his opponent Richard Fowler of Roseburg to win the District 23 Senate Seat. And Winston was no exception. Betty Fortino became the first woman mayor of the City of Winston. She edged out incumbent Harley Means by 18 votes.

Mrs. Fortino campaigned on the platform that Winston needed a change of leadership and direction. Change came, not only to Winston, but all across the country. Harley Means was stunned by the defeat and expressed that his support for the city's proposed comprehensive plan might have been his demise. He was a member of the city council for twelve and a half years and served as mayor for eight of those years. He was the first elected mayor of the city in 1979. Prior to that date all the city mayors were appointed by the elected councilors. Mrs. Fortino was qualified and ready to lead the city. She was the co-owner, with her husband, of Coast to Coast Hardware Store and taught at Umpqua Community College part-time. Her only political involvement at the time was her appointment to the Winston-Dillard School Board #116 Budget Committee. She served as mayor for one term and did not run for a second.

Photo: Courtesy Leif Photography

Marge Brady, another business woman, saddled up for the Winston mayoral race in November 1982. She was challenged by George Jacobs (deceased) who had retired from the Douglas County Sheriff Department in 1979. Mr. Jacobs served as Winston's police chief from 1963 to 1975. In the race he out ran Mrs. Brady to win the seat by a margin of 132 votes. However, by an unfortunate turn of events, the then chief of police Harold Forney suddenly passed away from a heart attack in January 1983. Mayor elect Jacobs called a special meeting of the newly elected city council. At that meeting he was sworn in as the mayor and then resigned from the position. He then accepted the position as the chief of police. The city council then appointed Mrs. Brady as the mayor. She was informed of their decision by phone and accepted. George Jacobs held the position as chief of police until his passing in November 1988. Mrs. Brady served as mayor for one term and did not run for a second.

Photo: Courtesy Leif Photography

For the next 26 years, the author is not aware of any woman of Winston who campaigned for the mayoral throne. But on November 2, 2010, Sharon Harrison became the savior for what appeared to be a disunited community. Many folks and organizations did not like the direction in which the city was going and the "Riverside Center dispute" exacerbated the tension. Mrs. Harrison, a native of this area for 32 years and co-owner of Harrison's Hardware True Value, challenged incumbent Rex Stevens. When the votes were counted, Mrs. Harrison crushed Mr. Stevens by winning 67 percent of the votes cast. Mr. Stevens, who sat on the mayoral throne for 10 years, was ready to turn the gavel over to Sharon and wished her the best.

Courtesy Leif Photography

As a point of historical interest, Harrison Hardware True Value was first called Coast to Coast Hardware Store and now operates out of the same building once used by Mrs. Fortino. True Value bought out Coast to Coast Hardware Stores. The Harrisons then changed the name.

The Brockway Store

Brockway Store 1890-2012

The historical Brockway Store stands at the corner of Highway 42 and Brockway Road as a landmark filled with archives of memories of long ago. This white structure with its high facade is 122 years old. In 1890 the store was built and operated by I. B. Nichols on the Old Brockway Road until his retirement in 1941, when his son Cyril "Sid" Nichols took over the business. However, in 1922 I. B. moved the structure to the intersection of Highway 42 and Brockway Road when the highway joined Pacific Highway in Winston, now called Highway 99.

This merchandise store was both a commercial and social "hub" for just about all the communities from Camas Valley to Green and Round Prairie to Lookingglass. The lower level was used for the store, and the upper level was used for multiple functions, like dancing etc. The store housed the post office for 66 years before the service was moved to Winston in 1956. I. B. Nichols was the postmaster for 51 of those years. Once a customer walked into the Brockway Store, he/she first saw a sign which read "If we don't have it, you don't need it." That was a true statement for that kind of store in that era. But, by the early 1900s, the Brockway Merchandise Store was the godfather of today's stores like the Wal-Mart and the Fred Myer of Roseburg, the difference being customers paid either in cash, gold dust, chickens, eggs, running errands or credit in which the customer's name was entered into a credit ledger. What was rather interesting is that every purchase and payment made by a customer was entered into a ledger, including the customer's name.

The store was designed to assist farmers and ranchers of the rural community as well as tourists going to and from the Oregon Coast. Customers came to the store to trade and buy merchandise. Some came only to pick up mail and socialize. What a difference between the Brockway Store then and the Wal-Marts and Fred Myers of today! The store had no refrigeration, sodas were kept cold in ice-boxes and the customer had to leave the bottle at the store. Prices of merchandise were a vast contrast with today's prices. For example: Levis jeans were $0.75 a pair, shoes $0.25 a pair, eggs $0.05 to $0.10 a dozen. With the advent of automobiles, the store got into the sale of gasoline. Since there were no trucks to haul the vats of gasoline, they came in carts hauled by horses.

By the end of the 1980s and the beginning of the 1990s, Brockway Store was getting stiff competition from major department stores in Roseburg. The Nichols Brothers Ranch Incorporated, of which the store was a part, decided to close the store. The permanent padlock on the doors ended a long chapter in the history of rural stores.

Civil Bend Pioneer Cemetery

The first cemetery in Civil Bend District, now Winston, was about a quarter mile northeast of the historic house located at 13224 Lookingglass Road. The cemetery was established on the John Cox Donation Land Claim in 1856. The first to be buried there was Thomas S. Gage, 18 years of age. He was killed in the Cow Creek Canyon during the Indian war in 1856. Many others were buried on that ridge shaded by oak trees. It is believed that

13224 Lookingglass Rd.

during a rain storm between 1875 and 1876, the graves slid off the side of the ridge. The remains were taken to Pleasant View Cemetery in Civil Bend District. In May of 1877 a corporation was formed, and the name was changed from Pleasant View to Civil Bend Pioneer Cemetery. (Note: As a point of historical interest, Douglas County Pauper's Cemetery shares the southeast boundary line with Civil Bend Pioneer Cemetery.)

References:
The News Review, *The Umpqua Trapper*, City of Winston Council Minutes, Civil Bend Pioneer Cemetery Records. Photos: By Leif Photography and the author.

CHAPTER THREE

WINSTON-DILLARD WATER DISTRICT

Prior to 1945 the agrarian population who lived in Winston and the Greater Winston Area got their usable water from wells, creeks or the South Umpqua River. But by 1947, with the great influx of migrant workers to the areas to work in the timber industry, the Winston and Dillard communities were growing by leaps and bounds. There were no garbage disposal sites, and household waste was burned, buried or indiscriminately thrown out. The evidence of the outhouses and leaking septic tanks stirred up concerns about the health and welfare of the communities, especially in that of Winston.

The Coos Junction Committee that was formed in April of 1948 to bring back postal services to the Winston Community reorganized to form a water district. In a small section of Dillard there was a water distribution system financed by Paul B. Hult and Cornelius C. Fosback. They were pumping water from the South Umpqua River to the Hult Lumber Mill and a few houses in close vicinity to the mill. The community of Dillard asked to join the Coos Junction Committee and soon after the name was changed to Winston-Dillard Water District Committee under the leadership of Marshall Haughn. Within a month of its formation the committee had a petition bearing 182 signatures ready to be filed with the county court. The Committee held a meeting at Dillard Grade School on August 16, 1948, before a packed audience, to discuss the proposed formation and at the same time to elect a five-man board of directors. The Committee had unanimous approval from the audience to form the

Winston-Dillard Water District

district. J. V. Long, attorney for the Committee, filed the petition, and the court set the election for October 5, 1948.

Disappointingly, voter turnout at the polls was not as heavy as anticipated. However, it came as no surprise when the votes were counted on October 5, 1948; the Winston-Dillard Water District incorporation was approved by an overwhelming majority of 181 to 5 votes. Only five registered voters filed to run for the board of directors. The electors were Marshall Haughn and Frank True of Winston and Paul B. Hult, Cornelius C. Fosback and Roy Gordon of Dillard. Ten days later, at the board's first meeting, each elected board member was given the oath of office by attorney J. V. Long. They elected Marshall Haughn as chairman, Cornelius C. Fosback as secretary and Paul B. Hult as treasurer. They read a letter from the court in which it confirmed the legality of the incorporation of Winston-Dillard Water District. They appointed a Budget Committee to draft a budget for the 1948 to 1949 fiscal year. They hired engineer James Daugherty to conduct a survey of the proposed water supply system in order to determine a cost on which to base a bond election. They discussed plans for two reservoirs, one in Winston and the other in Dillard. Seven months later they also hired the engineering firm A. D. Harvey and Associates of Medford to explore a test well for water in the Dillard Flats. The well was located about 200 feet from the South Umpqua River on Fred Burks' property and across from Moyer's Nursery.

By August of 1949 the Board ran into a roadblock with regard to bringing water to the district. Two exploration wells in the Dillard Flats did not have sufficient yield for commercial use. In January 1950 Roberts Creek Water District, located across the South Umpqua River from Winston, offered to sell water to the Winston-Dillard Water District. The Board accepted its proposal and set a bond election for $83,000 on May 16, 1950. The bond passed by an overwhelming majority of 235 votes to one vote. Unfortunately, through a technical error, the bond election was declared void. A recheck of the assessed valuation of the district revealed that the bonding capacity was only $78,000 instead of the $83,000 that was voted upon. Another election was set, and on June 16, 1950, the bond issue for $78,000 was approved by the voters. The First National Bank of Portland bought the $78,000 bond issue at an interest rate of 3.75 percent for the first five years and 4 percent thereafter for a total of 17 years.

In August of 1950 the Board, at its regular meeting held at the Community Center, approved a set of construction plans and specifications as presented by their engineer James R. Daugherty of Roseburg. They also called for bids for labor and material for constructing the proposed water distribution system. They scheduled a public meeting at Dillard Elementary School to apprise the residents of the district of the proposed contract with Roberts Creek Water District for purchasing water. About a week after the public meeting both Roberts Creek Water District Board and the Board of Winston-Dillard Water District signed a contract for 17 years. On August 28, 1950, the bids were opened, and the Board awarded the contract for the piping material to Armco Drainage and Metal Products Co. from Portland. The contract for the valves and fire hydrants was given to Renselear Valve and Co. from Seattle, Washington, and the contract for the excavating and laying of the pipes was awarded to R. B. Miller Co. from Salem.

The Board sent out notifications to all the residents in the district advising them to sign up for service connections as soon as possible so that the number of persons to be served would be known before construction began. An installation fee of $50 was charged upon signing the agreement. A very unusual dry spell in April 1951 caused many of the wells on the hillsides on the east side of Winston to go dry. The drought caused an unusual hardship on many families in the area. In May of 1951 Roberts Creek Water District began supplying water to Winston. The contractor expedited the project, and in the spring of 1952 the contract was completed. The contractor was applauded by various business places in Winston for the quick and efficient work. By 1954, with the growing population of both Roberts Creek Water District and that of Winston-Dillard Water District, the facilities at Roberts Creek were struggling to keep up with the demand for water. Winston-Dillard Water District constructed a 500,000-gallon tank on the hill north of Lookingglass Road, (that area is now known as Galaxy Drive) in November 1955.

It is interesting to note that in 1953, when Winston was incorporated as a city, it automatically withdrew from Winston-Dillard Water District. It purchased its water directly from Roberts

Creek Water District. However, in August 1955 the incorporated city voted 117 to 6 to again become a part of the Winston-Dillard Water District. On October 3, 1955, voters outside the city but within the Winston-Dillard Water District voted unanimously to include the City of Winston in the district by a vote of 11 to 0.

It became quite obvious that Roberts Creek Water District was having trouble meeting the demands for water from both districts. Winston-Dillard Water District Board decided to build its own filtration plant. In 1956 the Board presented the voters with a bond issue of $115,000 to construct a water plant along the South Umpqua River. On December 3, 1956, the voters approved the project. The board hired the engineering firm Cornell, Howland, Hayes and Merryfield of Corvallis to prepare the plans for the project. Archie Rice was the engineer in charge. In May 1957 the contract to build the filtration water plant was awarded to Lee Hoffman Co. Within eleven months, in April 1958, the plant was completed, and Winston-Dillard Water District became self-sufficient and discontinued purchasing water from Roberts Creek Water District. Before the plant was completed, the Board hired Lou E. Shigley as the plant superintendent in January 1958. In March 1960 the district built another water reservoir. In 1962 the community of Brockway voted overwhelmingly to join the Winston-Dillard Water District.

When the City of Winston posted a "Legal Notice" in *The News-Review* calling for a public hearing on October 18, 1971, at City Hall, regarding a proposal of the city's intention to withdraw from the Winston-Dillard Water District, the news stirred up a hornet's nest infuriating many people in the community. On the evening of the hearing, the city council's chamber was packed to the point of overflowing with many people standing outside in the hallway. The hearing opened exactly at 8:00 PM. Several citizens echoed their objections to the city's proposed intention to withdraw from the Winston-Dillard Water District. The citizens were: Elton Zuver, Art Greise, Ab Rice, Bart Hult, Lloyd Stutsman, Larry Zuver, Judy Zuver, Harold Shears, Glenda Kennerly, Lee Hunt and Stanford Buell. Many questions asked by the various speakers who opposed the proposed withdrawal were answered by City Attorney Carl Felker. He explained that "a municipality has the legal authority to withdraw at any time from any district of which it is a part." Even though there were heated opinions expressed, the hearing was orderly and ended on a very friendly note. The meeting adjourned with the City Council asking the Water Board to set a meeting between the Water Board and the City Council so that they could meet and discuss the issue further. The board and the city met twice and did iron out some differences that existed between them.

At the City Council meeting on November 22, 1971, Jim Richey, Chairman of the Winston-Dillard Water Board, asked the Council if they had come to a decision regarding their proposed intention to withdraw from the district. He told them that the Board needed to know urgently since they were preparing to present the voters with a bond issue to replace water mains along Highway 99 before the highway department began the widening and upgrading of the highway in July of 1972. The Council told him they would make a decision in the immediate future. Immediately after the adjournment of the City Council meeting, the Council held a special meeting to consult on the issue of whether they would withdraw from the Winston-Dillard Water District. City Attorney Carl Felker explained the role of the water district. He told the Council he felt they should withdraw from the district. He explained that the council would pay half or less in interest on the bond issues and suggested the council check on the interest rate on municipal bonds vs. single purpose bonds. The Council decided to make their decision at their regular meeting on December 6, 1971. The first item on the agenda for the December 6 meeting was the discussion on the proposed withdrawal from the Winston-Dillard Water District. The Council unanimously agreed to send a letter to the Winston-Dillard Water District expressing their intention to remain in the Water District. They also agreed to call a public hearing on January 17, 1972, to inform the citizens of their decision. In the letter the council stated "that their decision to remain in the Water District was in the best interest of the community as a whole and further pledged to support the district efforts."

With the growing demand for water from the district's customers, the 16-year-old plant, built in 1958, was reaching the point of obsolescence and could not handle the volume. The District Board, with the advice of their engineers, agreed to replace the old plant rather than modify it. They presented the voters with a bond issue of $480,000 to build a new plant and to replace distribution mains along Highway 99. On February 28, 1972, the district voters voted in favor of the bond issue by a vote of 120 to 40. The new treatment plant would provide for a two million gallon a day capacity, with provision to add additional units capable of producing another million gallons as the need was justified. The water mains along Highway 99 within the City of Winston were replaced, but the construction of the water treatment plant was delayed. The State Health Division, which is responsible for reviewing and approving plans for water treatment plants throughout the state, "red-inked" with disapproval the design of the proposed plant on three occasions. There were 14 technical items with design flaws the health department had issues with. One of the most serious was "the proposed filter rate, which health officials feel should be low to more effectively treat the poor quality water in the South Umpqua River." In August 1974 the water treatment plant went into operation adjacent to the old plant under the supervision of Elmer Mills.

By November 1975 Dillard and areas south of Dillard were experiencing low pressure in the mains. The two reservoirs in the district's distribution system were located on the northwest side of Winston. As a result of the heavy consumption of water usage in the Winston area, Dillard and areas south of Dillard were experiencing low pressure in the mains. Parametrix Engineering Firm of Eugene advised the district to build a million gallon storage tank in Dillard, upgrade the size of the main between Winston and Dillard and replace under-sized and leaking lines in the system for an estimated cost of $680,000 in order to alleviate the problem and improve the distribution system. The Board of Directors held a public meeting at the Junior High School in Winston in order to apprise the customers in the district of the problems and the proposed solutions.

According to the Coos-Curry-Douglas Economic Improvement Association (CCDEIA), the proposed Winston-Dillard water supply system upgrade was put on the top of a list of five possible construction projects that would be funded for the 1976-1977 fiscal year. The Economic Development Administration (EDA) was asked to contribute $544,000 of the total estimate of $680,000. In

June 1977 the Winston-Dillard Water Board rejoiced upon learning the district was given a federal grant of $544,000 for the upgrade and expansion of the water system. Ron Eachus, spokesman for the Economic Development Administration (EDA), told *The News Review* that "the expanded water system will save an estimated 200 jobs in local wood product industries. One purpose of the water system development is to make the area more attractive to new businesses and encourage established businesses to expand." The Board appropriated $136,000 of its funds together with the $544,000 grant to get the project done.

In May 1978 the Water District Board was pleased and proud with the operation of the district's plant and distribution system. It wrote a letter to the community to be read 25 years later, in the year 2003, about the district's status. That letter was placed among other letters and paraphernalia from other agencies and businesses in a capsule and buried in the parking lot of Winston City Hall. In the letter it spelled out that the district had 7½ miles of water line with 2½ million gallons of storage. It served 1622 dwellings through 1300 meters. It pumped 571,500 gallons of water in the summer and charged $6.50 per month for the first 4000 gallons of water consumed plus $.45 per 1000 gallons used in excess of the first 4000 gallons. A meter installation was charged at a rate of $200 for a ¾ inch meter.

In 1989 another controversy erupted between the City and the Winston-Dillard Water District. In January of 1988 at the City's Goal Setting Session, "consolidation of the utilities" was placed at the top of the list of goals the city wanted to accomplish. A year later, at the City Council meeting of February 21, 1989, the issue was brought up by Winston resident, Art Griese. The Council discussed the matter and authorized Ron Schofield, City Administrator, to contact the city's attorney Bruce Coalwell in order to find out the legalities with regard to consolidating both the water and the fire districts. When *The News-Review* broke the news the following day, Elmer Mills, Manager of the Water District, was soaking with rage. He told *The News-Review* Reporter, Tricia Jones, that "he hired Portland, Oregon Attorney Andrew Jordan, who is a specialist in representing special district's interest." Bill Belding, Assistant Fire Chief, became overheated saying: "he is ready to fight the takeover." He made it clear "that his board of directors would regard an attempt by the city to take charge of its fire services as a hostile takeover." Since Attorney Coalwell is the attorney for both the city and the water district, he declared a conflict of interest. The city did not hire an attorney but sought legal guidance through Eugene, Oregon Attorney Keith Marten. He cited five legal conditions necessary for the city to withdraw from the districts, which were published in *The News-Review,* March 12, 1989.

Rumors of the city's proposed "consolidation of the utilities" spread like wildfires throughout the districts. The City Council's meetings, normally poorly attended by the public, saw a dramatic increase in attendance. Water District Manager Elmer Mills and Assistant Fire Chief Bill Belding attended all their future meetings armed with tape recorders. The city was so embroiled at the time with pending disputes and litigation with the School District, the Police Association and Bremner Hills Co-op, the issue of "consolidation of the utilities" was placed on a back burner on the city's proposed agendas. However, a group of Winston residents, calling themselves "Citizens for Responsive Government" and "Citizens for Responsive Representation", upset with the city's modus operandi and the pending litigation against the city, filed a petition for the recall of Mayor Ken Hull and Councilor Gus Jennings. On November 7, 1989, Mayor Ken Hull and Councilor Gus Jennings were recalled, and Jim McClellan was appointed the Mayor and Gary Vess was appointed Councilor to replace Mr. Jennings. The issue of "consolidation of the utilities" was put to rest under Mr. McClellan's leadership.

By August 1999 the Winston-Dillard Water Board of Directors experienced a huge expansion of the district when the communities of Willis Creek and Rice Creek formed a "Local Improvement District" (LID), and joined said district. Safe drinking water in those communities had become very scarce with little or no water in the creeks in the summer and a high bacteria count in the winter. The majority of the people were buying water by the 50-gallon barrels or bringing home gallon jugs of water from their jobs each day. When the water district was approached regarding extending their main lines into those communities, the board made it clear that it did not have the funds to do so. However, the district encouraged those communities to form a

Local Improvement District (LID) in order to pay for the link to the district's mains. A group of residents from both communities, under the leadership of Linda Wells, with assistance from Stephen Mountainspring, managed to get about 144 property owners to sign the petition agreeing to form the LID. Umpqua Community Development Corp. assisted the group with the annexation process, and the Oregon Economic and Community Development Department contributed $1 million in grants and low interest loans. OECDD also financed the feasibility study. The final design called for nine miles of pipes, one pump station, fire hydrants, and two 100,000-gallon reservoirs at a cost of $3.1 million. At the commencement of the project in December 2002, OECDD was able to secure both federal and state grants totaling $1.7 million. Each property owner was then assessed about $6600.00. After several years of hurdling red tape and bureaucracy, in October 2003, the residents of Willis Creek and Rice Creek were celebrating the luxury of having safe drinking water.

Winston-Dillard Water Plant 2012

With the expansion of services into Willis Creek and Rice Creek, the district now has a population base of 8500 people. The Board is now focused on keeping up and meeting the required water quality standards as set forth by Oregon Health Division and the U.S. Environmental Protection Agency. It is planning to construct a new filtration plant to replace the old one built in 1974. The proposed plant will be capable of producing four million gallons of water a day. Construction of the new plant is projected to be completed February 2012 and will cost about $7 million.

As of December 2010 the Winston-Dillard Water District has about 2500 customers and pumps 1.4 million gallons of water a day in the summer months. It sells a ¾-inch meter for $2,305.00, and the average monthly bill for a customer is $37.38 for 7000 gallons of water.

References:
The News-Review, Winston-Dillard Water District Minutes, Winston City Council Minutes.

WINSTON-DILLARD FIRE DISTRICT

By 1950 the community of Winston, then called Coos Junction, was growing by leaps and bounds. The male "booster club" of business owners incorporated into the Winston Chamber of Commerce. All the communities in the area depended on Roseburg Fire District for assistance in the event of a fire. The number one item on the roster of projects for the Chamber of Commerce was to form a fire district. Without a quasi-body of its kind, the community was vulnerable to loss of lives and properties due to fires. The Chamber argued that a fire district would meet insurance and under-writers' standards and thus reduce the rate of fire insurance in the community. The Chamber directed Russell Turner to organize a meeting of the communities of Winston and Dillard in order to inform them of the Chamber's plans for a fire district for the area. At that meeting a Winston-Dillard Fire District Committee was formed, and twelve enthusiastic residents volunteered to serve on the committee. Arthur McGuire was elected chairman of the committee. Tentative plans were laid out for a fire district for Winston and Dillard. The plans called for a five-man board of directors, a fire pumper-truck and a proposed boundary that would include Brockway, Coon Hollow, Round Prairie, and would extend north to meet the south boundary of Roseburg Rural Fire District at Kelley's Corner in Green.

In December of 1951 the Fire District Committee called a meeting of the community at the Dillard School to discuss the proposed plans. The Committee invited Roseburg Fire Chief, W. E. Mills and State Fire Marshall, A. J. Butch, as guest speakers. The two fire experts spoke on the importance and the need for a fire district in a community of its size. After the proposed plans were explained, Chairman McGuire called for a vote from the residents who attended the meeting and received a unanimous vote of support from the 30 residents who attended to form the fire district of the area. The chairman then explained that the committee needed a petition of 25 percent or 200 names of registered voters and property owners as a minimum before that petition could be presented to the county court. The meeting ended with a slide show given by one of the representatives of firefighting equipment companies.

March 25, 1952, the Fire District Committee filed a petition of 207 certified signatures with the county court to form a Winston-Dillard Fire District. The county court set April 29, 1952, at 10:00 AM for the public hearing with regard to any objections to the proposed fire district. All the required filing fees were paid by the Winston Chamber of Commerce. At the hearing, Gilmer Griggs Lumber Company, with 18 acres of property, asked to be removed from the proposed fire district, but two other property owners west of Winston asked to be included in the district. With no further comments, the court set Monday, June 6, 1952, as the date for the election of Winston-Dillard Rural Fire Protection District. Seven candidates contested for five positions on the proposed board. After the votes were canvassed on the evening of June 6, 1952, Winston-Dillard Rural Fire Protection District was overwhelmingly approved by the voters with 65 votes for and five against. The voters also elected the Board of Directors for the district, with Roy Fisher tipping the scale with 57 votes, Forest Dean Collins with 53 votes, George W. Tipton 51 votes, Pat Manley 40 votes, and Cyril Nichols 40 votes.

At the board's first meeting of June 1952, Forest Dean Collins was elected as chairman and Bill Tipton, by a unanimous vote, was elected secretary and treasurer. For the remaining of the meeting the board focused on the budget and the purchasing of a 600 gallon fire pumper-truck. By August 1952 the voters approved a four mill tax to cover the cost of the truck and operating expenses for fiscal year 1952 to 1953. At that meeting they agreed to advertise for a fire chief and volunteers to staff the department. Between December 1952 and February 1953, the board appointed J. C. Welch as the fire chief of the department, accepted 24 volunteers for training and had taken possession of the fire truck that was housed at Welch Bros. shop. The board had enough money from its budget plus donations of material and labor to construct a fire building that would house the fire truck, office, kitchen and recreation room for the volunteer firemen. In June of 1953, while the fire building was under construction, the board sadly lost their Chairman, Forest Dean Collins, in a plane crash in the Rice Creek Canyon. Then, in April 1954, they suffered another disappointing moment when J. C. Welch resigned as chief of the fire department. Mr. Welch told the board that he had accepted the position of Captain of the Sheriff's Reserve for Civil Defense, and he recommended Robert Nichols, one of the trained volunteers, be promoted to the position of chief of the department. The board immediately appointed Robert Nichols Chief of the Winston-Dillard Fire Department. (The present Fire Chief, Robert Nicholls is not related to the Nichols mentioned above.) In December 1953 the City of Winston began holding its council meetings in the recreation room, and the Winston Chamber of Commerce began holding their regular meetings in the same room in April of 1954.

Community volatility and a near incidence of a neighborhood riot all started as a result of a difference in opinion between Fire Chief Robert Nichols and two Board members, Charles Hutton and Erv Gubser. However, over the course of several months, the differences developed into a mosaic of animosity. That animosity spread like a virus among the volunteer firemen, and subsequently it affected 15 of them and the community of Winston. On Wednesday July 13, 1955, Fire Chief Robert Nichols, together with 15 volunteer firemen, resigned from the department. The board delayed acceptance of Chief Nichols' resignation pending his replacement. Then on Friday night, July 15, 1955, the board unanimously accepted his resignation and appointed Barney Shepherd to head the department. Just as Mr. Nichols' resignation was being accepted, a mob from his neighborhood, the Suksdorf Orchard Area, began to vandalize his property. They threw rocks on his house and made attempts to overturn the family's vehicle in front of his house. Mr. Nichols' wife called in State Law Enforcement for protection. (The City of Winston did not have a police department at that time.) By the time the State Police Officers arrived, the violence had subsided. There were as many as 20 adults and children loitering in front of the Nichols' home. The presence of law enforcement caused the mob to disperse, thereby averting a riot in the area. The plea for a City of Winston Police Department was then on the lips of the community.

Saturday morning following the incident two delegations of citizens representing the Nichols' family and another representing the neighborhood complained to District Attorney, Robert Stults, in Roseburg, regarding the controversy. Both sides discussed possible legal action. But neither group signed a complaint before leaving the attorney's office. Talk of a petition to recall two board members, Charles Hutton and Erv Gubser, filtered through the area, putting another burden on the already fragile community. But, it was the psychological brilliance of newly appointed Fire Chief Barney Shepherd who restored harmony to the community. He first met with Mr. Nichols and discussed the situation regarding the future of the Fire Department. He picked up the department's records, the chief's badge, and shook Mr. Nichols' hand. With only three firemen left at the department, Chief Shepherd called a special meeting on Monday, July 18, 1955, at the Fire Department at 7:00 PM. His enthusiastic request was to sign up any person interested in becoming a trained fireman. He said that volunteers would be paid a stipend for each fire. Within an hour 32 men volunteered to join the Winston-Dillard Rural Fire Department. Chief Barney Shepherd was credited for bringing back the unity and stability to the department and the community of Winston.

Twenty-three years after the formation of the Winston-Dillard Rural Fire Department, it was showing signs of expansion, stability and professionalism with a fire rating of 7. Fiscal year 1975 to 1976, Anthony Vicari was then Fire Chief. He had been Chief since October of 1968 and had occasional disagreements with the Board's style of governance. The department had on its payroll 12 firemen, emergency medical team personnel and 16 volunteer firemen. It was also running federally-funded employees' Comprehensive Employment and Training Act - CETA. On May

6, 1975, it presented the voters with a fire district budget of $282,778, a sum far beyond the six percent limitation. When the votes were canvassed, the budget was defeated with some 298 voters opposing it and 246 supporting it. Following the defeat, the board met and reduced the budget by five percent. But that too was defeated on June 17, 1975, with 320 against the proposal and 300 supporting it. According to state law, fire districts and other special districts could hold an unlimited number of budget elections. For the third time, on August 5, 1975, the department presented the voters with a budget of $313,018 a total of $267,028 beyond the six percent constitutional limitation. The voters pushed that one over the cliff by a margin of three to one against the budget. The tally showed that 364 electors voted against the budget and 119 voted for it. In unrelated circumstances, that very evening, the Board held a special meeting to consult on "certain allegations of misconduct directed against Chief Vicari." They unanimously voted to suspend Chief Vicari from his duty as chief of the Winston-Dillard Fire Department. Ronald Boyd, next in rank to Mr. Vicari, became acting chief of the department. The attorneys who represented both the Board and Mr. Vicari agreed not to disclose any of the allegations of misconduct in the public hearing. However, the results of the fourth election on September 16, 1975, were no different. The voters rejected the budget of $251,921 with 198 persons voting yes and 268 voting no.

The next possible election to present a new budget to the voters was November 4, 1975; the department had a balance of only $11,857 in its account, but the cost of operating the department for one month was about $20,000. The Fire District Board held an emergency meeting at the Winston-Dillard Fire Department on Thursday, September 18, 1975. Before an emotionally charged audience, the Board unanimously approved a motion "to borrow $15,000 from the Fire Engine Replacement Fund in order to continue operating the department through September 30." After that date the Board would "suspend without pay all paid personnel with the exception of the secretary until a new budget is approved." Chairman John Thiems added that "if the budget is defeated at a future election, we will be in a position of having to sell the fire department equipment to replace the loan taken from the engine replacement fund." There was a moment of drama and anxiety, when the meeting was interrupted for a time when the emergency medical team was called to rescue a Winston resident who suffered a malfunction in his artificial heart valve. It had been noted that only 27 percent of the 1700 registered voters participated in the last election. Jack Patterson, Jr., chairman of Winston Jaycees, volunteered himself and his organization to circulate information to voters in the entire district to determine what they wanted in the way of fire protection. The meeting ended with a complex mix of emotions regarding the decision to suspend all the firemen.

On Monday evening, September 29, 1975, the Board and the Budget Committee met and reduced the budget to $230,000 for the November election. Again, that figure was still outside the six per cent limitation. They reduced the twelve paid fireman squad to a squad of eleven men. They found $24,244 in the general fund. They had a huge boost of confidence when a representative of the Jaycees organization reported that 351 taxpayers had signed the petition requesting the Board to continue full operation of the department. With the confidence they had found enough money in the district accounts, the Board then voted to continue full-time operation of the department until the November 4th election. In an abrupt 180 degree turn from the previous announcement, the Chairman of the district Board, John Thiems, announced that: "it's all but a certainty; the firefighters will have to be suspended as of midnight October 2, 1975." That decision came as a result of an emergency meeting held on Wednesday, October 1, 1975 to discuss the legal roadblock with using the funds found in the budget.

For the first time since its formation, residents and property owners in the Winston-Dillard Fire Protection District were left without a full-time firefighting and emergency rescue squad. At midnight Thursday, October 2, 1975, before a packed audience, the Fire District Board voted to suspend 11 paid professional firefighters and the emergency rescue unit. At the end of the heated debate, three members voted in favor, one voted against and the chairman did not cast a vote. William Hall, the Board member who voted against the motion, verbally tendered his resignation, left his volunteer fireman badge on the meeting table and walked out of the meeting. An article in *The News Review* stated, "officials believe the decision marked the first time in Oregon history a paid fire department was forced to close down because it lacked the fiscal budget." The chairman then announced: "Beginning today, the fire station business will be operated from 8 AM to noon and from 1 PM to 5 PM on weekdays by the dispatcher/secretary, Juanita Sawyer." The Board then appointed Jack C. Patterson, Jr. as chief of the volunteers, and Larry Wait was named assistant chief. They were both instructed to notify the other area fire departments in the event of a fire emergency. The fire alarm telephone was manned by Mr. Patterson, Jr. from his home when the station was closed. About 30 minutes after the official suspension of the paid firefighters and emergency rescue unit, the volunteer unit was called out to extinguish a fire at the Foursquare Gospel Church in Winston. Eight volunteer fighters responded, and the fire was quickly extinguished. Some damage was caused to the floor. The church, located at the corner of Highway 99 and Thompson Avenue in Winston, was under construction at the time. Investigators discovered that two road flares were the cause of the fire. There were no suspects nor was anyone charged.

October 9, 1975, one week later, after the suspension of the Winston-Dillard Firefighters, the skies lit up with glowing orange flames surrounded by mushrooms of black smoke about 100 feet in the air over Struthers Furniture Store and Warehouse in Dillard at about 10:29 PM. Fourteen volunteer firefighters from Winston-Dillard Fire Department and 16 firemen from Roseburg Fire Department, under the mutual agreement, responded to the fire. Struthers Warehouse burned to the ground, but the Furniture Store was saved. The company suffered about $240,000 in damages. Oregon State Police arson investigators were called to the scene while the buildings were still ablaze.

The Struthers Fire was still under investigation when another fire at Round Prairie Lumber Co., within the Winston-Dillard Fire District, broke out at 12:39 AM on October 20, 1975. The night watchman reported hearing a bang, and minutes later he saw the sawmill complex was engulfed in flames. He explained that the fire started as a result of a malfunction in the compressor room of the saw mill. The fire quickly spread into the dry lumber plant and went out of control. Twenty volunteers from Winston-Dillard Fire Department went to the scene with three pumpers, a tanker and a pickup truck. Under the mutual aid agreement, Winston-Dillard dispatcher called out three other fire districts to help. They were Roseburg Fire District, Douglas County District No. 2 and Myrtle Creek Fire Department.

The next day, October 21, 1975, at 7:00 PM at the fire station, the District Board Chairman, John Thiems, called a special meeting of the board at the request of Jack Patterson, Jr., Chief of the volunteer firemen. The meeting began with the usual tempo like many of its meetings. But, when Mr. Patterson, Jr. was given permission to speak, the meeting exploded into a verbal donnybrook of accusations and name-calling. Among the audience who attended the meeting were the suspended firefighters and Robert Nichols, president of the Firefighters Union Local 2091. There were even murmurs of a recall of the board from among the packed audience. Mr. Patterson, Jr. wanted to know why the board did not call out the 11 suspended firefighters during both the Struthers and the Round Prairie Lumber Co. fires. He was armed with copies of the Oregon statutes and the state's fire code that explained the rights and duties of the chief. Again, he emphasized, "Why was I refused an order to call back the paid men?" Chairman Thiems explained, due to the district financial crisis, there was no money to pay the men. He continued that he had been informed by the suspended firefighters that "if they were called back, at anytime during the suspension, that they would be considered to be back on the payroll for the remainder of the year." The Fire District attorney, Mark Hendershott, advised that "the volunteer chief has the power to request the paid men be called to the fire scene, but the board has the right to either approve or disapprove the request." In another outburst of rage and frustration, the board was accused of not giving its full support to the volunteers and did not try hard enough to seek emergency funding in order to avert the budget crisis. With the time registering 2 hours 30 minutes into the meeting and the meeting spinning out of control, Chair Thiems banged the gavel on the meeting table three times and called for a motion to adjourn the meeting.

Between October 21 and November 4, 1975, the board made every effort to inform and educate the voters about the budget and the importance of having a professional fire department in the district. The members examined the results from the 300 returned responses of the 1200 questionnaires mailed out to registered voters at the beginning of October. They were pleased that the majority of the residents who responded were in favor of a combined paid personnel and volunteer fire department. They held two public hearings on the proposed budget and agreed to present the voters with a budget of $229,617, a total of $188,852 outside the 6 percent limitation which needed voters' approval. They appointed Chris Lanham to replace William Hall on the district board. At its meeting on October 28, 1975, Glen Williams, a Winston insurance agent, was invited to explain how fire insurance on properties in the district would be impacted by a defeat of the budget on November 4, 1975. Mr. Williams explained, by use of a chart, that the district's rating would drop from a class 7 to a 10 and thereby would spike the rate of fire insurance on properties in the district. He concluded by saying: "It would be stupid to try to do away with the (paid) fire department and then pay more in insurance costs."

The Winston-Dillard Fire District Board breathed a sigh of relief when the results of the election on November 4, 1975, showed the voters approved the district's operating budget by a stunning margin of 610 in favor and 206 against. The suspended firefighters were called back on the job by midnight after the results were canvassed. The volunteer firemen, under volunteer Chief Jack Patterson, Jr., were relieved of the burden of responsibilities for the fire department. By November 5, 1975, the fire department personnel roster was comprised of the battalion chief, the fire marshal, three captains, four firemen and three CETA firemen, 30 volunteers and the dispatcher/secretary, Juanita Sawyer.

The investigation of the church and the Struthers fires was still ongoing. However, as a result of persistent rumors of suspicion involving the 11 suspended firefighters, that they might have started the fires, Lt. Duane Pankratz, officer in charge of the Roseburg headquarters, asked the 11 firefighters to take a polygraph test. Four of the suspected firefighters volunteered to take the test in Roseburg, including Don Boyd, acting Fire Chief. But five days later, the International Association of Firefighters Local 2091 informed the State Arson Squad that no more of the paid firefighters would take the polygraph test. The IAFF Local

2091 stated, "The request impinges upon their individual integrity and implies a suspicion of wrongdoing." It went on to say, "The Oregon State Police has assured the union that there is no reason to suspect a paid firefighter of arson or other involvement. The firefighters deny any involvement in any of the fires in the district during the recent suspension of the paid firefighters. They pledge full cooperation with Cpl. (Greg) Baxter in a complete investigation."

There had always been a struggle in getting voters' approval for an annual budget or tax base. But, on May 17, 1988, Winston-Dillard Rural Fire District submitted a tax base of $695,155 to the voters, and, to their surprise, 574 voted in favor and 570 voted against the tax base. After 35 years of trying, the measure passed on the first submission. The department breathed a sigh of relief after carrying that budgetary burden for so many years. However, there was a technical glitch made by the Elections Division. Some of the voters, who voted against the measure, were dismayed and furious. On June 6, 1988, Gay Fields, Douglas County Clerk, sent a letter to the members of the District Board. The letter that addressed the Board read:

> Enclosed herewith are the official final results of the Winston-Dillard Fire District Tax Base election held May 17, 1988. The canvass is complete and the results are official, however, we must inform you that an error occurred in the distribution of ballots in Precinct 55. It appears that the election board for that precinct did not distinguish between electors which were coded in the poll book as being in the fire district from electors coded in the poll book as being outside the fire district. By matching the ballot stubs with the poll book it appears that 154 electors that were in your district did not receive a ballot coded for the fire measure and 14 people out of the district did receive a ballot coded for the fire district measure. We cannot, of course, tell how the electors voted that received the incorrect ballots, as when the stub is removed, the ballots are the same. ORS 258 provides that any elector in your district has until June 27, 1988 to file a petition of contest in Circuit Court.

Fortunately for the Fire Department, after June 27, 1988, the results of the tax base election was considered final since no one had filed a petition of contest in the Circuit Court. From that date the department never looked back and set its compass on progress and professionalism. It expanded its limits to include a 50 mile radius with Winston as the hub and serves about 15,000 citizens. The district now provides an ambulance service that includes all of Camas Valley to the county line with Coos Bay and all the communities between Brockway, Olalla and Tenmile. It currently enjoys a class 4 protection rating. With an expansion and consolidation plan in action, it began saving funds to replace the 50-year-old obsolete fire station. By May 2004 the department had $3.1 million in savings, grants, loans and in-kind donations to construct its new fire station. In February 2005 the Winston-Dillard Fire Department took possession of its new building. It now stands as a landmark for one of the most functional and attractive fire departments in Douglas County.

Winston-Dillard Fire District built 2005

References:
The News Review 1952 - 2005, Fire District Scrap Book, Fire District News letter, Interviews with the chief and staff. W-DFD Logo: Compliments of Winston Fire District. Other photo by the author.

DISTRICT STATISTICS

WINSTON-DILLARD WATER BOARD OF COMMISSIONERS OCTOBER 4, 1948

Marshall Haughn	Chairman
Cornelius C. Fosback	Secretary
Paul B. Hult	Treasurer
Frank True	
Roy Gordon	

WINSTON-DILLARD WATER DISTRICT SUPERINTENDANTS

Lou Shigley	1958 – 1974
Elmer Mills	1974 – 2004
Jerry Kimbrell	2004 – 2004
Robert Young	2005 - Present

WINSTON-DILLARD FIRE BOARD OF DIRECTORS JUNE 1952

Forest Dean Collins	Chairman
Roy Fisher	
George Tipton	
Pat Manley	
Cyril Nichols	

WINSTON-DILLARD FIRE DISTRICT CHIEFS

J. C. Welch	1953 – 1954
Robert Nichols	1954 – 1955
Barney Shepherd	1955 – 1957
Mike Neeley	1957 – 1964
Earnest Adams	1964 – 1968
Anthony Vicari	1968 – 1975
Donald Boyd	1975 – 1975 Acting Chief
Dennis McGirk	1975 – 1976
Jerry Hall	1977 – 1998
William Belding	1998 – 2003
Stan Wagaman	2003 – 2004
Robert Nicholls	2004 – 2012
Ken McGinnis	2012 – Present

GREEN SANITARY DISTRICT FORMATION CONTROVERCY

The name of Mrs. John Lucas has long been forgotten in Green's history. However, her name should have been embossed on a plaque and hung in the office of Green Sanitary District in memory of her concerns for the health of the community, initiatives, volunteerism, and tenacity in getting the movement started to form a sanitary district. In spite of the hard work, insults, name calling and disappointments endured by the Board of Directors for almost eight years, she saw the district's objectives come to fruition. In January of 1963 Green Sanitary Facilities went into operation. It was a sigh of intense relief coupled with great jubilation for those who supported the movement.

Green Sanitary District Office

The year was 1954. Green was growing rapidly with an estimated population of about 1,500 people. Like many communities across the State of Oregon, Green had severe sewer problems. There were many leaking septic tanks and outhouses. But, most evident and disturbing, was sewer runoff from leaking septic tanks off Linnell Avenue onto the grounds of Green Elementary School and sewerage leaching into Roberts Creek by way of drainage ditches. Since Green was and still is not incorporated, the state brought pressure on the County Health Department to make that community have a sewer system. In the spring of 1954, Douglas County Health Department, with the aid of a representative from North Roseburg Sanitary District, held several meetings with small groups of the community.

A committee of 10 volunteers, headed by Mrs. John Lucas, went from door to door soliciting funds to pay for a feasibility study to determine if a sewer system was possible and affordable. The group, calling itself the "Green Sanitary District Committee," hired the engineering firm Cornell, Howland, Hayes and Merryfield from Corvallis, Oregon. The cost of the study was $500 for the survey and $200 for elections and filing fees. The Committee met their financial goals from donations and a talent show held at the Green Elementary School. The report from the engineering firm called for the formation of a sewer taxing district, a complete sewer system and a disposal plant. On July 20, 1955, a public hearing was held at the county courthouse on the matter of creating a sanitary district at Green. Judge Carl C. Hall presided over the hearing. There were no objections at the hearing to the proposed district. The court then set the date for the elections for September of 1955. Prior to the elections, at one of the public meetings at the Green School, the boundaries for the proposed district were set. It would serve 355 homes at an estimated cost of $355,000. That cost would be paid by taxes, a $3.50 monthly service charge, and the homeowners would carry the cost of the laterals to their property.

On September 7, 1955, the residents of Green voted overwhelmingly in favor of forming a sanitary district. That credit belonged to Mrs. Lucas and the Green Sanitary Committee for their hard work of inspiring the residents to vote "yes" for a district. The vote was 117 in favor and 42 against. Also, three members were elected to the sanitary board from the eight candidates nominated. They were Allen Petersdorf, 86 votes, Warren Engdahl, 85 votes and Richard Terrell, 60 votes. At the board's first meeting Mr. Petersdorf was elected president of the board. Attorney William D. Green, representing a group of residents from the western part of the district, presented the board with a petition of 52 names who opposed inclusion in the district. The group claimed their area was rural not urban and did not need a sewer system. The board accepted the petition. However, Edward D. Murphy, attorney for the district, explained that "the law does not provide for a portion of the district to withdraw from it." He told the group that the only solution would be to dissolve the newly formed sanitary district and then organize a new one. He explained that "an area can be annexed, but not de-annexed." One week later a committee of residents began circulating petitions calling for the dissolution of the sanitary district. They were opposed to the placement of the district's boundaries and the high cost each property owner would have to bear. In less than two weeks the committee presented the board with a petition containing 195 names calling for the dissolution of the district. According to state law, the committee had more than the 15 percent of the registered voters in the community necessary to call an election. Therefore, an election was scheduled for November 22, 1955.

For three consecutive weeks, the "Reader Opinions" in *The News Review* was the convenient forum for the residents of Green to vent their feelings for or against the dissolution of the sanitary district. Those who sought dissolution couldn't see 350 homeowners building a $367,450 sewer system while those favoring the continuance of the district countered by quoting the engineer's cost of $312 for the normal individual home hook-up plus a monthly service charge of $3.50. The heat of the controversy radiated in newspapers across the county. When the votes were counted on September 22, 1955, Green Sanitary District weathered the controversial storm by a margin of eight votes. Voters in the community turned down an attempt to dissolve the sanitary district. The votes were 163 against the dissolution and 158 in favor.

The Board of Directors began the year 1956 with a new president. Allen Petersdorf resigned from the board, and Warren Engdahl was elected as president. The Douglas County Court appointed James C. McCarty to fill the vacant position. The first item on the board's agenda for its first meeting of the year was another petition calling for the dissolution of the sewer district. About 16 percent of the 510 registered voters in the district had signed the petition. Edward Murphy, attorney for the district, explained that "the state law on sanitary districts is silent on the number or frequency of elections on the matter." The election date was called for February 2, 1956, at the Green Elementary School from 8 AM to 8 PM. Meanwhile, the board approved a contract with the engineering firm Cornell, Howland, Hayes and Meryfield to complete phase two of the engineering works which included surveys, test-holes, and preliminary designs of the sanitary sewers, the sewerage treatment facility, and preparation of cost estimates to serve as a basis for a bond issue. The board hired Ms. Orpra Rutan as secretary to the board. Again, during the days leading up to the election, the "Reader Opinions" in *The News Review* was used to "trash talk" those for and against the dissolution. However, the results were embarrassing and disappointing for those on both sides of the issue. The dissolution failed by one vote. Several recounts of the votes showed the tally as 187 to 186 against the dissolution.

Five weeks later Calvin Stroup, chairman of the Dissolution Committee, presented the board with another petition calling for the dissolution of the sanitary district for a third time. With no tax dollars to pay for those elections, a complaint was lodged with the court. Attorney General Robert Y. Thornton ruled: "there is no limit to the number of elections which can be held to dissolve a sanitary district, and that no way exists legally to make the petitioners pay for the election." Since cost was always the optimum word used by those debating against the formation of the district, the board proposed mediation between the district and the Committee for Dissolution in order to resolve the impasse. The Dissolution Committee rejected the board's proposal and countered with its own. It called on the board to abandon the sanitary district for five years. During that period, the board should prohibit the holding of public meetings, should stop all engineering designs on the proposed sewer system and dismiss the engineering firm, the attorney and the secretary. The Dissolution Committee argued that by holding the district in abeyance the community would continue to grow and would have increased in assessed valuation, and, therefore, it would be possible to have a sewer district at a cost affordable to all. The board rejected the committee's proposal, calling it illegal.

In response to the controversy surrounding the Green Sanitary District, the Douglas County Health Department sent a stern letter to the board regarding the health hazards in the community. The letter states: "It is the opinion of the Douglas County Health Department that continued building in Green area and disposal of household sewerage by means of septic tanks and subsurface disposal fields will only add to the existing nuisance and health hazard. Therefore, the policy of the department will be to render opinions that there should be no building allowed in the Green area until such a time as approved sanitary sewers are installed and approved sewerage disposal is provided." Another agency annoyed with the conditions in Green was the Federal Housing Administration. Its letter to the board stated that the area "constitutes a desirable residential area with the exception that inadequate disposal of sewerage within the area constitutes a health hazard and introduces into the area a serious value destroying element." The letter went on to inform the board that the FHA will "not favorably act on applications for mortgage insurance within the area until an acceptable sewerage system was put in place." The letters sent ripples of ambiguity among supporters for dissolution of the Sanitary District. The Committee for Dissolution responded in a release statement, charged that the agencies were "arbitrary and discriminatory" and insisted on having the district dissolved. A scheduled date of May 10, 1956, was set for the elections. Meanwhile, James McCarty resigned from the board and the County Court replaced him with Kenton L. Gum.

The district's engineering firm completed the preliminary report on the design and cost of the sewer disposal system. That cost was discussed in two scheduled meetings at Green Elementary School. In anticipation of the upcoming third dissolution election, the report enunciated concerns if the District didn't win by an overwhelming majority and expressed skepticism regarding the selling of a bond issue at a reasonable rate of interest. With regard to the cost of the entire system, which was comprised of the sewer mains and a treatment plant, the firm recommended that the district send its effluence to Roseburg to be treated at their new plant since it was less expensive than building a treatment plant in Green. The cost estimates for constructing a plant in Green gave a healthy edge to connecting to the Roseburg plant. They were $112,278 for the joint usage method and $134,900 for a separate sewerage treatment plant. The cost did not include the cost of maintenance of the plant. The total cost of the sewer mains was estimated at $195,794. The Dissolution Committee examined the preliminary survey for the possible sewer construction in Green but still held a firm stand on dissolution of the district citing "cost" as the main reason. Once again, the "Reader Opinions" was the launching pad for emotions from those on both sides of the issue. Green Sanitary District won the election on May 10, 1956, but by a slim margin of 226 to 217 votes. The Dissolution Committee was jubilant. They sent a letter to the editor of *The News-Review* expressing thanks and appreciation for the publication of all their articles. In the letter the committee thanked the voters who supported their cause.

With the support from the majority of the residents of the beleaguered sanitary district, the board sought advice from the engineers of the Federal Housing Administration and that of the State Sanitary Authority with regard to its future. It also received a letter from the County Building Department informing it of its decision to halt all building permits for new construction in Green until an acceptable sewer system was put in place. Suggestions from a meeting with the engineers gave the board a spark of confidence. It then called for a budget hearing for a sum of $7,711 for the 1956 to 1957 fiscal year, which included $2,996.52 for expenses already incurred. That proposed budget went to the voters and surprisingly passed with a comfortable margin of 183 to 110 votes on July 16, 1956. In a bold move Mrs. Lucas and the Committee in Support of the Sanitary District collected 261 signatures on a petition requesting a bond election to raise money for construction of sewer facilities. On August 27, 1956, the board held a remonstrance hearing of the property owners within the five proposed sub-divisions of the district. According to state law, Ed Murphy, attorney for the district, informed the board that "a two-thirds remonstrance against the proposed sewer by the property holders in any of the five sub-divisions is necessary to keep that sub-division out of the Sanitary District." At that meeting the Board received 30.4 percent of remonstrance letters from the five sub-divisions.

The first glimmer of good news came to the troubled sanitary district when it learned via its engineering firm that it had been qualified for a grant of 30 percent of the total cost of construction of sewerage treatment and related facilities according to a new Federal Water Pollution Act. The grant was secured through the State Sanitary Authority. It was approximately $36,000 for the proposed pump station and force main to deliver the effluence to the Roseburg treatment plant. Unfortunately, federal grants were contingent on the financing of the entire project whether by sale of bonds or by loans. The district was given until December 1957 to sell the bonds.

The Committee in Support of the Sanitary District presented the board with a petition requesting an increase in the membership of the board from three to five members. The board voted in favor and had the measure placed on the ballot for the December 1956 election. Supporters for the sanitary district were surprised and rather perplexed to see Calvin C. Stroup, chairman of the Dissolution Committee, seeking a position on the board. Of the six candidates who competed for two positions on the Board, William J. House drew 120 votes and Leland A. Stadig received 110. On the advice of their engineering firm, Cornell, Howland, Hayes and Merryfield, the Board signed a contract for 25 years with the City of Roseburg to receive and process effluence from Green sanitary system. The contract called for Green's Board to pay the City of Roseburg an annual lump sum of $2,000 per year and an additional cost of $15 per million gallons of effluence for a year's total not less than $1,000. The contract would have become null and void if the sewer system was not built in Green within two years from the signing of the contract.

In an ambitious and audacious move, the board voted to change the assessment method of financing the proposed sewer construction project by putting the entire cost of the construction into a general obligation bond issue. The intent was to ease the burden of payment on the residents of the district. It then called for a remonstrance hearing on the proposed change. It received four remonstrance letters, but they ran into stiff opposition at the hearing from representatives of two mills, Umpqua Plywood Corporation and United States Plywood Corporation, with threats of moving out of the district. They called for a re-evaluation of the proposed financing method. Those mills made up 43 percent of the assessed valuation, and the revised plan of financing would have hit them the hardest. The plan called for industries and utilities to carry most of the load of amortizing the $320,000 bond issue. However, from the content of the two remonstrance letters from the mills, the board adopted a compromise on financing the debt service on the proposed bond issue for the sewer construction. The compromise came in the form of an ordinance. It set the sewer service charge at $4 per month to affect a lower millage rate against property owners. Also, it increased the proposed bond to $355,000, which would be amortized through a property levy for 25 years. The board then set the date of the bond election for Monday, May 20, 1957.

After the votes were counted on Monday night, the $355,000 bond election was approved by the voters with an overwhelming majority of 209 to 93 votes. This result brought an atmosphere of joy and celebration mixed with utter surprise. The president of the Sanitary Board thanked the voters and pledged expediency in getting the sewer system to the district. The board's attorney was given the task of advertising the sale of the $355,000 bond. Both the bond and stock market were in a slump, and as a result there were no offers to buy the bond. At the time of the advertisement of the bond, the opposition to the sewer district came alive and that helped to keep the bond buyers away. The board held a budget hearing for $4,455, the amount that was needed to operate during the 1957-1958 fiscal year. On July 1, 1957, the voters of the Green District again approved the proposed budget by a vote of 58 to 24.

Green Sanitary District was facing terrible odds: a severe depressed bond market and a vociferous opposition. The district was given another month's extension until January 1958 to have the bond sold to be eligible for the grant. A glimmer of hope came but quickly disappeared. The Federal Housing and Home Financing Agency agreed to loan the district the $355,000. This was made possible through a bill in Congress, which called on agencies like the HHFA to make loans to small communities with a population of less than 10,000 that were struggling to get loans. The controversy over financing the sewer system in Green reignited. The Committee for Dissolution of the district responded with a petition of 59 names and a letter asking Director L. R. Durkee of the Agency in Seattle, WA, not to approve the loan because it was too costly and unaffordable. The committee took their fight one step further. It sent letters to state senators Neuberger and Wayne Morse explaining their case. The senators promised to look into the matter. In response, the Sanitary Board's president Engdahl rebutted with a long letter to Director Durkee. He outlined the necessity for the financing, the health hazards the community was facing and gave a breakdown of the engineer's cost for each property owner. He also meticulously outlined the history of the formation of the district and the three dissolution elections the district survived. He concluded by rejecting the inflated cost and false assertions given to him by the opposition. The Opposition Committee made a telephone call to Director

Durkee and personally told him again its side of the controversy. In response, Mr. Durkee told the committee that the agency's policy was "not to make loans where opposition was strong." While waiting for a decision from the Housing and Home Financing Agency regarding the loan of $355,000, the State Sanitary Authority granted Green Sanitary District a second extension of time before losing $36,000 in federal funds. The time was dependent on the decision reached by the Housing and Home Financing Agency.

On July 7, 1958, Green Sanitary Board received a disappointing letter from the Federal Housing and Home Financing Agency denying the district the loan of $355,000 for the sewer system in Green. Acting Director A. F. Moberg, cited community opposition to the sewer project as the main reason, but also expressed high cost as another factor considered in the agency's denial of the loan. And, unfortunately, the district lost the $36,000 in federal grant aid. The board was stunned by the rejection and the loss of the grant, but nevertheless continued to function with optimism. On the other hand, the committee opposing the sanitary district wallowed in a pool of "wait and see" attitude. The Green Board again advertised the $355,000 bond for sale. The December 1958 election for two directors, whose terms had expired, was poorly attended. Director Robert Boehm was re-elected for three years with 50 votes and Floyd Warner was elected with 40 votes for three years taking Kenneth Gum's position. Gum had declined reelection.

With just one month left on the two-year contract with the City of Roseburg for receiving and processing sewer effluence from Green, supporters of the district packed the Roseburg council chambers with a petition seeking a continuance on the contract. Ed Murphy, attorney for the District, addressed the Council. He gave the Council a briefing on the district's misfortune for the past two years and begged the Council for an extension on the contract. In May of 1959 the Roseburg City Council approved to extend the original contract for another two years. It was a decision that brought applause and joy to the Green residents in the council chambers.

The month of May was surely a lucky month for the troubled sanitary district. State Senator Daniel Dimick informed the Green

Board of Directors through its secretary that Governor Hatfield had signed into law a bill giving sanitary districts the opportunity to make application for the sale of bonds directly to the State of Oregon. The bill was brought before the legislature by the Douglas County delegation of Senator Dimick and Representatives Al Flegel and W. O. Kelsay. The new state bill, the first of its kind, allowed any sanitary district in the state struggling to sell its bonds on the open market to be able to sell those bonds to the state if the bonds were approved for investment. The Green Board of Directors wrote Senator Dimick a letter expressing thanks and appreciation for getting the bill passed. In the letter the board expressed its appreciation by saying, "we feel that it would be of much help to sanitary districts like ours, faced with difficult financial problems." Money for such bonds came from earmarked funds called the Sanitary District Sewerage System Revolving Fund. Later on, the legislature revised the law to permit a county court to purchase bonds from sanitary districts. The year of 1959 slid away with very little accomplished except for the re-election of two board members in December.

The headache of financing the sewer construction project for the district was about to go away, but the pain of the opposition was still present. Green Sanitary Board made a request that the county buy the $355,000 bond for construction of its sewer system. Since Green was unincorporated, the court referred the application to District Attorney Avery Thompson for a ruling on its legality. The district attorney consulted the attorney general on the matter who advised that the action was legal if a master plan was used. The purpose of the master plan, his letter explained, was "to make certain of coordination of agencies of community development and to avoid inefficiencies, inconsistencies and waste." The court called on Green Sanitary Board to prepare a "master plan" and to explain the method the district hoped to use in disposing of its sewerage. The board immediately did, and enclosed a copy of the contract it had with the City of Roseburg. The board became infused with confidence and felt assured of a positive decision from the court. On the other hand, the opposition was very vocal and disruptive at it meetings. Mrs. Margaret Cross, then leader of the opposition, told the board that its group had hired an engineer to examine the cost of construction and found it way out of line since it had been based on 1957 estimates. The board responded by giving her a copy of the revised estimates prepared in January of 1960 by its engineering firm of Cornell, Howland, Hayes and Merryfield. The estimates were 11 mills for 25 years, a $250 connection fee and a $4 a month sewer service charge. Once again, the "Reader Opinions" in *The News Review* became the center stage to sound off emotions and hostilities for or against the sewer system in Green.

With the advent of new technology, Green District learned about a new and inexpensive form of sewer treatment called the oxidation pond or sewerage lagoon treatment system. It was an engineering design to purify sewerage through natural process. That kind of sewer treatment was being used at Klamath Falls with much success. State sanitarian T. M. Gerow of Grants Pass described the lagoon system to the board and a group of Green's residents. He gave a slide show of a lagoon at the Green Elementary School and explained that the system was virtually self-maintaining and was odorless when operating properly. He explained that cost of installation of a lagoon for disposal and treatment of sewer waste was far less than that of building a sewerage treatment plant or piping sewer effluence three miles to Roseburg as had been planned. He told them that the land, which was estimated at 20 acres for the size of the Green community, would be the most expensive item of the construction complex.

The board, with the approval of its engineering firm, made its decision in the first meeting in January 1961 to use an oxidation lagoon system to solve its sewerage waste problem. It also voted to hold another bond election, since it had been about four years since the residents of the district had voted and had passed the $355,000 obligation bond issue. The board's decision had to do with the many changes that had taken place within the district and an improvement in the bond market. It set the date of the election for April 24, 1961, and began an aggressive campaign to inform the residents of the community. Ken Luderman, a director of the board of the district, was a guest speaker at the Douglas County Realty Board's first meeting of 1961 and used that opportunity to promote the acquisition of a sewer system in Green and the scheduled election for the $355,000 obligation bond to construct that system. In an unprecedented gesture Dr. John Donnelly,

Douglas County Health Officer, sent a letter to *The New-Review* urging the residents of Green to vote "yes" on the $355,000 obligation bond in the scheduled election on April 24, 1961. He described the conditions as "deplorable" and cited a high propensity for the spread of several internal virus diseases including infectious hepatitis as a result of the existence of several unsanitary conditions in the district. The opposition, which had dwindled in size, fired back with a letter to the editor of *The News Review*. It claimed the cost was too high, especially in light of high unemployment in the district. The letter especially called attention to US Plywood's closure of its operation in Green, leaving the residents to pick up that defunct company's share of the taxes.

Voters in Green Sanitary District again approved the floating obligation bond for construction of a sewer system by an overwhelming majority of 236 to 85 votes. The Board of Directors was thankful and celebratory and promised to have the sewer system built and in operation within 18 months. On the other hand, the results of the election were a stunning disappointment for the opposition, and it gradually dropped its fight with the district. Again, the board offered the bonds for sale, and unfortunately, after several months on the market, had only one offer at 5.04 per cent. The interest was too high and the board rejected it. About a week after the board rejected the offer, State Treasurer Howard C. Belton notified the district that the state would consider purchasing the bond at the rate of 4.5 per cent if the board would consent to the state's conditions in the form of a resolution. The conditions were:

- "The state treasurer will consider only general obligation bonds in which all affected property is made security for the bonds.
- The district will contract no other debt without permission of the state treasurer so long as the bonds remain unpaid.
- The district will continue service and connection charges so long as any of the bonds are held by the state unless approval of the state treasurer is obtained for any change."

The Board took the necessary legal steps to make its bonds suitable for the state, and within two weeks it adopted the state's conditions as stipulated in the form of a resolution and had it delivered to State Treasurer Howard Belton.

Then, in August of 1961, a memorable month for the Board of Directors, the State Treasurer, Howard Belton, agreed to buy the bonds. He called a meeting with all five board members and staff of the District, the County Court, County Commissioner Elmer Metzger, Dr. John Donnelly, Douglas County Health Officer, and George Gratke, President of Roseburg Chamber of Commerce. They consulted on: the current unsanitary conditions in Green District, the district's struggle to get funding for the past six years, the resilience of the community and its ability to have a sewer disposal system, the district's potential for growth (being a bedroom community for Roseburg) into an area of moderate-priced homes largely financed through FHA insured loans. However, what the assemblage of that meeting did not know was that Mr. Belton had investigated the situation in the area prior to the meeting. He first sent a staff member who had come to the area unannounced and spoke to some residents of the District, business members and bankers in Roseburg. After reporting his findings to Mr. Belton, he again sent a different employee of the department to investigate, but that time identifying himself as a staff of the State Treasury Department. Mr. Belton informed the group that his strategy used was to be sure he was investing tax-payer dollars wisely. Judge Jackson and Commissioner Metgzer told Mr. Belton that it was their opinion that Green would have an exceptional future as a residential community if sanitary disposal facilities were developed. They further noted the construction of a sewer disposal facility would immediately improve the value of properties in the area and therefore would make it possible to refinance property by its owners if necessary.

Then, in October 1961, Green Sanitary District scored yet another victory in its efforts to construct a sewer disposal system. U.S. Senator Maurine Neuberger informed the board that the Department of Health, Education and Welfare had approved a grant in the sum of $52,170 for construction of a sewerage stabilization pond and pump stations for the district's proposed sewerage disposal system. The board located and purchased the site for the oxidation ponds across the river from the district on the north side of the South Umpqua River. That area was chosen since it was out of sight and would not be a nuisance to the community. The District Engineering Firm began the survey for the road to the ponds, the sewer mains and the sewer easements. The year ended on a good note for the district with the re-election of two board members whose terms on the board had ended. They were Floyd Warner and Kenneth Luderman.

On a cold and rainy night in February 1962, the Green Elementary School was packed with over 100 residents from the District. They came to get a progress report and see the construction plans for the proposed sewer disposal system. There was a polite demeanor about that crowd as opposed to those of the past. There were no loud talking and "name-calling" in an effort to intimidate one side or the other. The assemblage in the room came with eagerness to learn from their board members and the engineers when the system would be ready for use. In the room was a panel of experts to explain the various facets of the project. The panel was made up of: Gordon Carlson, the new attorney for the district, Robert Harris of Douglas County Title Co., Lee Wimberly of Commercial Abstract, Engineer Don Hall, representing the firm Cornell, Howland, Hayes and Merryfield, and all five board members of the district. The board had received only 20 percent of the easements it needed for sewer mains that would be laid on private property; therefore, Floyd Warner, chairman of the board, made another request for more easements. He explained that it was far less expensive to lay sewer mains on private property rather than in road and street right-of ways. He predicted that the project would be ready for construction bids in March 1962.

As promised, Green Sanitary District advertised bids to construct sewer mains, sewerage stabilization ponds, pump stations, and a pressure main according to the design plans and specifications prepared by the engineering firm, Cornell, Howland, Hayes and Merryfield. In April the board awarded the contract to Selmar A. Hutchins of Roseburg from a list of 10 bidders for a contract sum of $400,052.98. The Roseburg contractor had the lowest bid. The engineer's estimates were $418,110. In July State Treasurer Howard Belton came to Green to get a first-hand look at the project in progress. He was very impressed and congratulated the board and the district on the work. He expressed delight at the large number of people who already had paid their connection fees in advance. He was also impressed by the large number of homeowners and low number of rentals in the district.

Finally, by mid-January 1963, Floyd Warner, Chairman of the Board of Directors, announced that the long awaited sewer system was completed and ready for use. He emphasized that homeowners and businesses would first have to apply for a permit before connecting to the system. Green Sanitary District's office then was located at the rear of Roberts Creek Water District office. At the end of the meeting, he expressed thanks and gave praise to the board, the secretary Ms. Rutan, and all those who assisted in making the district and the facility a reality. He especially pointed out Mrs. John Lucas and the committee for their hard work and perseverance for those long eight years.

Green Oxidation Lagoon 1963-1981

References:
The News Review 1954 -1963, Green Sanitary Records, Roberts Creek Water District Pamphlet. Photo of the Sanitary Lagoon donated by: Green Sanitary District and the other by the author.

Snapshots Along the Umpqua   89

CHAPTER FOUR

FROM COOS JUNCTION TO WINSTON

The area of Dillard, Brockway and Winston, as we know it today, was once called Civil Bend District. Local legend claims that the area was so called as a sarcastic gibe because the behavior of the people attending the horse-racing games in the district was raucous and uncivilized. In 1875 unexpectedly and for reasons unknown, the fairgrounds and racetrack closed. Later, in 1882, Reverend John Dillard gave permission to Southern Pacific Railroad Company to lay railroad tracks and build a railroad depot on his property, and the company named the railroad station and surrounding area Dillard. In 1889, when postal services were re-established to the western section of Civil Bend District (now named Brockway); the name was changed from Civil Bend District to Brockway. This was in honor of the distinguished pioneer Beman B. Brockway who was a resident of Civil Bend District at the time. In 1893, when postal services were established in the home of Pioneer William Chauncy Winston, the northeast section of Civil Bend District was renamed Winston. The service was discontinued in 1903 due to insufficient customers, and the area was then served by the Camas Valley mail route out of Roseburg. Most of the area's residents made their living from farming and raising stock. In addition to growing vegetables, the Winston family operated a ferry near their home on the South Umpqua River between Winston and Roseburg. A bridge was later constructed in 1890 downstream from the ferry.

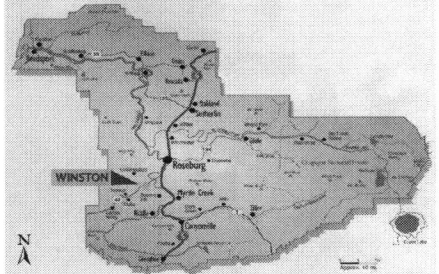

The education of children was very important to the pioneers in the Winston Community. In 1878 Winston School District No. 48 was formed and a one-room school was built on a knoll

Winston School 1890

overlooking the area now called Sherry Street. By 1914 the school was too small, and a bigger one was built on an acre of land donated by J. H. Booth located on the southeast corner which is now Brosi Road and Highway 99. By 1940 that school was too congested for the volume of students, and District No. 48 agreed to consolidate with Dillard District No.116.

Between the early 1900s and the middle 1940s Orchard Tracts in the Winston valley (today known as Winston Section Road) was the envy of Douglas County. The beautiful Orchard Tract was subdivided into parcels ranging from five acres to 30 acres, thus attracting higher income residents from the county. Among the residents in the tract were three doctors - Dr. Hoover, Dr. George Baker and Dr. George Bradborn. The houses in the tract exhibited architectural flair ranging in styles from Queen Ann to simple bungalows. Many of the houses, including the Winston home built in 1878, are still livable. Today some of the houses in that area are included on the county's register as historic places.

By 1913, when the footbridge over the South Umpqua River connecting Dillard to communities like Kent Creek, Willis Creek and Brockway was replaced with a wagon bridge, Dillard became the hub for those communities and of Winston. (See the books - *Memories of Long Ago* and *The History of Dillard* by Sherley Clayton.) The very few residents who lived in Winston at the time shopped and socialized in Dillard, Brockway and Roseburg. In 1920, when the north-south Pacific Highway, later called Highway 99, was completed, it finally gave Winston a direct link to Dillard. The two-lane highway was only 16 feet wide then. In 1922 the Coos Bay Highway, later known as Highway 42, intersected Pacific Highway at Winston, thus connecting it with Tenmile, Camas Valley and Coos Bay on the Oregon Coast. Soon after the merging of the two highways, Charlie McGinnis opened a blacksmith shop at the junction on the north side of Coos Bay Highway. That section of Winston was soon referred to as Coos Junction. It was so called since horse and buggy taxis picked up passengers at the junction who came there from the coast and areas west of Winston to take them to Dillard to catch the train to Portland.

In 1923 Otis Hopple started a campground business at the junction on the south side of Coos Bay Highway where Abby's

Pizza and Astro Service Station are today. He rented cabins to migrant workers who came to the area to work harvesting fruits. However, it should be noted that the majority of the migrant workers did get their room and board from the farmers of the orchards at which they worked. In the 1930s, during the acute years of the Great Depression, the price of the fruit and vegetable market tumbled. Some of the farmers in the area defaulted on their loans and, as a result, lost their farms. The farmers throughout Douglas County suffered another setback during the early stages of World War II when the price of prunes fell so low that they were losing money harvesting their crop. That demise worsened when prune trees from Glendale in Douglas County to the Willamette Valley in Lane County developed a disease and most of the trees died.

At the end of World War II there was a great surge in the timber industry in Oregon, and Douglas County led the state in timber revenues. The county experienced an influx of migrant workers from California (nicknamed the dust bowl people), Texas, Arkansas, Kentucky, Oklahoma, and Missouri seeking employment. Unfortunately, there were no housing accommodations in Winston or Dillard to handle the volume of workers who came there seeking employment in the woods and in the sawmills. Immediately, farmers and large land owners began capitalizing on the opportunity. Lands were subdivided into house lots; horse barns and chicken coops were partitioned into rooms and campgrounds and auto-courts were developed along Highway 99.

By 1948 there were over 1000 people living within a half-mile radius of the Coos Junction area. That explosion in the population precipitated the formation of a committee to handle basic needs of the community. The committee first focused on requesting postal services to the area. A post office was immediately established on July 21, 1948, not in the name of Coos Junction but in that of Winston. According to an article in *The News Review* dated June 17, 1948: "The department refused to use the name Coos Junction, because of possible confusion of that name with Cave Junction and Coos Bay". (Due to the over-crowding of many of the facilities which housed the Winston Post Office the service moved five times between 1948 and 2012.)

With rapid commercial growth along Highway 99 in the early 1940s, there were more than 25 businesses. However, they had no potable water, and the committee's next task was to tackle this issue. Paul B. Hult of Dillard, owner of the Hult Lumber Company, and Cornelius Fosback, also a businessman of Dillard, joined the Coos Junction Committee in an effort to form a water district. The committee collected the necessary petitions, and on October 1, 1948, the Winston-Dillard Water District was incorporated.

In 1949 a group of community-minded residents of Coos Junction started a community club. The group borrowed money from Charlie White to purchase seven and one half acres of land and built a community center. All the materials and labor for the 40' x 90' structure were donated by merchants, lumber mills and friends. The structure was designed to house a kitchen, a snack-bar, and a large hardwood dance floor, which was also used as a skating rink for children. The Community Club held its first dance in August of 1949. Dances were held every Saturday night thereafter. By December of 1949 the club was able to pay off its debt to Charlie from membership dues and revenues from the dances. The club held several discussions about developing the rest of the land into a park. In 1951 it agreed to sell it to Douglas County Parks Department. Coincidentally, following on the heels of that sale and maintenance arrangements, Mrs. Ulah Winston, wife of Harry A. Winston, donated five acres of land adjoining the club's parcel to Douglas County in honor of her late husband, who passed away in July of 1952. In addition, she gave the county the funds to develop a picnic area with a pavilion. In August of 1971 the Winston City Council renamed the park "Winston Community Park" instead of "Harry A. Winston Park" The Community Center was expanded several times over its 59 years of usage. With similar enthusiasm and spirit of volunteerism, a new community center was built in January of 2008, and the old one was demolished. This community park is located west of Edgewood Street, east of Grape Street and north of Thompson Avenue.

In the early 1950s Coos Junction, like many communities in Douglas County, was experiencing serious sanitary problems with outhouses and leaking septic tanks. The area had no garbage disposal facility, and house trash was indiscriminately thrown out.

The devastating flood of October 1950 exacerbated the misery of the sanitary conditions in the area. The State Sanitary Department approached Martin Suksdorf, owner of the Suksdorf Orchard Tract, to form a sanitary sewer district. Martin organized a committee and began investigating the feasibility and affordability of a sewer system for the area. Livability problems began to shake up the community when school bus drivers refused to go on certain streets to pick up children because the roads were impassable and dangerous. A sewer stench began coming from the open ditches on Highway 99, and bar-room fights were out of control. The opening of the Wigwam Dance Hall in 1949 and the Benetta Theater in 1950 on Highway 99, which were social outlets for the community, often created problems since there was no law enforcement in the area to uphold civility. Two churches, the Four Square Gospel Church on Jorgen Street, established in 1949, and the Christian Church on Gregory Street, which started in 1950, were not enough to bring about social and environmental order to the community. However, in June of 1952, Dr. Frederick A. Bracker, osteopathic physician and surgeon, brought a glimmer of hope to the area when he opened an emergency hospital and clinic with ambulance service on the southeast side of the junction of Highway 99 and Highway 42. In 1954 Dr. Bracker sold the hospital and clinic to Dr. Fletcher.

The newly formed Chamber of Commerce, whose mission at the time was: "let us boost the community," began to address such problems and many more. Just about everyone in the community depended on Roseburg Fire District for assistance in the event of a fire. Hence, the chamber formed a Winston-Dillard Fire District Committee. That committee was to inform the residents of the importance of a fire district, and, as a result, a lower rate of insurance. From the efforts of a door-to-door campaign, the committee collected the necessary signatures to file with Douglas County Court. In the election of June 6, 1952, the residents voted to form the Winston-Dillard Rural Fire District by an overwhelming majority.

Soon after the fire district was formed, the Winston Community Club met with the Chamber of Commerce to discuss incorporating Coos Junction into a city. In November of 1952, the Chamber hired Attorney Dudley Walton, of Roseburg, to come to the Community Hall to speak to the residents about the benefits of incorporation. More than 100 people jammed the meeting venue to hear Mr. Walton speak. He opened with a paradigm speech on the value of incorporation and said: "It would cost more in the long run for the Winston community to form its own sanitary, fire, water and road district than to incorporate." At the end of his talk, members of the audience participated in a question and answer session that resulted in a majority in favor of incorporation. The camaraderie and receptivity at the meeting energized the Chamber members and the Community Club to form a Coos Junction Committee. The newly formed committee prepared a pamphlet outlining 12 fundamental benefits to be gained from incorporating into a city. They are:

1. Sanitary sewers: Preliminary plans have been designed and tentatively approved for a sewerage system and disposal facilities. Incorporation would make these possible this year. Both the state and the county health departments have assured Winston that they'll aid an immediate construction when either the area incorporates or a sanitary district is established.
2. Street paving. Local government could improve streets with the aid of state and government funds available to corporations.
3. Storm drainage. This is part of the paving problem and local authority could handle it.
4. Street lighting. This would be simpler to secure if boundaries are established and the power to franchise granted.
5. Police protection. A system of officers on call immediately could be established.
6. Zoning restrictions. These could be formulated to protect investments and ban poor construction.
7. Traffic control. The "wide place in the road" treatment would be ended, with speeding controlled and fines imposed.
8. New business. As soon as health authorities remove existing bans new firms would spring up.

9. More homes. These would be possible when FHA and GI loans were available to builders.
10. Property value increase. The official status of an incorporated community would bring this about.
11. State highway and government funds. These are available to corporations in proportion to population.
12. Insurance rate decrease.

They then embarked on a house-to-house campaign to apprise the residents of the progress regarding incorporation and to distribute the pamphlets. The Chamber of Commerce hired Civil Engineer James R. Daugherty to prepare a map of the proposed boundaries for the incorporation. Several public meetings were held at the Winston-Dillard Water District office for property owners to express their likes or dislikes for the proposed boundaries. One of the meetings, according to Mr. Daugherty, was to determine "who wants in or who doesn't." Residents living in the Winston Section Road Area and those northwest of Highway 99 asked to be removed. A few home owners who lived close to the center of the proposed city wanted to be out. Mr. Daugherty pointed out that they couldn't stay out unless they lived on the fringes. He went on to explain: "We can't have islands." The meeting erupted into heated discussions from opponents who opposed the proposed incorporation. However, by the end of the meeting a hand vote was taken showing a majority in favor of the proposed city. The Incorporation Committee collected the necessary signatures for the petition needed to file with Douglas County Court. The Chamber of Commerce then hired Attorney Harrison Winston to prepare and file the Winston incorporation petition. The court set the election for April 16, 1953, at the Winston-Dillard Water District office. However, backers of the Winston incorporation suffered two setbacks when

Coos Junction 1950

the dates of the election were changed on two occasions. The first was due to a faulty boundary description, and the other was a conflict with a Winston-Dillard Water District bond election. Finally, on June 12, 1953, the Winston incorporation proposal passed 159 to 57. On June 21, 1953, Douglas County Court made it official. The City of Winston then became the twelfth incorporated city in Douglas County. For the next 60 days, 12 men and one woman squared off in a door-to-door campaign vying for the five city council positions. On August 25, 1953, the first Winston City Council was elected. The five elected candidates with the highest votes were: Paul Bender 164, Frank True 122, Ed B. Welch 103, Martin Suksdorf 100 and Roy Fisher 96.

The newly elected City Council immediately formed a united bond. They withdrew the city from the Winston-Dillard Water District and the Winston-Dillard Fire District. They held their first meeting at Frank True's Grocery Store on September 21, 1953. A lighted lantern was placed outside the store to inform the public as to where the meeting was being held. The next four meetings were held at private establishments, and again the lighted lantern was used as a marker. However, with the completion of the Winston-Dillard Fire District building on Highway 99, the council accepted the use of the Fire District meeting hall on December 21, 1953. Between September 1953 and December 1954 the following is a snapshot of some of the important decisions the city council arrived at. They:

- Appointed experienced businessman Paul Bender as mayor of the city of Winston and hired Harrison Winston as the city's attorney.
- Authorized a census to be taken in Winston so that the city could receive its share of highway and liquor revenues. A population of 1,960 was established for the new city.
- Issued franchise contracts to the companies of Pacific Power, Pacific Telephone and Telegraph, garbage disposal and taxi service.
- Hired Dean Guyer as city recorder and Jim Tabor as municipal judge.
- Passed Ordinance #1 calling for an election to remain with Winston-Dillard Fire District. In the election, held on

November 10, 1953, the canvassing of the votes showed 61 votes in favor and no vote against the proposition.
- Divided the chores of running the city among four council members.
- Agreed to buy water from Roberts Creek Water District.
- Hired retired Roseburg City Manager W. A. Gilcrest to assist the city in getting a charter, budget and other city affairs started.
- Joined the League of Oregon Cities.
- Accepted the streets and sewerage network at Ford, Hart and Peach-South Slope Subdivision from Baer Construction Company for one dollar. (The 44 houses at South Slope Subdivision were financed by Kenneth Ford for his supervisors and foremen in 1952. The sewer plant, which was located on Highway 99, became a nuisance to the community.)
- Began the selection process of finding an engineering firm to conduct a survey and feasibility study for the city's proposed sewer system.

The year of 1955, with a population of 2000, was quite a challenge for the "young" city council, but in spite of the many difficulties encountered, their achievements were commendable. The experience gained from the training given by W. A. Gilchrest gave them the confidence to consult and tackle serious problems. They appointed Frank True as the new mayor of Winston and welcomed J. V. Ryder as the new member of the council who replaced Martin Suksdorf. The following is another sampling of their accomplishments. They:

- Hired Lee Altendorf as the new municipal judge at the resignation of Jim Tabor.
- Organized a planning commission in March of 1955.
- Rented an office on Highway 99 and three months later established a city hall sinking fund. (The office was in the area now owned by "In and Out" restaurant.)
- Passed Ordinance No.19 setting an election date of August 16, 1955, to determine if the city residents wished to annex and become a part of the Winston-Dillard Water District.

- Hired Ben Scheele as the first police chief on July 25, 1955. (An incidence of an "almost riot" on Gregory Street on July 16, 1955, when the County Sheriff had to be called in to restore peace and order, forced the council to make that urgent decision.)
- Passed Curfew Ordinance No. 21 calling for minors under the age of 18 years to be off the streets by 10:30 p.m. except Fridays, Saturdays and Sundays when the curfew hour is midnight.
- Hired H. J. Kleve as city recorder to replace Dean Guyer.
- Hired Lloyd Tumlin as the first building inspector for the city.
- Winston voters approved the city's budget of $60,908.40, after the second attempt, by 100 yes votes and 72 no votes on June 21, 1955.
- Voters passed the first City Charter on August 16, 1955 by 117 yes votes to 6 no votes. The charter called for a name change from Coos Junction to Winston.
- Received an overwhelming victory from the voters on the $265,000 bond issue to construct a sewer collection and disposal system for Winston.
- Received a resounding majority in the election of August 16, 1955, in favor of the proposition to return to the Winston-Dillard Water District.
- Hired engineering firm Cornell, Howland, Hays and Merryfield to furnish engineering and surveying plans for the sewer collection and sewage disposal system.
- Received assistance from the Chamber of Commerce to prepare and install 67 street signs in the city.

At this juncture, redundancy is necessary in order to understand the following paragraph. It should be noted that between August and September of 1953 the history is unclear as to what transpired between the newly formed City Council and the Winston-Dillard Water Board of Directors. But the following actions indicated a rift had developed between the two governmental bodies. The City withdrew from both the Winston-Dillard Water District and the Winston-Dillard Rural Fire District. The first City Council meeting conducted on September of 1953 was held, not at the water district office, but at Frank True's Grocery Store annex on Highway 99. That action called for a lighted lantern to be placed outside the store to inform the public as to where the meeting was being held. The next five meetings of the council were held at various private establishments, again with the lighted lantern informing the public as to where the meetings were taking place. On November 10, 1953, the City of Winston voted 61 to zero to return and become a part of the Winston-Dillard Rural Fire District. On December 21, 1953, the Winston City Council held their meeting at the Winston-Dillard Fire meeting hall, the first public venue since its formation. The City of Winston remained out of Winston-Dillard Water District, purchasing its water directly from Roberts Creek Water District until August of 1955 when the city voted 117 to 6 to again become a part of said water district. However, the rift continued to deepen and later turned into controversy when the city posted a legal notice in *The News Review* on October of 1971 calling for a public meeting to discuss whether the city should remain in the Winston-Dillard Water District. The meeting took place at City Hall on October 18, 1971 before a packed audience. Many of the citizens who addressed the council were outraged and expressed their desire to remain in the water district. In a special meeting held the following week the council voted to remain in the above mentioned water district. Nevertheless, the friction remained a subtlety.

References:
The News Review 1948–1955, *Land of The Umpqua* by Stephen Dow Beckham, Winston City Council Minutes 1953-1971, *Growing Up With The* West, by Erma Gourley, *Stories Of Early Settlers and Dillard, Oregon* by Shirley Clayton, *Memoirs of the Winston Family* by Harrison Renner Winston

Snapshots Along the Umpqua   100

WINSTON MAYORS

1953-1955
Paul K. Bender

1955-1957
Frank O. True

1957-1959
Roy M Fisher

1959-1961
William D. Schell Sr.

1961-1963
Alfred Daniels

1963-1967
Normal A Lee

1967-1969
Erwin Gubser

1969-1971 & 1973-75
Jim Suiter

1972-1973 & 1975-81
Harley R Means

1981-1983
Betty Fortino

1983
George Jacobs

1983-1985
Marge Brady Charas

1985-1987
William Zuver

1987-1989
David Van Dermark

1989
Ken Huff

1989-2000
Jim McClellan

2001 - 2011
Rex Stevens

2011 - Present
Sharon Harrison

Courtesy: Leif Photography

WINSTON COUNCILORS

1953　　　Frank True (President)
　　　　　Ed Welch
　　　　　Roy Fisher
　　　　　Martin Suksdorf

1954　　　Frank True (President)
　　　　　Ed Welch
　　　　　Roy Fisher
　　　　　Martin Suksdorf

1955　　　Paul Bender (President)
　　　　　Roy Fisher
　　　　　Ed Welch
　　　　　J. V. Ryder

1956　　　Paul Bender (President)
　　　　　Roy Fisher
　　　　　Ed Welch
　　　　　J. V. Ryder (Resigned August 1956)
　　　　　William D. Schell, Sr. (Appointed August 1956)

1957　　　William D. Schell, Sr. (President)
　　　　　Art Griese
　　　　　Don Hatch
　　　　　Ed Welch

1958　　　William D. Schell, Sr. (President)
　　　　　Art Griese (Resigned September 1958)
　　　　　Don Hatch (Resigned July 1958
　　　　　Ed Welch
　　　　　Russell Turner (Appointed July 1958)
　　　　　Walter E. Brown (Appointed September 1958)

1959　　　A. B. Peterson (President)
　　　　　Russell Turner
　　　　　Arthur Hill
　　　　　Walter E. Brown

1960　　　　　　A. B. Peterson (President, resigned July 1960)
　　　　　　　　Glen Ryder (Appointed July 1960
　　　　　　　　Russell Turner
　　　　　　　　Walter Brown (Resigned July 1960)
　　　　　　　　Arthur Hill (Died May 1960)
　　　　　　　　Otto Jones (Appointed May 1960)
　　　　　　　　Milford D. Waters (Appointed September 1960)

1961　　　　　　Otto Jones (President, resigned September 1961)
　　　　　　　　Norman Lee
　　　　　　　　Harry Van Dermark
　　　　　　　　Glen Ryder (Resigned January 1961)
　　　　　　　　Waldo Jack Cooper (Appointed January 1961)
　　　　　　　　Dixie Meglason (Appointed September 1961)

1962　　　　　　Harry Van Dermark (President)
　　　　　　　　Jack Cooper
　　　　　　　　Dixie Meglason
　　　　　　　　Norman Lee

1963　　　　　　Marvin Green (President)
　　　　　　　　Erv Gubser
　　　　　　　　Harry Van Dermark
　　　　　　　　Alfred Daniels

1964　　　　　　Marvin Green (President)
　　　　　　　　Erv Gubser
　　　　　　　　Alfred Daniels
　　　　　　　　Harry Van Dermark

1965　　　　　　Erv Gubser (President)
　　　　　　　　Roy Fisher
　　　　　　　　Norman Slack
　　　　　　　　Marvin Green

1966　　　　　　Erv Gubser (President)
　　　　　　　　Norman Slack
　　　　　　　　Marvin Green
　　　　　　　　Roy Fisher (Resigned October, 1966)

Larry Vang (Appointed October 1966)

1967   Erv Gubser (Appointed Mayor April 1967)
Harley Means (President, appointed April 1967)
Marvin Green
Al R. Hooten (Appointed April 1967)
Larry Vang (Resigned August 1967)
Paul Holland (Appointed August 1967)

1968   Harley Means (President)
Marvin Green
Paul Holland
Al Hooten

1969   Harley Means (President)
Marvin Green
Erv Gubser (Resigned May 1969)
Larry Zuver (Appointed May 1969)
Al Hooten (Resigned November 1969)

1970   Harley Means (President)
Marvin Green (Resigned January 1970)
Larry Zuver
Doyle Sisco (Appointed January 1970)
Robert Duey (Appointed January 1970)
(Student Councilman – Steve Van Dermark)

1971   Jim Suiter (President)
Larry Zuver (Resigned February 1971)
Robert Duey
Parker
Ray Shaw (Appointed February 1971)
(Students Dorris Adams and Mark Hanson)

1972   Jim Suiter (President)
Robert Duey
Ray Shaw
Parker

1973	Robert Duey (President) Harley Means Ray Shaw (Resigned September 1973) Gary Spellman Joanne Riley (Appointed September 1973)
1974	Robert Duey (President) Joanne Riley Gary Spellman (Resigned October 1974) Harley Means James Ford (Appointed October 1974)
1975	Joanne Riley (President, resigned April 1975) James Ford (President from April) Louis Parkel Lloyd Johnson (Resigned April 1975) Walt Lindner (Appointed April 1975) Vivian Borges (Appointed April 1975)
1976	James Ford (President, resigned August 1976) Vivian Borges Louis Parkel Walt Lindner Art Griese (Appointed August 1976)
1977	Louis Parkel (President) Walt Lindner Vivian Borges Donald Shepherd
1978	Louis Parkel (President) Vivian Borges Donald Shepherd (Resigned March 1978) Walt Lindner (Resigned April 1978) Marjorie Brady (Appointed March 1978) George Goodwin (Appointed in April, resigned in July) Roy Fisher (Appointed July 1978)

1979   Marjorie Brady (President)
Vivian Borges
Erv Gubser
Daniel Seitz

1980   Marjorie Brady (President)
Vivian Borges
Daniel Seitz
Erv Gubser

1981   Marjorie Brady (President)
Erv Gubser
Steven Fisher
Daniel Seitz (Resigned July 1981)
Robert Duey (Appointed July 1981)

1982   Marjorie Brady (President)
Erv Gubser
Robert Duey
Steven Fisher (Resigned July 1982)
Jim Buckanan (Appointed July 1982)

1983   Erv Gubser (President)
Dennis Mills
Marjorie Vaughn
Jim Buckanan (Resigned July 1983)
Mary Lea Weinberg (Appointed June 1983)

1984   Erv Gubser (President)
Dennis Mills
Mary Lea Weinberg
Marjorie Vaughn

1985   Dennis Mills (President)
Marjorie Vaughn
Mary Lea Weinberg
Brian Otten (Resigned October 1985)
David Van Dermark (Appointed October 1985)

1986	Dennis Mills (President)
	Marjorie Vaughn
	David Van Dermark
	Mary Lea Weinberg (Resigned October 1986)
	Floyd Ledbetter (Appointed October 1986)
1987	Floyd Ledbetter (President)
	Dale Hudson (Resigned May 1987)
	Ron Cleveland
	Ken Hull
	Hazel Pettijohn (Appointed July 1987)
1988	Floyd Ledbetter (President)
	Hazel Pettijohn
	Ron Cleveland
	Ken Hull
1989	Floyd Ledbetter (President, resigned February 1989)
	Gus Jennings (President, recalled November 1989)
	Don Roberts
	James Milton (Appointed February 1989)
	Hazel Pettijohn
	Gary Vess (Appointed December 1989)
1990	Don Roberts (President)
	James Melton (Resigned February 1990)
	Bonnie Tufts (Appointed March 1990)
	Gary Vess
	Hazel Pettijohn (Died August 1990)
	Connie Robinson (Appointed November 1990)
1991	Don Roberts (President)
	Gary Vess
	Bonnie Tufts
	Connie Robinson
1992	Don Roberts (President)
	Gary Vess

                Bonnie Tufts
                Connie Robinson

1993   Don Roberts (President)
                Gary Vess
                Bonnie tufts
                Steve Smart

1994   Don Roberts (President)
                Bonnie Tufts
                Gary Vess
                Steve Smart

1995   Gary Vess (President)
                Christine Whalen
                Steve Smart
                John Steinfelt

1996   Gary Vess (President)
                Christine Whalen
                Steve Smart
                John Steinfelt

1997   Gary Vess (President)
                Christine Whalen
                John Steinfelt (Resigned November 1997)
                Chuck Johnson

1998   Gary Vess (President)
                Christine Whalen
                Chuck Johnson
                Donald Kuyper (Appointed February 1998)

1999   Gary Vess (President)
                Chuck Johnson
                Rex Stevens
                David Van Dermark

2000   Gary Vess (President)

                Chuck Johnson
                Rex Stevens
                David Van Dermark

2001   David Van Dermark (President)
                Bev Heyer
                Larry Wait
                Laura Duncan (Appointed February 2001)

2002   David Van Dermark (President)
                Bev Heyer
                Larry Wait
                Laura Duncan

2003   Larry Wait (President)
                Bev Heyer
                Laura Duncan
                Dick Hayes

2004   Larry Wait (President)
                Bev Heyer
                Laura Duncan
                Dick Hayes

2005   Laura Duncan (President)
                Dick Hayes
                Ken McGinnis
                Lucy Watson

2006   Laura Duncan (President)
                Dick Hayes
                Ken McGinnis
                Lucy Watson

2007   Ken McGinnis (President)
                Dick Hayes
                Christine Glen Knutson
                Chris Berquist

2008	Ken McGinnis (President) Dick Hayes Christie Glen Knutson Chris Berquist
2009	Christie Glen Knutson (President) Ken McGinnis Dick Hayes Sandy Lipphardt
2010	Christine Glen Knutson (President) Ken McGinnis Dick Hayes Sandy Lipphardt
2011	Christine Glen Knutson (President) Ken McGinnis Dick Hayes Sandy Lipphardt
2012	Christine Glen Knutson (President) Ken McGinnis (resigned 8/2012) Dick Hayes Sandy Lipphardt

Snapshots Along the Umpqua   110

CITY OF WINSTON ADMINISTRATORS 1969-2012

Al R. Hooten
1969-1972

Jim Herbison
1973-1974

Dale E. Ennor
1974-1982

Dave Waffle
1982-1987

Ron Schofield
1987-1990

Bruce Kelly
1990-2004

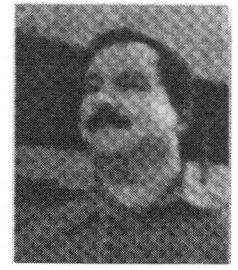

David Van Dermark
2004-Present

Photos: The News Review

CITY OF WINSTON STAFF

WINSTON POLICE CHIEF

Ben Scheele	1955 – 1959
Ray Oliver	1959 – 1961
Bill Hale	1961 – 1963
George Jacobs	1963 – 1975
Harold Forney	1975 – 1983
George Jacobs	1983 – 1988
Bruce Justis	1988 – 2004
Jamie Greer	2004 – Pro tem
Scott Gugel	2004 – Present

WINSTON CITY ATTORNEY

Harrison Winston	1953 – 1956
Karl Felker	1956 – 1971
Dean Heiling	1971 – 1972
Ron Pole	1972 – 1973
Bill Wolke	1973 – 1987
Bruce Coalwell	1987 – Present

WINSTON MUNICIPAL JUDGE

Jim Tabor	1953 – 1955
Lee Altendorf	1955 – 1957
H. J. Kleve	1957 – 1972
Darrell Johnson	1972 – 1979
Ralph Rawson	1979 – Pro tem
Darrell Johnson	1979 – 1986
Gerald Snyder	1986 – 1987 Pro tem
Gloria McGinnis	1987 – 1996
Andrew Johnson	1997 – Present

PUBLIC WORKS-STREETS/SEWER

Larry Exceen	1957 – 1957

Marvin White	1957 – 1963
Marshall Holmes	1963 – 1968
Marvin White	1967 – 1968
Dennis Mills	1968 – 1976

PUBLIC WORKS SUPERINTENDENT

Jim McClendon	1976 – 1979 Pro tem
Mike Parker	1979 – 1984
Jim McClendon	1984 – 1987
Eric Wilson	1987 – 2005
Jennifer Sikes	2005 – Present

AREA NEWSPAPERS

The Enterprise	1950s -1960s
The Winston Wire	1966 - 1967 (Editor: Ray Melton)
The Herald	1982 - 1982
Winston Area News	2000 - 2006 (Editor: Rosemary Smith)
Winston Reporter	2007 - 2007

CHAPTER FIVE
Biographies

THEODORE "TED" BENEDICT, JR.

The name Ted Benedict has been and will remain a fixture in the history of Tenmile, Oregon. Everyone knew him, and he knew just about everyone in that community. He was once owner of the Tenmile Store, postmaster, school board member, defacto law-enforcement officer, fire chief, and local historian. But most of all he has left a legacy of love, leadership, humility and steadfastness for the communities of Reston, Olalla, Porter Creek and Tenmile. This legendary citizen passed away at the age of 82. As a gesture of appreciation, the community of Tenmile honors his life with a gazebo and a plaque at his graveside in the Tenmile Cemetery. It is the first of its kind at that cemetery.

Courtesy of Tenmile Post Office

Ted was born in The Dalles, Oregon, on September 15, 1923. He was the son of Theodore "Dode" and Orelena Benedict. His sister Betty preceded him in death. He spent his early childhood in Ester, California. He later returned to Springfield, Oregon with his parents when he was a junior and graduated from Roseburg High School in 1941. Soon after graduation he was drafted into the US Navy during World War II. He was deployed to the Pacific region soon after Pearl Harbor was attacked. Ted was a navigator and a mechanic. He was decorated with the Distinguished Flying Cross and the Navy Unit Commendation. He was also deployed in South Korea during the Korean War for a short while in 1950. After his discharge from the US Navy, he moved to Modesto, California and worked for United Air Lines. While he was in the US Navy, he became close friends with Don Pack. In 1956 Don passed away from cancer. He left behind his wife Ava and two children: Bill, eleven and Nancy, seven. Before Don succumbed to the disease, he asked Ted to take care of his family. In 1958 Ted married Ava

Pack at a ceremony in the Methodist Church in Modesto, California and happily took on the role of stepfather to her children. In the words of his daughter Nancy Pack Peters, who is filled with ebullient pride about him, "Ted was absolutely the most wonderful father; always patient and compassionate." He and Ava had no children of their own, but his joy and satisfaction was to see her and his children happy.

In 1952 Ted came to Tenmile to take over the Tenmile Store from his father who was quite ill. His dad had owned and operated the store for 13 years, and Ted performed the same role for 22 years. Ted fell in love with the business and the community. The following year he was made postmaster of the Tenmile Post Office and he served in that position for 25 years. In 1958, soon after his marriage to Ava, she and the children came to Tenmile to join him. He was very ambitious and resourceful. In addition to operating the store, he planted and logged timber on 140 acres of land he and Ava owned.

In the early 1960s the name Ted Benedict became synonymous with the Tenmile Volunteer Fire Department. In 1962 he spearheaded the group that organized the first fire department. They raised funds for the fire truck and equipment by holding ice cream socials and a door-to-door campaign soliciting endorsement for the department. Ted was the one who went to Yoncalla, Oregon to pick up the department's first truck. He donated the land in front of his store to build the first firehouse. He was the fire chief for almost 28 years and captain for several years after retiring from the position as fire chief. As chief, he documented every fire in which he officiated in very clear, concise and legible handwriting. In 1965 the Tenmile Volunteer Fire Department received state recognition for its outstanding performances in fire prevention. About 1977 the department was experiencing financial hardship, operating with about 20 to 30 volunteers, and was approached by the Winston-Dillard Fire Department to join their district. They turned down the invitation because they wanted to continue being self-autonomous. Ted, with his leadership and diplomacy, encouraged the volunteer department to form a local fire district. He was involved with the door-to-door campaign collecting signatures for the legal process. In January 1982 Douglas County

Court gave its approval to the area to form the Tenmile Rural Fire District.

Ted was very diplomatic and had the finesse to handle difficult problems. He was always called upon to arbitrate any family disputes in the community. He was recognized as a law enforcement officer without a badge. He was also involved in many social activities. To name a few: In the 1960s he became a member of Winston-Dillard School Board and served for several years. Since Ted was aware that many of the less fortunate friends in his community benefited from the support of the Winston-Dillard Food Pantry, he volunteered hundreds of hours to the establishment. He donated $100.00 a month via the Methodist Church to the Food Pantry to purchase flour. He drove his pickup truck for several years collecting food for the pantry from Roseburg.

But his altruistic spirit was clearly demonstrated when he organized the restoration of the Tenmile Cemetery. Because of years of neglect, the grounds were overgrown with weeds and shrubs. Headstones had been broken, and some graves were unidentifiable. He cleaned the entire site. With the aid of the outdated map, he conducted a survey of the entire gravesites and prepared a new set of drawings of the layout of the cemetery. Done in perfect architectural lettering, this map is now used by the Cemetery Committee to identify graves and empty spaces. When he was chairman of the committee, he had been quite vigilant not to allow that respected site to revert back to the point of neglect.

Gazebo honoring "Ted"

Plaque honoring "Ted"

Ted was a family man in the true sense of the word and created the time to be with them. They went on holiday trips and picnics. He played with his grandchildren and great grandchildren. In the words of his loving wife Ava "as long as his family was happy, he was happy." About the year 2003, Ava became ill with a crippling disease which impaired her mobility. Ted took care of her until he became very ill himself. Diane Schiro, his caregiver, said: "even in the end, he thought about his family." Ted Benedict, Jr. passed away on January 30, 2006.

References:
The News Review, Tenmile Fire Dept. Scrap Book, Interview with friends and family. Photo of Ted: Courtesy of Tenmile Post Office and the photos by the author.

BEMAN B. BROCKWAY

It is rather interesting that the Pioneer Hon. Beman B. Brockway (as he was referred to in his later life), in whose honor the community of Brockway was named, never lived in Brockway, but in Winston on Lookingglass Road on a knoll just northeast of Cary Street. Mr. Brockway built and lived in his mansion in 1860 until his death in 1905. That road was then named Roseburg-Myrtle Point Stage Road. Prior to 1882 the areas of Winston, Dillard and Brockway were called Civil Bend District. The division of the Civil Bend District began in 1882, when the Oregon and California Railroad Company constructed railroad tracks and a railroad depot on John Dillard's property. In gratitude for his generosity for the right-of-way, the Company called the depot Dillard. In 1889, when Civil Bend Postal Service was reestablished, the people of the District called it Brockway in honor of the highly respected and loved Beman B. Brockway. And, in 1893, when postal service was established in the home of the Winston family, that area became known as Winston.

Mr. Brockway was born in upstate New York, in Chautauqua County, on February 12, 1829. His parents were Horace and Eliza Brockway. They had four children: Henry, Beman, Burban, and Mary Ann. In 1852, at the age of 23, Beman and his brother Burban went to Naperville, Illinois to join a wagon train to cross the plains to come to Oregon. The journey lasted for six months before ending in Josephine County. For the next six years they were employed mining gold in both Josephine and Jackson Counties and were quite successful. In 1858 they relocated to Douglas County and invested in 610 acres of land, lying about one mile west of the Winston Bridge (today referred to as the Green Bridge). Beman returned to his mining operations while his brother attended to growing wheat and raising stock. While the brothers were living and mining in Josephine County they both served in the Rogue Valley Indian War and were involved in the battle of the Meadows.

Courtesy of Douglas County Museum

About 1860 Beman joined his brother on the ranch. They made extensive improvements to the farm, adding fruit orchards to the wheat and cattle operations. As a result, they developed a very successful farming operation. Beman's home was the largest house in the Civil Bend District and was considered a landmark for several years before it was destroyed by fire in 1951. In 1870 he married Mrs. Margret A. Rice, a widow. They had no children, and in 1881 she passed away at their home in the Civil Bend District. He laid her to rest next to her first husband at the Willis Creek Cemetery. In 1879 his brother sold his interest in the farm and moved to the city of Roseburg, leaving Beman with 325 acres of farm land to manage. He married Mary F. Drew, a native of Iowa. They had three children: Edith, Charles, and Mary.

Mr. Brockway was of medium height and always wore a beard. He was a Republican, a leader in his community, Civil Bend District, and also of the county. He always sponsored Fourth of July celebrations, and, in 1887, three days of the District Fair was held on his farm. He held the office of county commissioner, and in 1880 he served one term as a representative of Douglas County to the state legislature. He and his brother sold two acres of land for $25 to the Association of Civil Bend Pioneer Cemetery in 1877. He was made a member of the Founding Fathers of the association. On September 18, 1896, Mr. Brockway was struck with embarrassment when his brother Burban was arrested and charged with assault by beating Charles H. Fisher with a cane. Mr. Beman B. Brockway passed away on March 2, 1905, and was buried at Civil Bend Pioneer Cemetery.

References:
The News-Review, *The Umpqua Trapper* 1975 vol. X1 #1, Portrait and Biographical Record Of Western Oregon, The *Winston Wire* January 1968, Articles by Shirley Clayton. Circuit Court Records Box 57, Vault 107-109 November 1896. Douglas County Museum Records. Photo: Courtesy of Douglas County Museum.

GEORGE BROSI

He did "everything" with rapidity. He held the record for the 100 yard dash at Douglas High School for several years. He handled the plow and the harrow with speed and dexterity. It was always a phenomenal experience to watch George as he operated any piece of farm equipment. He was community minded. Where ever there was a community project he was there to help. He was a true "handy-community-man."

George was born in Roseburg, Oregon, on March 2, 1937. He was the only child of Marcus "Kelly" and Rose Davis Brosi. He married Gaylyn Bradley of Seattle, Washington on September 16, 1961. The couple had three children: Debbie, Mark and Becky. All his children graduated from Douglas High School. Mark went on to Willamette University to study mechanical engineering.

Courtesy of Leif Photography

George was a student of the first graduating class at Douglas High School in 1956. He was also an eye witness to the drowning of two of his classmates, Frank Collins and Avery Morgan, at Sunset Bay in May 1954. He played all sports in high school, but it was in track and field that he dominated with his speed. After graduation from high school, he worked on the farm with his dad for a short time and went to work for Pepsi-Cola Bottling Co. In February 1977 his Dad Kelly passed on and George inherited the farm.

The history of farming runs through the veins of the Brosi family. They are of German descent and came to Oregon from Missouri in the late 1800s. In 1907 George Brosi's grandfather bought about twenty five and a half acres of land in the Winston Section and farmed that land until his passing in 1932. He also built his home in 1913, and his great grandson Mark now lives there with his family. On the other hand, "Kelly's" uncle never married and owned a large ranch in Lookingglass Valley. He also owned a prune orchard on Lookingglass Road. He passed away in

August 1932. (The Ark of the Covenant's property sits on part of the orchard.) "Kelly" inherited his father's estate and continued the farming until his passing in February 1977. George and Gaylyn became owners of the home and the farm. They formed a corporation of "Brosi Orchards" with approximately 100 acres of diversified farmlands that included the original twenty five and one half acres purchased in 1907. Unfortunately, George and Gaylyn's marriage did not keep up with the quality and growth of the farm and ended up in divorce court in 1986. George never remarried but lived with Juanita Sawyer for several years. She preceded him in death. Mark Brosi now owns the farm, and in 1996 he renamed it "Brosi Sugar Tree Farms" comprising 142 acres. In 2007 Brosi Farm was registered as one of Oregon's century farms.

Brosi Sugar Tree Farms

George's volunteering contribution to the community of Winston was phenomenal. In 1974 he was one of the many citizens of Douglas County and Oregon who showed their concerns for saving Wildlife Safari from going into bankruptcy. He donated his time and equipment to the park by grading and seeding various grazing fields. In an effort to see Winston and Dillard become better and more livable communities he applied for membership on the Park Board and served both officially and physically for several years. He was involved in the development of the Community Park, the Riverbend Park and the Riverbend Park picnic area. He did all the grading and seeding of the areas in front of and adjacent to the outdoor theater at the park. He was elected to the Winston-Dillard School Board and the Winston-Dillard Fire Board. He served for several years on the Winston-Dillard Water Board of Directors. On February 23, 1998, George was speechless before hundreds of community guests when his name was announced as the recipient of the First Citizen Award by the Winston-Dillard Area Chamber of Commerce. Brosi Orchard Road which runs from Highway 99 to Winston Section Road was named in the family's honor.

By February 1989 George experienced a deceleration in the pace of his life. He received a successful heart transplant at the Oregon Health Science University Medical Center, the first in his community to receive that kind of surgery. The procedure took seven and half hours and cost $55,000. It was the community of Winston and Dillard he loved dearly who began a fund raising campaign to assist with his medical expenses. He went on to enjoy the next 20 years of his life before passing away at a care giving facility on May 27, 2008.

References:
The News Review, Winston Park Board Minutes, Interview with Family members. Photo of George: Courtesy of Leif Photography and the other photo by the author.

THE BURKS FAMILY

The name "Burks Fruit Stand" has become synonymous with the community of Dillard. Fred Burks was only five years of age when he came to Douglas County, Oregon with his parents Abraham and Arizona Burks in 1903. But upon his passing away at age 81, Fred Burks and his wife Lena Jane Burks left a legacy of professional farmers and a roadside produce stand of fruits and vegetables for the people of Douglas County.

Fred was born on July 10, 1898, at Machines, Washington. He grew up on his parent's farm in Brockway, Oregon and attended the Brockway School District #16. He was tall with red hair and always wore a smile. He was the seventh child of his parents' ten children. He became quite close to his father, and at age 10 he was helping him with many farm chores. Unfortunately, his father's untimely death at age

Courtesy of Douglas County Museum

52 devastated Fred. He was only 13 at the time and wore the sorrows for many years. He continued working on the farm until, at age 18, he joined the US Army during World War I. He was discharged from the military in September 1919, and in November of that same year he married his sweetheart, Lena Jane Laurance. Soon after they were married, the couple left his mother's farm to seek work in Portland. They leased a restaurant, but after several months into the business they decided to give up the lease. They left Portland and found work on a ranch in Eastern Oregon. Fred was a stockman, and Lena cooked and did odd chores for the ranch hands. It was on the ranch they both realized that farming was what they knew and loved best. They returned to Brockway and purchased 16 acres of land from his mother. They lived with his mother until they built their own house.

Lena, like Fred, was just a little girl of four years when she came to Dillard, Oregon with her parents and siblings in 1903. She was born on May 16, 1899, in Riverside, North Carolina. Her parents were George Baker and Barbara Ellen Laurance. Her parents had 14 children. She was beautiful with long black hair. She attended the Dillard two-room elementary school. Just like her husband Fred, Lena was only 16 when she suffered the loss of a parent. Her mother, Barbara Ellen Laurance, passed away in 1915. Lena wasted no time in sharing the role of motherhood with her sister Jess in the Laurance Family. They took on the household chores of caring for nine brothers and sisters and a 10-day-old baby sister. At age 20 Lena was ready for her own motherhood. She married Fred Burks in a ceremony in Roseburg on November 16, 1919.

Fred and Lena cleared the 16 acres and planted an orchard. They also built a small cottage on the farm for them to live. On November 29, 1921, Lena gave birth to their first child. They called her Wilma Mae, but nicknamed her "Billie". The ambitious couple leased land in Dillard from her father, G.B. Laurance, and began the truck-farming business. Lena was selling fruits and vegetables from both farms while Fred was hauling produce to the Oregon Coast covering Coos and Curry Counties. By 1926 that grafting of ideas between Fred and Lena blossomed into a landmark farm business. They leased farm land in Garden Valley, built a bigger home and put up a fruit stand on Highway 42 about two miles west of Coos Junction (renamed Winston).

On November 9, 1933, their second child David was born during the peak of the Great Depression. With hard work and perseverance the family business survived that economic blizzard. In the middle of the 1940s, their farm business had an upsurge. Between 1946 and 1948 an influx of migrant workers came to the Umpqua Valley to work in the timber industry. As a result, Fred and Lena's farm business had an upswing in profits. In 1946 they moved the fruit stand on Highway 42 and built a larger one on Highway 99 in Dillard. It was known and advertized as "Burks Blue Fruit Stand."

Burks Blue Fruit Stand-Dillard 1946-2011

In October 1960 Fred and Lena celebrated 33 years in the roadside fruit and vegetable stand business. By then, their "sought-after" peaches, apples, melons of all kinds, corn, tomatoes, pumpkins, etc. were in markets in Salem, Portland and as far north as Seattle. At the celebration, their son David and wife Donna had already become partners in the family business. Fred and Lena were affected by the floods of 1950 and 1955, but never forgot that landmark storm of 1964. The flood waters destroyed many of the fruit trees, and the famous blue fruit stand floated away. However, the fruit trees were replanted and the fruit stand was rebuilt.

In 1969 the couple celebrated their 50th wedding anniversary. Between 1968 and 1970 they bought the estate of the late William and Ruth Blair of Dillard. They lived in the estate house for a few years and later built another house, but on a hill far above the flood plain. Lena Jane Burks passed away on September 11, 1973 at age 74. Fred remarried Mary Lamb, a widow, in 1974, and, after five years of that marriage, Fred passed away in January 31, 1979. Fred and Lena are buried at Civil Bend Pioneer Cemetery in Winston.

David K. Burks:
David K. Burks was born in Roseburg on November 9, 1933. He attended Dillard Elementary School and graduated from Roseburg High School in 1951. At 18, David had the resemblance of his father. He was tall with red hair and blue eyes and very friendly. At a very young age he knew he wanted to become a farmer. He enrolled at Oregon State University majoring in agriculture, but dropped out after one year. He reasoned that his parents could teach him everything he wanted to know about farming. In June of 1954 David married Donna Fromdhal at the Lutheran Church in Roseburg. They purchased 12 acres of farm land from his parents and planted a variety of fruits and vegetables. They leased 14 acres of river-bottom farmland in Winston Section from Mrs. Harry Winston. On that farm they planted pole beans for the cannery in Roseburg. The young and ambitious couple leased another 10 acres in the Garden Valley area. There they planted cantaloupes for the Portland market. In 1955 David was drafted into the US Military and served his country in Germany. After a few months there, Donna joined him. He was discharged after 18 months. Soon after his return, David and Donna went into partnership with his parents. With David and Donna on board, they expanded the business with more varieties of produce. They hired more workers, especially bean pickers. During the height of the bean market, the family planted over 60 acres of pole beans. The couple never had children of their own, but adopted Michael David in March of 1959 and Mary Jane in June of 1961.

In 1969 David became involved with Winston-Dillard Melon Festival through the Lions Club. In a *News Review* article dated September 13, 1973, it quoted that "Around this time each year Burks becomes to Winston-Dillard Melon Festival what Babe Ruth was to the New York Yankees." Burks farm has been supplying the Winston-Dillard area with melons (watermelons and cantaloupes) since the festival first started in 1969. Every year the farm contributes several tons of melons.

By the mid 1970s the Burks family and the other 90 truck farmers in the Dillard Area had lost the greater portion of the melon market in Oregon to California growers. David concentrated on growing and selling fresh produce from the family's produce stand in Dillard, Coquille and Empire on the coast. By the early

1980s, there were only six truck farmers growing melons in the Dillard area. After graduating from high school, Michael David became a farmer and a partner in the Burks produce farming business.

References:
The News Review, Memoirs of Fred's Family by Ruby Laurence Wetzell, Historic Douglas County Oregon, 1982, Civil Bend Pioneer Cemetery Records. Photo: Courtesy of Douglas County Museum and the other by the author.

SHERLEY CLAYTON
Very few people in the Winston-Dillard Area have ever heard of him; and those who have may not be aware that he was a historian dedicated to preserving the history of the early pioneers who settled this area. On September 24, 1966, at age 68, Sherley Clayton was honored with the "Henry Clinton Collins Award for the Collection and Preservation of Local History" at a ceremony held at the Oregon Historical Center in Portland. He received the award for his book *Memories of Long Ago* published by the Douglas County Historical Society in 1956. The award consisted of a certificate and an undisclosed sum of money granted by the Oregon Historical Society and by Mr. and Mrs. Donald F. Menefee of Eugene. The Manefee's contribution was in memory of her father, the late Reverend Clinton Collins, an Episcopal Minister in The Dalles, Oregon. Rev. Collins devoted much of his time in preserving Oregon's history.

Photo: Courtesy of The News Review

Sherley W. Clayton was born on April 3, 1898, in Roseburg, Oregon. His parents were Grant and Eva Estella Clayton who homesteaded in the Kent Creek Area. His brother Elzie was five years younger. When Sherley was four years old he developed blood poisoning from a cat scratch. He became terribly sick, and a doctor in Roseburg recommended amputating the hand in order to alleviate the pain and suffering. His parents refused and took him to see Dr. Taylor, who was stationed at one of the placer mines in Olalla. Dr. Taylor cut into the festered wound on his arm with a razor and drained the poison from the wound. Within a few days Sherley became well and was out playing with his friends.

By the time Sherley was at the age to attend school, the Kent Creek School District #56 had discontinued. For that reason, in 1905, his parents moved to Roseburg. His father worked for Finis Dillard in real estate, and his mother worked as a seamstress. However, in June 1910, the family bought a section of the old Kent Place across the river in Dillard from Annie Kent and returned to the area they loved. They began stock raising and truck gardening. They were well known for growing huge melons, tomatoes and flowers. Sherley and Elzie tended sheep. Sherley continued his schooling at Dillard Elementary School and later graduated from Roseburg High School.

At a very young age Sherley developed an insatiable appetite for history. He was always eager to listen to his mother tell stories of days gone by. She was knowledgeable and was a source of information for the community. Later on, Sherley followed in his mother's footsteps and became an historian for the Umpqua Valley, especially in the Winston-Dillard Area. He has written hundreds of essays about the lives of early settlers and events spanning a period between 1850 and 1969. He always wrote with a pinch of philosophical flair. It was not known whether he had a vested interest in the newspaper *The Wire* published in the Winston-Dillard Area, but he wrote historical articles about Winston and Dillard in every issue between 1966 and 1969 before the newspaper stopped publication.

Sherley never married nor had children but left a legacy of historical footprints along the Umpqua Valley. His works: *Memories of Long Ago, The Story of Dillard, The Story of the Kents, The Story of the Rices, The Story of Grant and Eva Clayton*, etc. can be found at the Douglas County Museum and the Douglas County Library. Sherley Wallace Clayton suffered for several years from a degenerative disease, which crippled him before he passed away on December 27, 1971 at his home in Dillard, Oregon. He was buried at Civil Bend Pioneer Cemetery in Winston.

References:
The News Review, Sherley Clayton's writings. Photo by *The News Review*.

DILLARD FAMILY

Dillard Train Depot 1882

The Dillard Railroad Depot, located on the grounds of the Douglas County Museum off the I-5 Corridor, stands as a replica of Rev. John Dillard's legacy. In gratitude for his generosity of a right-of-way through his property for the railroad tracks, the Oregon and California Railroad Company named the train station and the area "Dillard." Rev. John McCord Dillard passed away on June 12, 1893, in the community of Dillard. He was buried at Civil Bend Pioneer Cemetery in Winston

Rev. John and his wife, Jane Grey Dillard, were married in Springfield, Missouri in January 1832. They were both 19 years of age. They had three children: William Martin, James McCord, and Finis Winfield. He was a Presbyterian minister, farmer and a skillful handyman, and she was a seamstress. The family often thought of immigrating to the State of Oregon, but the cyclone disaster that hit Springfield in 1849 and destroyed their house expedited their decision to leave immediately. They arrived in Oregon in the fall of 1850 and temporarily settled in the Salem area.

In the spring of 1851 the Reverend and his friend James Burnett went prospecting for gold in Jacksonville, Oregon and Yreka, California and at the same time they were looking for a permanent place to settle. (The discovery of gold in those areas, which began about 1848, attracted an influx of immigrants from the East Coast, the South and the Midwest.) Within a short span of time, they were quite successful with each grossing over 22 pounds of gold dust. (The market price of gold then was $15.00 an ounce.) In 1852, while returning to join their families, Rev. Dillard purchased 640 acres of land in the Dillard Valley (then called Civil Bend District) for $800.00 in gold dust from John Slooper. Mr. Slooper was the owner of the property under the Squatter's Rights Act. John Burnett took out a Donation Land Claim at Round Prairie, four miles south of Dillard. Mrs. Dillard, in the absence of her husband, for almost two years, worked as a seamstress making men's trousers for a company in Salem. Upon the return of Rev. Dillard and Burnett, they encouraged many of the families who came on the covered-wagon train with them to come to Douglas County. Those families were: the brothers John and James Cox and children, Joseph Gage, Louis Dozer Kent, James and Michael B. Belieu, Will Sebring and Will Cochran. The above mentioned families all filed Donation Land Claims in the neighboring vicinity of Dillard.

The Dillard Family immediately began to make improvements on their property. Because of rumors of possible Indian attacks, they built their two-story dwelling on a hill east of the present Southern Pacific Railroad Tracks and filled the walls with dirt. In addition, they built a blacksmith shop, a granary and a barn. With his experience as a farmer, he kept the family well provided with food. He planted grain, raised cattle, hogs and sheep. He made ham, bacon and lard. He made salt from a salt spring found on the property. He later went on to set up a refinery to make salt in commercial quantity. He and his sons hauled the farm's produce to the market in Scottsburg, on the Umpqua River. In the Indian War of 1855 to 1856, Rev. Dillard and his eldest son, William, volunteered to fight at the Olalla Fort. How long they stayed at the fort is unknown. (The fort was set up to protect the settlers in the Olalla area against Indian attack.)

Rev. Dillard returned his attention to preaching the gospel. He organized a Presbyterian Church in the Civil Bend District, the first of its kind in Douglas County. He later built a modest-looking church at the base of Mt. Bragg. This area is now known as Brockway. In 1854 he assisted the settlers at Willis Creek with the construction of a school for the area. His son Finis, who was then five years of age, attended that school, but unfortunately it was burned by the Indians in the fall of 1855. (Willis Creek School District #14 was one of the first schools to be operated in this area.) In 1883 Reverend Dillard produced 16,000 bushels of grain. Jane Dillard preceded her husband in death in November 1883, and the Rev. John Dillard passed away in June 12, 1893. They were both buried at Civil Bend Pioneer Cemetery in Winston.

Rev. Dillard's first son William was born on November 16, 1833, in Springfield, Missouri. He filed a Donation Land Claim on property adjacent to his father's on both sides of the South Umpqua River. William never married and worked as a miner throughout Douglas County. His untimely death came when he suffered a ruptured appendix at age 49.

James McCord, the Reverend's second son, was born on September 14, 1842. He married Mary Ellen Cox, daughter of James and Sarah Cox, (pioneers to the South Umpqua Basin.) They had two sons and two daughters. He lived and worked on his parents' farm until the late 1870s. In 1880 he was elected County Commissioner. That same year he purchased a farm across the South Umpqua in Civil Bend District, now called Brockway. In 1881 he was appointed postmaster and justice of the peace of Civil Bend District. He moved back to Dillard and opened the first merchandise store. When postal services came to Dillard in June 1884, he was appointed postmaster, and the service was operated from his store. James McCord Dillard passed away on April 16, 1900. (As a point of historical interest, their daughter Jennie married Samuel C. Miller in 1890. The couple bought Reverend John and Jane Dillard's 1000-acre farm and built their home on Pacific Highway, now called Highway 99.)

Jennie Dillard Miller's house built -1913 at 9197 Highway 99

Rev. Dillard's last son Finis was 94 years of age when he retired from the Douglas County Sheriff's Department. At the time of his retirement, he was the oldest law enforcement officer in the United States. He was born on March 29, 1849 in Springfield,

Missouri and was one year old when he came to Oregon with his parents. He attended the Willis School District #14 for about a year and then transferred to the Brockway School which was closer to Dillard. He finished his education at Umpqua Academy at Wilbur. He married Amanda Frances Cox, sister to Mary Ellen Cox on October 15, 1871. The couple had one son, who died in infancy, and two daughters. They lived on his parents' farm for a while before buying a 320-acre farm on the west side of the South Umpqua River, across from his parents' farm. While living on the farm with his parents, he was very helpful in the production and sale of salt from a salt well found on the farm. In 1882 he contracted to supply beef to the Southern Pacific Railroad camps that were constructing railroad lines between Roseburg and Glendale. He continued the wholesale and retail selling of beef until 1890 when he sold the farm and moved his family into Roseburg.

Finis joined the Douglas County Sheriff's Department and served under Sheriff Samuel C. Miller. In 1898 he quit the sheriff department to run for the chief of police position of Roseburg. (The position of chief of police then was a political one.) He beat his opponent P.C. Ream by one vote. He served as chief for five years. He had a passion for law enforcement. He spent four years as a guard at the Victory Gold Mine in Cow Creek Canyon. He returned to the Douglas County Sheriff's Department and served as a deputy until his retirement in 1944. Finis W. Dillard passed away at the age of 96 on January 31, 1946, in Roseburg. He was buried at Civil Bend Pioneer Cemetery in Winston.

References:
The News Review, Douglas County Museum Records, *Story of Dillard* by Sherley Clayton, Civil Bend Pioneer Cemetery Records. Photos: by the author.

KENNETH FORD

There is no doubt that Kenneth Ford, nick-named "Pappy", was Oregon's iconic blue collar businessman of the 20th Century. His dedication to hard work, his philanthropic kindness and his belief in education impacted communities across the state, especially those of Roseburg, Winston and the greater Winston area. That legacy will no doubt continue to shine into the future. Mr. Ford summed it up best by saying:

> People have been so good to me that I want to give back to them. This company, the timber industry, my friends and family, and the employees are the ones who will carry on when I am gone. You are now the torch-bearers, and you must understand your responsibility to mankind.

Kenneth Webster Ford was born on August 4, 1908 in Asotin, Washington, a farming community on the Snake River. Kenneth was the only son of three children. His younger sisters were Edith and Lois. He was tall and stern-looking with long arms. His parents were Ora and Clair Ford. Ora was a mill operator and farmer from St. Cloud, Minnesota. His mother, Clair, was a schoolteacher from Galt, California. The family operated saw-mills in Idaho and then in Lebanon, Oregon. At age 16, while working for his dad, Kenneth learned about the value of hard work in the timber business. Kenneth graduated from Lebanon High School with a high GPA. His dream as a child was to run a dairy farm on the Oregon coast. After graduation he attended Oregon State Agricultural College for one semester but quit to rescue one of his dad's sawmills.

Photo: Courtesy of The Ford Family Foundation

In the early 1930s, Kenneth and his dad came to Roseburg to set up a sawmill, but with the Great Depression affecting most businesses, they were unsuccessful. Kenneth returned to Roseburg in January of 1936 with his wife, Hallie, and built a sawmill on Diamond Lake Boulevard. From then on he never looked back but developed a vision and tenacity for the industry. He bought several thousand acres of repossessed timberlands from the county for as little as two dollars an acre. Mr. Ford, unlike the previous owners, kept the taxes paid, and at the same time negotiated to cut timber on federal lands for as little as a dollar per 1000 board feet. He understood every aspect of the logging and sawmill business. He built roads and bridges and sometimes helped Hallie with the cooking at camps when necessary. He felled trees and set chokers. When a piece of equipment broke down, he fixed it. He installed new machines at the plant and maintained them. A plaque on his office wall that characterized Kenneth reads: "The world owes you a living. But you have to work hard to collect."

Kenneth met Hallie Brown in the summer of 1933. She was introduced to him by his sisters, Edith and Lois, who were all teachers. All five of them, including Edith's husband, went on a road trip across the country. They visited areas like Boston, New York, Chicago, New Orleans and Florida. Kenneth and Hallie were married in Lebanon, Oregon, the following year, 1934, at the Methodist Church. They had two children, Allyn and Carmen. (Allyn is now president of Roseburg Forest Products and Chairman of the Board of the Ford Family Foundation. Carmen worked for Linn-Benton Community College in Albany and sits on the Board of the Ford Family Foundation.) Kenneth and Hallie lived a very frugal life style. Even in the 1940s, during the post World War II timber boom when he was sitting on the throne of wealth, they were renting a duplex house in a middle class neighborhood at 1385 Madrone Avenue, Roseburg. In 1956, the couple moved to another apartment at 415 Madrone Avenue, Roseburg, and resided there until 1969. He drove an old Buick car and took his lunch to work in a brown paper bag. The

Photo: Courtesy of Douglas County Museum

couple divorced in 1972. Hallie moved to Salem and became a trustee of Willamette University for 32 years until her passing in 2007. She and Kenneth founded the Ford Family Foundation. In November of 1982, Kenneth Ford married Bonnie Stanley in the First Presbyterian Church in Portland. In 1983, they built and lived in a modest home at 480 SE Summit Drive, Roseburg until his death in 2007.

After World War II, the housing market soared and so did Ford's profits. In 1946 he built a new sawmill complex at a convenient location near the Southern Pacific Railroad tracks close to the South Umpqua River in Dillard. The plant occupies about 2.2 miles, fronting both sides of Highway 99. When a section of the Roseburg plant burned in 1948, Dillard became, and still is, the center of operations. In 1970 this facility became the world's largest manufacturer of wood products. With an expansion and consolidation plan set into action, his empire made Kenneth Ford the wealthiest man in Douglas County and the state. In the early 1980s, the prominent business magazine, *Forbes Fortune 400*, named three Oregonians to the list of wealthy Americans. The financial trio was: Kenneth Ford, Phillip Knight of Nike Inc. and Howard Vollum of Tektronic Inc.

Roseburg Forest Product in Dillard

Between 1936 and 1996, Ford expanded and consolidated his empire fifty-seven times, a phenomenal milestone for any businessman in Oregon's history. A few changes he implemented were: the building of a wood chip facility at Coos Bay to enable the company to ship wood chips to Japan, an enterprise that was once dominated by Weyehaeuser and Georgia-Pacific, the purchases of Colonial Pacific Leasing Corp, the Ford Industrial Plant in Portland, Kimberly-Clark Corporation in Northern California, comprised of two sawmills and 300,000 acres of timber lands, a purchase that stunned the timber giants Weyehaeuser and Georgia-Pacific and the purchase of IP Timberlands which became Smith River Lands. In June 1982, at the beginning of the recession, Ford, then 74 stepped aside due to an ailment and hired John Stephens as the president of the company. Stephens came to Roseburg Lumber Co. with ten years of experience as vice president of International Paper and nine years with the international accounting firm of Arthur Anderson & Company.

Prior to the mid-1940s, Douglas County's economy depended on agriculture. There were very few sawmills in operation. But with the surge in the timber market after World War II, the sawmill business took off throughout the county. By the middle of the 1950s, Douglas County led the state in timber receipts and still continues today. The surge in the timber industry caused a housing problem for Ford's employees. He created accommodation opportunities in Dillard, known as the Ford Addition, and another in Winston, known as South Slopes. At the South Slopes Subdivision, he constructed 44 two and three bedrooms houses. Today that area is known as the Ford, Hart and Peach Lanes Subdivision. Those homes were built specifically for his supervisors and foremen. By 1975 the Roseburg Lumber Company 4000 employee weekly payroll dominated the area. The company became a vital contributor to the economy of Roseburg, Winston, Dillard and all of Douglas County. In 1985 Roseburg Lumber Co. changed its name to Roseburg Forest Products.

Aaron Rose founded the town of Roseburg, but Kenneth Ford developed it. In 1957 Ford and his wife Hallie set up a charitable foundation, known as the Ford Family Foundation. For the past 53 years the foundation has donated millions of dollars to communities in Roseburg, Winston, Douglas County, across the State of Oregon and in northern California. It has funded programs such as the Douglas Community Hospital, the Roseburg YMCA, the Douglas County Library, the Ford Family Center at Umpqua Community College, the Doernbecher Children's Hospital, Phoenix School, the Winston Community Center, the Student Center and administrative offices at the College of the Siskiyou in Weed, California and a host of others. It has donated money to many agencies serving the poor and needy. The Foundation has a special interest in helping schools, both elementary and secondary. It also has a four-year college scholarship program for talented Oregon students.

Kenneth Ford did not finish college. However, he was highly decorated with scholastic, business and civic awards before his passing in February 1997. In 1985, he was awarded an honorary Doctor of Letters degree by Kanto Gakuin University in Yokohama, Japan. The university is a sister institution to Linfield College in McMinnville, Oregon. Ford was a trustee of Linfield College for 25 years. He was chosen First Citizen of Roseburg in 1958 and Lumberman of the Year in 1960. He received the Governor's Corporate Excellence Award in 1984, the Salvation Army's "Others" Award in 1993, and the Harry Merlo Award in 1996. Douglas County Commissioners named a road "Kenneth Ford Drive" off Stephens Street in his memory in 2009. Kenneth "Pappy" Ford passed away on February 8, 1997. He left behind the largest independent manufacturing forest business in the United States, and that famous plaque that hangs in his office still encourages his family, friends and employees to carry the torch for future generations.

References:
The News-Review, Douglas County Museum, *The Register Guard, West Coast Lumberman,* The *Woodsman, The Oregonian.* Photo of Mr. Ford donated by "The Ford Family Foundation" Compliments of Douglas County Museum Re: Men falling timber. The other by the author.

WILLIAM "BUD" BETTS GLEN III
The useful adage of "action speaks louder than words" is very true in describing Bud Glen's contribution to the Winston-Dillard Community. He carried a calm demeanor and listened more than he spoke. But, when it came to getting a project done, he was all "action" and dependable. He and his wife Jane owned and managed Glen Construction Co. As a contractor he was quite knowledgeable and operated both his D6 Caterpillar bulldozer and front-backhoe with great skill and confidence. In July 2011 the Winston City Council honored Bud Glen by renaming Riverbend Park Picnic Area, - "Bud Glen Playground."

William Betts "Bud" Glen III was born on July 17, 1937, in North Hollywood, California. He was the son of William Betts, Jr. and Myrtle Pittman Glen. He was the oldest of three children. His siblings are Charles and David. In 1947 the family moved to Coos Junction, Oregon (renamed Winston). Bud attended elementary schools in Winston and Dillard and was a student of the first graduating class at Douglas High School in 1956. He witnessed the tragic drowning of two of his classmates, Frank Collins and Avery Morgan, at Sunset Bay in May 1954. It took several years for that incident to be erased from his mind. After graduation, he assisted his parents with their grocery store and Dew Drop Inn Cabins at 304 NW Main Street. In 1957 he married his sweetheart Judie McGuire. The couple had five children: Christie, Judie, Dana Mae (deceased) and twins Peter and Sadie. Unfortunately, they were divorced in 1962.

In 1966 Bud remarried Jane Lowery at Carson City, Nevada and lived there for about a year. At the time of the marriage Jane had two girls from a previous marriage. They are Kim and Dawna. Between 1976 and 1979 Bud built three subdivisions in Winston and one in Roseburg. The one in Roseburg is called Christie Court, the name of his first daughter Christie Glen Knutson. Glen Court in Winston is located east of Glenhart Ave. and south of Lookingglass Rd. and named for the Glen family. Jole Allen Court is located on the east side of Winston off Tokay Ave. and was named for his first grandson, Jole. Bud, his wife Jane and James Richey, Jr. formed a partnership to build Parkway Subdivision. That subdivision is located east of Thompson Ave. and west of Edgewood St. At this subdivision he named one of the courts Dawna Court which is the name of one his step-daughters. About 1981, he and Jane took their contracting business on the road. They

Photo: Courtesy of the Family

handled contracts in California, Alaska and Hawaii. In 1994 they returned to Winston and started an equipment and tool rental business and kept the business until his untimely passing on April 23, 2002. Six years later, Jane left this plane of existence, on May 3, 2008, to join her husband Bud.

In 1951 Bud joined the US National Guard Reserve and served his country until he was honorably discharged in 1962. He was a member of various organizations such as: the Moose Lodge, the Elks, Freemasons and the Shriners. He served on a posse for Douglas County and was a member of the National Rifle Association. In 1995 he became involved in serving the Winston-Dillard Community. He was elected to the Board of Directors of Winston-Dillard Water District and served in that position for several years. In 1996 he was appointed to the Winston Park Board. It was while serving on the Park Board that his passion for volunteering became alive and noticeable. A large portion of Riverbend Park development can be credited to Bud. He built the seating area in front of the Riverbend Park Theater. That project entailed cutting, spreading, grading, and compacting over 4000 cubic yards of topsoil donated to the city by Roseburg Forest Products. He cut and leveled all the parking areas at the park. He excavated, graded and modified Riverbend Park access roads. He loaned his forklift to the Winston Public Works Department to install all the Glu-Lam Beams and roof joists during construction of the Riverbend Park Theater. In 1997, when Keith Walsh donated seven acres of river property adjacent to Riverbend Park to the City of Winston, Bud converted that blackberry, logs-bound riparian property into a beautiful picnic area. He cut and graded a circular access road at Civil Bend Pioneer Cemetery in Winston. At the Winston Dillard Area Chamber of Commerce annual banquet in February 1998, his volunteerism and generosity to the community of Winston and Dillard was recognized, and he was given the Humanitarian Award.

Bud's legacy of contributing to Winston-Dillard's status as a healthy and livable community is shining through his daughter, Christie Glen Knutson. She has been a member of the Winston City Council since 2007.

References:
The News Review, Interview with family, Winston Park Board Minutes, Winston City Council Minutes. Photo: Donated by family.

JEPTHA GREEN

The only time he took a real vacation was in 1876 when he and his wife attended the Centennial celebration in Philadelphia, the city that hosted the 100-year celebration of American cultural and industrial progress. But Jeptha Green was a "workaholic". He began work at sunrise and ended after sunset. Even though he was crippled for the last two years of his life, he was still tending to the farm. When he passed away at age 82 he owned about 3000 acres of farmland. He was a blacksmith, farmer and stock raiser.

Jeptha was born in 1828 in Richland, Ohio. He came to Oregon in 1851 by way of the Oregon Trail and spent a year and a half in Yamhill County, Oregon. In 1853 he moved to Douglas County and took a Donation Land Claim about four miles south of Roseburg along the South Umpqua River. That area is now known as Carnes Road. In 1854 he built a two story house with nine rooms. In 1882, when the Oregon-California Railroad extended its line from Roseburg to Ashland, the company established a depot about four miles south of Roseburg and called it "Green Siding". Later on, residents of the area dropped the word "Siding" and just called the area Green.

3856 Carnes Rd. Built by Olive Green Castle

Jeptha married Mary Mitchell in October 1858. (She preceded him in death in April 1891.) The couple had five children. They are: Robert Green, Olive F. Castle, Roscoe N. Green, Rosa B. Green, and Ellis M. Green who died at an early age.

Snapshots Along the Umpqua 139

Green has a long history of commercial enterprises and may be one of the first areas in Douglas County to begin shipping produce and livestock from the area. Jeptha donated the land to build Green Elementary School on Carnes Road. In 1888 he was the reppreventative to the Oregon State Legislature from Douglas County. Jeptha passed away on June 12, 1911 and was buried in Civil Bend Pioneer Cemetery in Winston.

Jeptha Green's family: Eva Castle wife of Jeptha's grandson.

Photo: Courtesy of The News Review

References:
The News Review, Douglas County, Oregon Probate Records Volume 7. Photos: *The News Review* and the author.

FRANK HART

Frank Hart was not born in Oregon, but upon his passing in August of 2007 in Eugene, Oregon, he left behind a legacy unprecedented in Oregon's history. That legacy is a 600-acre Wildlife Safari Park in Winston, a park dedicated to the preservation and conservation of animals. But, most of all, he exuded a passion and love for animals that captivated the entire region.

Frank Ronald Hart, Jr. was born on July 25, 1923, in Los Angeles, California. He was the grandson of German immigrants. He attended South Pasadena High School and graduated in 1940. Upon graduating, Frank enrolled at Pomona College as a pre-law student. In college he played varsity football and tennis.

But when Japan attacked Pearl Harbor in 1941, his studies were interrupted. He enlisted in the US Army in 1943 and was sent to Germany with the First Infantry Division. His Division captured Aachen, the first German City to surrender. Frank was decorated with the Silver Star Medal for Gallantry for his role in the mission. When the war ended, he assisted with managing a prison camp near Nurenburg. In 1946 he received an honorary discharge from the Army and returned to Pomona College where he graduated in 1947. While in college he met his wife, Barbara Ann Frisbee, and they married soon after their graduation. Frank returned to law school but dropped out when Barbara became pregnant with their first of four daughters: Louise, Nancy, Fran, and Mary. In February of 1949 he went to work as a salesman for Walker & Lee, in Anaheim, California, a small real estate business with about 15 employees. Frank was good at whatever he did and worked his way up the corporate ladder to become general manager of sales.

By 1972 the firm had grown into a huge real estate conglomerate with 1300 employees in 65 branch offices in California, Arizona,

Photo: Courtesy of The News Review

Texas, Nevada and Hawaii. Frank, then president of the company and chairman of the board, encouraged his board to diversify its holdings. The purchase of a 600-acre savannah-like area surrounded by rolling hills to create a Wildlife Safari Park near Winston, Oregon was one of its diversifications.

As a boy Frank enjoyed hunting rabbits and birds, and that appetite grew into a passion as he became older and more prosperous. He made over 40 hunting trips to Africa and Asia. He was also a member of a private duck hunting club in Chiloquin, Oregon. However, over the years of taking hunting expeditions, he became aware of the tremendous threat to wildlife, not only in Africa, but in most parts of the world. Many wild animals were either on the endangered roster or extinct due to the rise in human population. Frank made a 180-degree turn from hunter to conservationist. So, in 1972, when South Umpqua Investors approached Walker & Lee Real Estate Company to develop its 2300-acre land near Winston, Oregon, Frank seized the opportunity. He encouraged the firm to purchase 600 acres and develop a wildlife animal park. Before the purchase was finalized, Frank hired a firm to conduct a marketing study. The results were positive, and Wildlife Safari was created.

In the beginning the park suffered from many setbacks due to mismanagement, loss of animals, animal parasite problems and a decrease in tourism due to the OPEC oil embargo of 1974. Those problems plunged the park into a deep financial hole. By the fall of 1974, Walter & Lee Real Estate Company was experiencing unforeseen financial problems of its own and decided to sell the park or close it. Frank disagreed and argued that Wildlife Safari was worth saving. He gave up his six-figure salary and traded his stocks in the company in exchange for the park and its debts. In January of 1975, Frank and his wife Barbara became owners of Wildlife Safari Park. He moved to Winston with his family to take over management of the park. Under his leadership and charisma, the park slowly began to prosper. Unfortunately, there was another set back in 1979 when the country experienced a second oil crisis, and Frank suffered a heart attack in Utah while traveling with a load of animals from the Denver Zoo. He decided to switch the park from a profit-making venture to a non-profit corporation. That move opened wide the gates for grants, gifts, memberships and education.

In 1980 Wildlife Safari obtained the status of a 501 (c) (3) non-profit foundation and was to be overseen by Safari Game Search Foundation, Inc. The Foundation absorbed the existing park and its debts. Frank stepped away as owner and was hired as managing director at a salary of $15,000 a year. By 1986 American Zoo and Aquarium Association accredited Wildlife Safari as a top zoo in the United States. In 1993 Leonard and Vivian Goodwin, who were friends of Frank and shared his vision, became strong financial supporters. Upon Leonard's passing in 2006, he left the park a substantial endowment. Frank credited Wildlife Safari's success to the selfless dedication of his underpaid employees and his volunteers. He was executive director and chairman of the board of directors for 20 years and was on the board until his passing. Frank was involved with several organizations in Roseburg and Winston. To name a few: he was a member of both the Chamber of Commerce of Roseburg and Winston and that of the Rotary Club of Roseburg.

Frank's steadfast devotion and his undaunted love and dedication for the animals at Wildlife Safari landed him a few awards: He received the Governor's Corporate Excellence Award. The Significant Award for the Cheetah Breeding Program was bestowed upon him. And, the Council of Economic Development for Oregon crowned him Man of the Year for 1989. At age 84, he sustained a fractured neck from a fall in his house and never recovered from it. Frank Ronald Hart, Jr. Founder of Wildlife

Safari passed away on August 3, 2007. In his memory, the Discovery Theatre at the park was renamed "Frank Hart Theatre."

References:
The New Review 1971- 2007, *Midday At Oregon Oasis* by Steve Cohen May 1984, *Lions, Tigers Bears Oh, My*! by Steve Sinovic. Photos: The *News Review* and the author.

AL R. HOOTEN

He is a man of many talents - farmer, businessman, builder, intarsia designer, storyteller, historian - all laced with an infectious laugh.

Albert Roy Hooten was born on July 20, 1927, in Los Angeles, California. He is the son of James and Irene Hooten. He was eight years of age when he came to Douglas County with his parents to start a dairy farm in 1935. The family purchased a farm in the Winston Section Road area (today called Hooten Road). Al attended Roseburg High School and graduated in 1944. While at Roseburg he played football and was an outstanding quarterback. After graduation he attended Oregon State College (now known as Oregon State University) studying architecture. Unfortunately, after one year he dropped out of college to work on the farm due to his father's untimely death. In 1948 he married his high school sweetheart, Mary Sullivan. The couple has four children: Peggy, Cathy, James and Danny and 15 grandchildren.

In 1964 the Hooten Family suffered yet another misfortune when their dairy farm business went into bankruptcy. Al went to work for Roseburg Lumber Company in Dillard as a welder. He is always proud to admit that his inspiration for quality of service and perfection came by watching the late Kenneth Ford "can do" attitude. He went on to work for Mattis Construction Company. In 1966 he became a member of Winston City Council and resigned from his post in 1969 when he was offered the position of city administrator of Winston (he was the first in the city's history.) He was selected from a short list of 41 applicants. He left Winston to work for Wildlife Safari Game Park as the general manager in 1972. He held that position for four years. In 1976 he was hired as the first city manager of Brookings, Oregon, and in 1978 the city of Sutherlin hired him as their city manager. He held that position until 1981 when he accepted the position with Public Works Department of Roseburg as Director of General Services. He held that position for three and a half years when F. G. & T. Construction Company offered him a high paying position with the company. He continued to work for various construction companies until his retirement.

Al was 71 years of age when his artistic creativity attracted the public's attention. His woodcarvings of birds and animals progressed into intarsia master pieces. Umpqua Valley Art Center displayed and sold many of his pieces within Douglas County and across the United States. Some of his intarsia art pieces can be seen hanging in the office of the Cow Creek Tribe of Umpqua Indians. In 1999 Al was appointed to the Umpqua Valley Art Center Board of Directors. While serving on the board he played a vital role in improving the condition of the center. The board was highly appreciative for the new look of the center in 2003. In 2005 the city of Roseburg wanted to replace its logo. The city commissioned Al to do an intarsia of woods for the logo. He made the logo using 350 pieces from seven different types of wood. It weighs 40 pounds. When the police and fire building in Roseburg was completed, the city again hired Al to do another intarsia of the city's logo for the building's lobby. That was another magnificent piece of intarsia art work.

City of Roseburg Logo in the Council Chamber

In 2008 a committee representing Winston Area Community Partnership (WACP) hired Al to do an intarsia wood design for the

Snapshots Along the Umpqua 145

new Community Center in Winston. He produced a work depicting the timber and farming community of Winston utilizing 1623 pieces from 14 different types of wood. It is on display in the lobby of the Community Center and will certainly be recorded as a masterpiece of wood intarsia.

Throughout Al's life in Douglas County he has contributed and still donates much of his time to the communities of Winston and Roseburg. To name a few: he was a member of the board of Umpqua Valley Arts Center for nine years. He served on the Winston Budget Committee during the 1980s, and in 1990 he became a member of the Winston Planning Commission. At the time of the publication of this book, at age 85, he was still serving on the Planning Commission.

Al Hooten's skillful and artistic ability will no doubt be recorded in the historic archives of Douglas County. However, the communities of Winston, Roseburg and Lookingglass will always remember that charismatic personality ready to tell a story.

Logo display in the lobby of the Roseburg Fire and Police building

Intarsia wood design in the lobby of the Winston Community Center

References:
The News Review, interview with Al. Photos: by the Author.

Snapshots Along the Umpqua

DOROTHY F. HULT

She had a passion for life, all life, and lived it to the fullest. She was intelligent, beautiful, sophisticated yet feisty, forceful, philanthropic, and an outspoken Democrat. As a spotlight to one of her legacies, the name Dorothy F. Hult will always remain synonymous with Umpqua Valley Humane Society in Douglas County.

Dorothy Frear Hult was born on November 2, 1916, in Roseburg, Oregon. She was the daughter of Floyd and Hazel Frear, who were prominent pioneers of Douglas County. Her only sibling was Donald J. Frear, who preceded her in death. She went to Roseburg High School and graduated in the top 10 percent of her class in May 1937. She attended Oregon State University and earned a Bachelor of Secretarial Science Degree in 1939. Soon after graduation she married her childhood sweetheart, Harrison Renner Winston. He was drafted into the Air Force in 1943 and was sent to the Philippines, and she moved to California and worked as a legal secretary. On his discharge from the military in 1946, the couple moved to Roseburg where he opened a law firm.

In May 1947 she gave birth to Renner H. Winston. Her marriage to Harrison ended in a divorce in 1954. On March 15, 1955, she married divorcee Paul B. Hult, in Cave Junction. Paul was the owner of the Paul B. Hult Lumber Co. in Dillard. She moved to Dillard and raised her son Renner and Paul's sons Ralph and Nels. She also joined her husband's business. Paul's sudden death in May 1970 devastated Dorothy. Coupled with that devastation was the burden of running the lumber company. After two years of shuffling multiple chores, she sold the company to Roseburg Lumber Company.

Courtesy: Leif Photography

In 1975 Governor Bob Straubs of Oregon appointed her to the State Fair Board of Commissioners. As a board member she attended many horse and rodeo shows and was quite vigilant with regard to the ill-treatment of animals. Dorothy was not only a mouthpiece for all animals, but a generous donor too. She was the cofounder of Umpqua Valley Humane Society in Douglas County in 1953, and was a volunteer secretary for over 40 years. The chapter was comprised of former Mayor Al Flegel, Dan Keohane, John Young and Zana Brodahl. One of her biggest accomplishments was the passing of the 1958 National Humane Slaughter Law. Her persistence and determination with the Oregon Legislature made Oregon rodeo games the safest in the nation. In 1977 she was honored by the American Humane Association and by the Humane Society of the United States in Washington D.C. for her outstanding dedication to the cause. In 1985 she was elected to the National Board of Directors of the American Humane Association and served for several years. Dorothy flew to New Orleans in 1992 to receive a Lifetime Achievement Award for her generous time and resources. After her passing in 2008, the American Humane Society for the Protection of Children and Animals, headquartered in Colorado, commemorated her passing by hanging a plaque on the wall of the boardroom in her honor.

Both she and her husband Paul were very much involved in the communities of Winston and Dillard. They donated materials to many projects in the community, especially to Douglas High School. They donated the materials for the first grandstand at the high school's track and field and the material that built the school's snack bar. It did not come as a surprise to her family and close friends when Winston Area Community Partnership, WACP, named the new library the "Paul and Dorothy Hult Library." She was involved with the Winston Branch of the Douglas County Library when it first came to Winston in 1964 and was located on Main St. She was one of the first directors of the board and served for two terms, one of which

Grand Marshall Melon Festival 1999

she served as president. She donated money and material to construct an annex at City Hall which housed the library from April 1967 to September 1983. When WACP began the campaign to build a new community center and library in Winston, Dorothy donated $145,842.00 to the project. She passed away one month after the Center was dedicated.

Dorothy had a passion for music as well, all kinds of music, especially jazz. She began playing the piano at a very young age. She attended the Christian Science Church in Roseburg and played the organ at services and Sunday school. It was at the church she developed the confidence and the ear for music. She had an enormous repertoire of different genres and wrote many songs herself. In 1964 she won an international song writing contest with the song, "She is a Beta Sigma Phi." That song is still sung by members of the Beta Sigma Phi Sorority throughout the world. She served as president of the Beta Sigma Phi Chapter in Roseburg and was the only Oregonian woman to be awarded the International Award of Distinction Degree. She played with a combo band at the Skyroom in Roseburg on Saturday nights for three years. Every Monday evening for about three years she held a musical quiz program at the V.A. Hospital in Roseburg for the patients. Those sessions were well appreciated by the patients.

Every moment of her life was spent serving her family and the community. She was a member of the Umpqua Watershed Resources Development Association and was a vocal advocate for the Days Creek Dam Project. She received several letters of appreciation from Senator Mark Hatfield for her vocal support of the project in Douglas County. In 1958 Governor Holmes sent her a letter of gratitude regarding her acceptance of membership to the Board of Employment for the Physically Handicapped. In 1982 the Winston-Dillard Chamber of Commerce celebrated her accomplishments with the honor of First Citizen Award. Like her husband Paul, who preceded her in death, she was a member of the Democratic Party and was quite proud of it. She served as vice chairman for several years. In 1959, when Ted Kennedy campaigned in Roseburg on behalf of his brother John, he was a guest at her house in Dillard. Later John F. Kennedy sent her a letter of appreciation for the hospitality given to his brother.

Whenever Dorothy had to address an audience, she was enthusiastic and flamboyant in her delivery and articulated her message very well. As a charter member of the Roseburg Toastmistress Club, she helped many of her co-members develop good speaking techniques. She was involved with just about every organization in Roseburg. To name a few: she was a charter member of Alturas Club and received the prestigious Member Emeritus Award, a member of Daughters of the Nile, member of Douglas County Museum and Umpqua Valley Arts Association, and member of the American Association of University Women. In 1999 she was the Grand Marshall of the parade for the Winston-Dillard Festival Association. On February 28, 2008, at age 91, Dorothy F. Hult said farewell to this plane of existence but left behind a legacy of accomplishments that has been recorded in Oregon's history.

References:
The News Review, Bio from family, Interview with Dorothy Hult. Photo: Courtesy of Leif Photography and family.

PAUL B. HULT

He may have been the most flamboyant and charismatic businessman in Douglas County for the 20th Century. He was handsome, intelligent, wealthy and generous. He was always dressed in a suit. He was a Swedish Lutheran, but not a Republican. He was a Democrat and loved it. He preached his democratic philosophies to all his friends and generously contributed to the financial welfare of the party in Douglas County and Oregon. He was a diehard fan for NASCAR racing and never missed watching a Memorial Day Indianapolis

Photo: Courtesy of the Family

500 race. He was the cousin to Nils Hult. (The "Hult Center" in Eugene, Oregon, is named in honor of Nils and his wife Jewel Hult.)

Paul Barton Hult was born the son of a sawmill family, Oscar Barton and Kim Marie Hult, on January 3, 1909, in Colton, Oregon. He was married to Mona Patchen Hult in July 1935. The couple had four children. They are: John Barton Hult, Mary Jeanette Hult, Ralph Steven Hult and Nels Thomas Hult. In 1945 Paul left his father's sawmill business in Tyee on the South Umpqua River to set up his own sawmill in Dillard, Oregon. He joined partners with Louis R. Andrus, and by October 1945, with six employees, Andrus & Hult Lumber Co. went into operation. In 1949 W.O. Kelsay, Douglas County State Representative, became a partner with 33 percent partnership. (Mr. Kelsay had an impeccable knowledge in the sawmill business.) In 1950 Paul was running the company by himself since Andrus ventured into a different sawmill operation.

By 1953 Paul was climbing the ladder of wealth and prosperity, but his marriage to Mona was sliding down a different ladder into divorce court. On July 6, 1954, the couple was divorced. Mona moved to Eugene with three of the children. John was already 18 and remained in Dillard. Paul married Dorothy Frear in March 15, 1955, at Cave Junction, Oregon. Dorothy had one son from her previous marriage and raised two of Paul's boys, Ralph and Nels, who had returned to live with their dad.

In 1956 Paul incorporated the company in the name of Paul B. Hult Lumber Co. Between 1950 and 1970 he expanded, consolidated and modernized the company several times. In 1960 the company purchased the office building of Green Valley Lumber Co. that had moved its business to Myrtle Creek. Paul transported the building to Dillard and renovated it into a first class office. He and the office staff moved out of the Southern Pacific Railroad Depot that had served as an office since 1945 when the first mill was built across from the Dillard Post Office on Highway 99. Between 1959 and 1970 he was president of K & S Cut Stock Lumber Co., an affiliate of Paul B. Hult Lumber Co. That company specialized in precut lumber for housing such as joists and rafters. At his sudden passing of a heart attack in May 1970, his wife Dorothy was left to run the company. In February 1972 she appointed H. A. Paetz as president of the company. Two months later she sold the company to Roseburg Lumber Co. in Dillard, Oregon.

Paul was quite influential in the area. In 1948 he was elected to the first Winston-Dillard Water Board of Directors. He served on the board for 10 years. He also served on the Winston-Dillard School Board for nine years. In 1953 Paul was president of the School Board when Douglas High School was being built. It was during the era of McCarthyism. The School Board selected Howard Glazer (who passed away in 2010) as the architect to build the school. Mr. Glazer, with the consent of Paul, incorporated three large ceramic murals into the design of the school, expressing the country's most civilized beliefs. At a time when the country was experiencing horrific persecutions, those murals became a symbol of anti-McCarthyism. The tiles were donated by a ceramic firm in Portland, and Paul paid the artists. In 1953 he was elected director of Western Forest Industries. In January 1959 Governor Robert D. Holmes appointed Paul to the State Board of Forestry. He served in that position for nine years. And, for 16 years, he was a director of the West Coast Lumber Inspection Bureau. He was a member of the Board of Trustees of Douglas Community Hospital.

In October of 1956 there was a lot of political hot air heating up in Washington, D.C. and Dillard, Oregon. Republican Senator Barry Goldwater of Arizona called on the Senate Election Sub-Committee to investigate a contribution of $434.00 donated by employees of Paul B. Hult Lumber Co. to Wayne Morse's campaign fund. Wayne Morse was a well-known democratic senator from Oregon. Mr. Hult defended the gesture as legal. He explained that 31 employees of his company who were supporters of Senator Wayne Morse volunteered to work a half day on Saturday, September 15, 1956, and donated their wages to Senator Wayne Morse's campaign fund in Douglas County.

Old-timers still remember Paul's kindness and generosity. Between 1945 and 1950 there was a great influx of migrant workers to Douglas County seeking employment in the timber industry. There was a scarcity of housing in both Dillard and Winston. Paul always assisted his workers with building materials when asked. His workers had his permission to take containers of safe drinking water to their houses. He donated much of the building material for the first Community Center built in Winston in 1949. He also donated material and money for the construction of the Winston Library in April 1967. Douglas High School could always depend on Paul B. Hult Lumber Co. for help with any of their athletic projects. The company donated all the material for the first grandstand and snack bar.

Paul was a member or supporter of just about every service organization in Douglas County. To name a few: He was a member of the Lutheran Church and a dependable financial supporter; he was a member of the Roseburg Shriner's Club, the Country Club and the Elks Club; he was president of the Winston-Dillard Kiwanis Club and was a member of the Board of Directors of the Umpqua Flying Club. At the time he was chairman in 1951 the club had only four aircraft.

Paul Barton Hult died on May 13, 1970. Thirty-eight years after his passing the Winston Dillard community, through Winston Area Community Partnership WACP, dedicated the new Winston Library as the "Paul and Dorothy Hult Library."

References:
The News Review, Interview with Dorothy Hult. Photo: Donated by Dorothy Hult.

GEORGE BAKER LAURANCE AND FAMILY

Reverend John Dillard and his family founded Dillard, and the town was given his name. Samuel C. Miller, who married Mr. Dillard's granddaughter, bought the Reverend's estate of 1000 acres and laid out the town. But G. B. Laurance and his family put Dillard on the Oregon map.

When George and Barbara Laurance were living in Ashe County, North Carolina, about the end of the 19th Century, their vision was to make sure that none of their sons would go away to work in the coal mines in West Virginia. (Most of the young men in that area went off to work in the mines after graduating from high school.) With the little knowledge George had learned of Douglas County, Oregon, the family was determined to leave North Carolina to seek a better life for their children. Some of their relatives and friends had tried to discourage them from leaving, telling them that Oregon was underdeveloped, with long and arduous winters. However, the negative comments about Oregon did not blur their vision. In March of 1903, after two weeks of traveling from North Carolina, George and Barbara with eight of their children stepped off the Southern Pacific Railroad train at Dillard. That community had a population of only 100 then. The family spent a week at the Dillard Hotel, owned and operated by Mr. and Mrs. Mark Howard. Within a few days of their arrival, G.B. and Barbara bought 22 acres of farmland from Samuel C. Miller.

Photo: Courtesy of The News Review

G.B. was a handyman, experienced farmer, a Democrat, and was known for his pleasant smiles. His father, Andrew Jackson Laurance, had taught him many of the techniques of farming. They farmed corn and tobacco. As a young boy, G.B. was capable of planting long and straight rows of corn and tobacco and brought that experience with him to Dillard. With the help of his sons, he built a house for the family and then concentrated on gardening. He bought several hundred strawberry plants from the Coon family and planted about seven acres. In the spring of 1906, G. B sent his first shipment of strawberries to Portland, Oregon for sale. He soon became the respectable truck gardener and horticulturist in the area, growing cauliflower, watermelons, cantaloupe, strawberries, tomatoes etc. on more than a hundred acres of land in Dillard. For many years much of his produce was shipped to Portland and Seattle, Washington. In 1907 G. B. and his family became the center of hospitality for distressed families in the area. A Southern Pacific Railroad train crashed into another train about two miles south of Dillard and caught on fire. The fire jumped the train tracks into the neighboring fields. The evacuated families were taken to the home of the Laurance family.

G. B. and Barbara had 14 children, seven boys and seven girls. Unfortunately, three of his girls died during early childhood. But on January 24, 1915, the stress of caring for eleven children fell on G. B's. shoulders when Barbara suddenly died 10 days after giving birth to her 14th child. She was only 44 years of age. The whole family was in grief and was devastated, since most of the domestic chores and the stability of the family had been carried by Barbara. Their daughters, Lena Jane and Jessie May, took over the domestic chores and the caring of their 10-day-old sister.

By the 1950s G.B. had seen the reality of his dreams: all his sons and a few of his daughters became renowned farmers in Douglas County including his last son Bert Joseph who was County Treasurer for 24 years. Members of the Laurance family owned farmlands in Melrose, Dillard, Garden Valley, Dixonville, Roberts Creek, Round Prairie, Myrtle Creek and Olalla. Towards the end of his life G.B. lived alone at Roberts Creek but always looked forward to the weekly visits from at least one member of the family. On April 17 each year, the family always congregated to celebrate his birthday. On June 23, 1960, George Baker Laurance passed away at age 93. He left behind a generation of Laurances whose children became farmers and professional citizens. In 1983 his granddaughter, Julia Laurance McNeese, won $1 Million in the Canadian lottery.

Bert Laurence:

The Douglas County Democratic Party was very proud of Bert Laurance, the last son of G.B. when he defeated Republican candidate Oliver Johnson in the 1956 general election for the seat of County Treasurer. He was the first Democrat to hold that position in many years and did so for six terms. Bert was born at Mercy Hospital in Roseburg on October 2, 1908. Like his dad, he always carried a pleasant smile. He attended elementary school in Dillard and Winston and graduated from Roseburg High School in 1926. In high school he excelled in math, baseball and football. He was the first freshman at Roseburg High School to earn the Athletic Letter "R". After graduation he played baseball for the Dillard ball team and earned many trophies for his skills in that sport.

As a young boy Bert developed the skills of farming from his father and his brothers. At age 17 he rented a plot of farmland from his dad and started his first gardening business. He also worked for one of his brothers picking tomatoes in Garden Valley. In June 1944 he married Virginia Buell in Vancouver, Washington. The couple moved to Crescent City, California where he found a job logging timber. His brother Jim also worked for the same company. At the logging camp they both played baseball for the camp ball team. Bert was the catcher and Jim the pitcher. About 1940 he and Virginia returned to Dillard and started farming. They first rented farmlands but later purchased property in Melrose and Dillard. They diversified their farming techniques, planting fruits and vegetables. They opened a fruit stand at North Bend, Oregon where they sold much of their produce. They operated that produce stand for 11 years. Bert and Virginia had two children, Pamela Jane and Nick Joseph. When the kids were older, they too helped on the farms. Both of their children are college graduates.

In 1956 Bert was approached by a few of his democratic colleagues to run for the position of County Treasurer. He agreed, even though he had no political experience. To his surprise, he defeated the Republican candidate, Oliver Johnson. Bert went on to win the seat for the next 24 years. However, he never gave up his career as a farmer. Upon his retirement, from the treasurer's position, the Winston-Dillard seniors gave him a surprise party with his family and friends. Bert Joseph Laurance passed away in December 1982.

Joseph A. Laurance:

On November 8, 2006, Joseph A. Laurance, better known as "Joe", won Douglas County Commissioner Position No. 2 in the general election. He defeated Republican Dan Hern by about 3017 votes. For Joe the victory came as no surprise since he worked hard on the campaign and had been trained in the field of political science at Southern Oregon University. He campaigned on grassroot issues which seemed to have resonated with the voters. According to *The News Review*, "Laurance becomes the third Democrat to win a seat on the Board of Commissioners in the last 30 years." On January 2, 2007, Joe Laurance took the oath of office as Commissioner of Douglas County Position No. 2. A couple minutes later, his jubilant wife Ricci crowned the ceremony with a toast of sparkling cider.

He is the son of Danford and Edith Heinbach Laurance and the great grandson of G.B. Laurance. Danford and Edith had four sons: Joe, David, Mark and Eric. Joe was born in Roseburg in January of 1950. Joe's parents were loggers and moved on several occasions, even out of state, for their business. So, between grade school in Dillard and his graduation from Roseburg High School, Joe attended several schools in Oregon and California. In 1968 he volunteered for the US Navy. During his four years in the service, he was deployed to Viet Nam on three occasions. Upon his honorable discharge from the US Navy, he attended the University of Southern Oregon. He received a Bachelor of Science Degree in Political Science and a minor in Economics. At the University he met his lovely and brilliant wife, Ricci Borg, who earned a Bachelor of Science Degree in Radiology in 1972. In June 1973 Joe and Ricci got married in Klamath Falls. The couple have three children. They are: Michael, Timothy, and Kristi. All three of their children are college graduates. They also raised three foster children: Morgan, Megan and Sarah.

Joe has brought with him to the Commissioners' office a wide range of leadership skills and experiences. He is a farmer and produce businessman. He owns a successful log-hauling trucking business. He is an airplane pilot and was manager of North Bend Municipal Airport in the 1980s. During that period he also served as assistant manager to the Medford Municipal Airport. He is approachable and compassionate, and he articulates his thoughts quite effectively. He was the coordinator of ABATE of Oregon. Between 2001 and 2003, he made three trips to Washington, DC to lobby funds to help bring about motorcycle safety nationwide. He was successful in obtaining $25 million for the program. He is an active member of Hucrest Community Church of God. Joe's compassion came alive when he joined the volunteer staff for Casa De Belen. This is a transitional housing facility dedicated to helping homeless teens and families with teens find a safe place to put their lives back together. Joe Laurence's achievements are another luminary in that vision of G.B and Barbara Laurance about 103 years ago.

References:
The News Review: 1950 – 2012, The Family memoirs by Ruby Laurance Wetzell, Historic Douglas County, Oregon, Douglas County Cemetery Records, Douglas County Museum Records. Photo: by *The News Review*. Douglas County Elections Records.

BERNICE MCCLELLAN

The burning desire to share and the selfless devotion to help the less privileged, epitomizes the love Bernice carries in her heart and the infectious smile she wears on her face when greeted. She is the type of individual who thinks of her community every waking moment. Bernice Royer McClellan was born in Pendleton, Oregon, on June 16, 1938. She is the daughter of Clarence and Reha Royer. She is the only girl in a family of three brothers. After graduation from Pendleton High School, she enrolled as a freshman at the University of Oregon in 1956. The friendship between herself and Jim McClellan developed when she worked in the cafeteria on campus. She was a junior when she decided to put her career on hold in order to marry Jim. On December 27, 1958, they were married in the Methodist Church in Pendleton, Oregon. In April 1960 Tom McClellan was born, and in July 1961 Barbara

Courtesy of Leif Photography

McClellan, commonly called "Barb", was another addition to the family. Bernice became a stay-at-home mom. But in Glendale, Oregon, where Jim accepted a position as principal at Glendale High School, her appetite for volunteering became evident. As soon as Tom and Barb were in school, she became an active leader for the Glendale 4-H club teaching home-making skills. She also became an active member in the Glendale Scholastic and Cultural Recognition Program, G.S.C.R.P. This is an organization that is actively involved in raising funds to give scholarships to kids, especially those who need help with their college education. She was a volunteer for G.S.C.R.P. for five years before leaving to come to Winston, Oregon.

On arrival in Winston in 1971, she joined the Civil Bend Parent Club. A year later she served on the Douglas County 4-H Home Economic Planning Committee and did so for many years. She joined the Roseburg Chapter of Altrusa International. This is a women's service club whose members use their energies and expertise to develop social projects to better their communities. While she was a member, she held official positions as district secretary and director of the club for two years. Altogether, she was a member for 10 years. She was on the board of the Douglas County Humane Society and was a membership director. By 1974, Wildlife Safari Animal Park in Winston was facing deep financial troubles. Bernice volunteered as a docent giving tours to the tourists. She was later employed as an executive secretary to the manager. With her quickly learned skills about the park's business she was doing multiple jobs. She spent 10 years at the park before resigning.

Her roster of volunteerism is quite long. She was a member of the Winston Park Board from 1989 to 2007 and was an active helper with the construction of Riverbend Park Outdoor Theater. She was a member of the Winston-Dillard Area Festival Association and held many official offices with the organization. She served on the Winston-Dillard Rural Fire District Budget Committee on several occasions. She has served and still is serving on the Winston-Dillard Water District Budget Committee. She is a member of the Winston-Dillard Area Chamber of Commerce and was director of the Visitors Information Center for 12 years. Her proficient skills with the English language are always sought in proofreading the writings of her colleagues and friends. In February of 1989, both she and her husband, Jim, were honored with the distinguished Award of the First Citizen of Winston-Dillard Area. With her burning desire to help less privileged families in the area, she volunteered to work for Winston-Dillard Food Pantry. In 1985 a few members of the Dillard Methodist Church started the organization. In 1989 the organization was restructured as a community supported food pantry, but still operates from the church. Every year the food pantry assists thousands of needy families with emergency food boxes. Bernice wears many hats in that organization. She is the director, and writes grants and letters to various charitable foundations. She picks up donated food and helps with the preparation of the emergency food boxes. In June 2011 the Winston-Dillard Area Chamber of Commerce honored Bernice and her husband Jim with the distinguished honor of Lifetime Achievement Award for their long and dedicated service to the community. The chamber punctuated the honor by calling it "The McClellan Award." That was the first and highest award ever given to anyone in this valley by the Chamber. History will always remember Bernice Royer McClellan for the humanitarian comfort she bestowed upon her community.

References:
The News Review and interviews with Bernice, Pamphlet: *Neighbor Helping Neighbor.* Photo of Bernice: Courtesy of Leif photography.

JIM MCCLELLAN

He writes under the name of "Curmudgeon" and loves it! But, according to Webster Dictionary's meaning of curmudgeon, James C. McClellan, better known as "Jim," is the very opposite. He is a man of integrity. He is considerate and altruistic. In 1989 both he and his wife Bernice were named male and female First Citizens of Winston at the Winston-Dillard Area Chamber of Commerce Annual Banquet. They were the first husband and wife to receive that meritorious award in the same year. In 1997 he was chosen as an outstanding community leader in the America Hometown Leaders Award by the National Center for Small Communities (NCSC).

Jim was born at Santa Maria, California, on April 25, 1930. He is the son of Charles and Helen McClellan. He has a younger sister, Kathleen Thomas. He graduated from Ventura High School in Ventura, California in 1948. While he was in High School, he was nicknamed "McPelican." After graduation he attended Ventura Junior College for one year. In 1955 he graduated from the University of Hawaii with a BA Degree in General Business. While he was doing his undergraduate studies, between 1951 and 1954, he joined the U.S. Coast Guard Reserves. He immediately transferred to the University of Oregon to work on his Masters Degree in Business. During his post-graduate studies he switched his major from business to general studies. In 1958 he graduated with a Masters Degree in General Studies. At the University of Oregon he met Bernice Royer, and they were married on December 27, 1958, in the Methodist Church in Pendleton, Oregon. They have two children, Tom and Barbara, and three grandchildren: Mark, Scott and AJ.

Courtesy of Leif Photography

Jim's resume spans 31 years of experience in the field of education. He first began his career as a teacher at Mohawk High School, in Mohawk, Oregon, in 1958. Two years later he became principal of the school. His record of success in small high schools was quickly recognized and appreciated, and in 1962 he was selected for the position of Principal/Superintendent at Monroe Union High School in Monroe, Oregon. In 1964 he accepted the principal position at Glendale High School in Glendale, Oregon. At Glendale he learned and developed a different method of teaching beginning reading. It is called the Initial Teaching Alphabet or ITA. It is a phonics based approach to reading. The method was introduced to the preschoolers in Glendale. However, the State Board of Education did not want to use the ITA method statewide. The Glendale preschool staff continued to use the method on a voluntary basis and had four and five-year-olds reading within a few months. The State Board of Education, on learning and investigating Glendale's preschoolers' success, gave the district permission to use the ITA method. In 1971 Jim accepted the Reading Coordinator's position at Winston-Dillard District #116 Public Schools. He was in charge of the reading curriculum for grades 1 through 12. He also acted as a consultant for the teachers in the field of reading and helped them solve reading problems. He worked in that position until 1975 when he was appointed to the position of Special Projects Coordinator. In 1988 Jim became Administrator Assistant for the District and held the position until his retirement in June 1989.

In 1986 he served on the committee that designed and placed the cheetah sculpture at the intersection of Main St. and Douglas Blvd. in Winston. Between the mid 1970s and the present, Jim had his footprint of volunteering in just about every organization in Winston and Douglas County. To name a few: He was chairman for Douglas County Interagency Council that was created for a few school districts. He chaired the meetings for Battered Persons Advocacy, Umpqua Regional Council of Government, R.S.V. P. the Salvation Army and several other similar agencies. In the late 1970s he became a member of the Board of Winston-Dillard Rural Fire District. He was Chairman of the Board for seven years of his eight years as a member. He was very instrumental in assisting with the design of the logo for the City of Winston and that of the Chamber of Commerce. Soon after retirement both he and Bernice started a company called B & J Data Service. In July 2005 he was sworn in as a member of the Board of the Winston-Dillard Water

District, and in 2007 he was elected president of the board and is currently in that position.

Jim's political career with the City of Winston began when he became a member of the Planning Commission. As a member he was quite outspoken and critical of decisions, or lack thereof, made by the City Council on several occasions. He served two terms. Unfortunately, the City Council rejected his application for the third term. In November 1989 the mayor and one city councilman were recalled, and Jim soon became the stratosphere for Winston politics. The then lame City Council appointed him as mayor by a unanimous decision on December 4, 1989. In accepting the position he said, "I want to get more people involved in city government." He served in that mayoral position for 11 years. Under his leadership he made city government transparent. He shored up the estranged relationship between the city and the Winston-Dillard Water District and developed cohesive working relationships between the city and all the inter-government agencies. On the dismissal of the then City Administrator, in 1990, he served as acting City Administrator without pay for six months. He helped the former Police Chief, Bruce Justis, create a Traffic Safety Commission and served as chairman for several years. In the late 1990s, he played a leading role in helping the Winston-Green Wastewater Treatment Plant obtain control from Douglas County. The county operated the facility for several years before releasing control to both Winston and the Green Sanitary District. He was the driving force behind the City of Winston to extend the Urban Growth Boundary to include Wildlife Safari, a move that protects the view-shed of the park. In 2003 Jim was again appointed to the Planning Commission and soon became president of the Commission. But again he ran into the wrath of the City Council, and his application for reappointment was denied in 2007.

At the Chamber of Commerce Banquet, before an audience of 210 people, where Jim and his wife received the First Citizen Awards, the presenter, Lloyd Stutsman, a friend of Jim's, described him as "loud, opinionated, very hard-headed and difficult. But he can't be described as one who doesn't have the community at heart." "Loud" may be an overstatement, but history will always remember Jim as selfless, steadfast, and an icon of volunteerism. He spends most of his time serving his community:

He served as treasurer of the Winston Kiwanis Club and the Winston-Dillard Festival Association Inc. He was president, treasurer and tourism director for the Winston-Dillard Area Chamber of Commerce. He served as chairman of the Pacific Power Customer Advisory Council. He was a member of Douglas County Employer Council and chaired those meetings. He served as president of Douglas County Teachers Credit Union which is now Cascade Community Federal Credit Union. He has spent and continues to spend thousands of hours manning the Visitor's Center and writing the Newsletter for the Winston-Dillard Area Chamber of Commerce. On Friday June 24, 2011, the Winston Dillard Area Chamber of Commerce awarded him and his wife, Bernice, a Lifetime Achievement Award for their selfless years of service to the community. The chamber punctuated the honor by naming all such honors given in the future "The McClellan Award."

With Jim's knowledge and experience with the different aspects of life in Winston, he built and maintains a website in order to keep the public informed. His insatiable love and devotion for his community will always be remembered.

References:
The News Review, Winston City Council Minutes and interview with the author. Letter from: NCSC - National Center For Small Communities. Photo of Jim, Courtesy of Leif Photography. The other photo by author.

MURIEL MO NICHOLS

As destiny may have designed it, Mo Nichols claims that she has come full circle now living in Winston and the greater Winston area for the past 30 years. That circle began with her birth on a farm in Argyle, Minnesota, on July 23, 1945. Argyle is a small town in northwestern Minnesota whose motto is: "Small town living, big city access." At a very early age, Mo was helping her parents on the farm. At age 11 she was already caring for the animals and operating the farm equipments. At age 18, before leaving for college, she had developed the necessary skills to manage the farm by herself. However, she swore to herself that, once she left Argyle, she did not want to step on another farm again.

Muriel Mo Jorgenson Nichols is the daughter of Loren and Jeanette Jorgenson. She is the eldest of four sisters and one brother. She attended grade school in Argyle, and in 1963 she graduated from Argyle High School, Valedictorian of her class.

Mo was very active in high school and in her senior year was editor of the school newspaper. She immediately went on to attend Moorhead State College in Minnesota and graduated with a B.S. Degree in Elementary Education and a minor in Special Education in 1967.

Soon after graduation Mo accepted a teaching position with the Bloomington, Minnesota School District. That same year she was offered a better position teaching third grade at Colorado Springs, Colorado School District. However, in 1969, she seized the opportunity to teach in her field of specialty when she accepted the job as an elementary special educator and supervising student teachers in Willmar, Minnesota. She worked in that position for two years. In 1970 Mo moved to Renton, Washington and taught elementary special education for ten years. During that period she took a year of sabbatical leave to attend the University of

Courtesy of Leif Photography

Washington where she earned a Masters Degree in Special Education in 1978.

In 1980 Mo's career swung 180 degrees. She met and became friends with Dr. Paul Hoot who was then owner of a 200 acre cattle ranch off the Hoover Hill Road about five miles west of Winston, Oregon. She accepted the job of managing the ranch for him. She did so from 1980 to 1984. It was during that period she met her husband Dick Nichols at a cattleman's conference. By 1984 she had enough of the ranching business and went back to the classroom. She accepted a teaching position with the Roseburg School District teaching elementary special education. After seven years with the district, Mo retired from teaching in 1992.

On July 31, 1987, Muriel Mo Jorgenson married Richard "Dick" Nichols in a quiet memorable ceremony in his backyard of the Nichols Brothers Ranch Inc. at 700 Old Brockway Road in Brockway. Dick's passion for community development soon ignited Mo's, and soon after her retirement she became aflame. Her claim to fame came in August 2001 when the Roseburg Park Board honored both her and her husband by renaming the popular summer concert venue at Stewart Park "Music on the Half Shell" the "Nichols Band Shell." What an honor, but a deserving one. Mo spent thousands of hours assisting in the development and launching of the annual musical summer concerts. This is a summer program that is attended by thousands of people each year. No sooner was the Roseburg program up and running when the couple launched a similar program at Riverbend Park in Winston in 1997. The summer event is called Riverbend Live. As soon as Riverbend Live season ends in the fall, Mo and Dick begin to plan for the next year's summer concerts. She wears several hats on that committee. She is the secretary, the grant writer, logistics organizer and a fund-raiser.

Mo's enthusiasm for volunteering is quite evident from the list of organizations in which she is a member. It would be fitting to name a few: She is a member of the Fourth of July Celebrations Committee in Winston. She is a member of both the Winston-Dillard Area Chamber of Commerce and Roseburg Chamber of Commerce. She is a member of the Board of Umpqua Community College Foundation. She is a member of Ford Sons and Daughters Scholarship Interview Team. In 1999 Mo was one of the founding members of Winston Area Community Partnership – WACP. This is a non-profit organization whose mission is to develop and better the entire region of Winston and the greater Winston area. From its inception, a noticeable difference to the Winston community became evident. In 2008 WACP constructed the new multi-purpose Winston Community Center at a cost of $4.7 million. Mo was one of the leading fund-raisers for that project.

The area kids' dream of having a skateboard park in Winston became a reality when Mo Nichols agreed to spearhead the project. Prior to her coming on board, the project suffered from lack of funding to meet its objective. Mo began a fund raising campaign by writing grants and seeking donations from businesses and local citizens. She personally raised more than $100,000 for the project. The project met its goal of $350,000, and in July of 2008 the area kids celebrated the birth of the Winston-Dillard Skate Board Park at Riverbend Park. That same year, on February 25, 2008, at the 30th Annual First Citizen Banquet of the Winston-Dillard Area Chamber of Commerce, Mo Nichols was given the prestigious award of First Female Citizen of Winston-Dillard Area for the year 2007. The ceremony was held at the new Winston Community Center. That hard working farm girl from Argyle, Minnesota who said "thank you" to the audience when she delivered the Valedictorian speech at her high school graduation class in 1963 is the same hard working farm lady from Brockway who said "thank you" to the audience of about 300 invitees who witnessed the ceremony.

References:
The News Review, WACP News Letter, Chamber of Commerce Bio of Mo. Photo Courtesy of Leif Photography.

RICHARD "DICK" NICHOLS

On November 15, 1996, the historic curtain was lowered on the Nichols Brothers Inc. ranching business. It was a sad day for the family and for Douglas County too. The family had operated a 2200-acre ranch spreading across communities of Brockway, Porter Creek and Tenmile. It was registered as the largest, and one of the oldest, ranches in Douglas County and the state of Oregon. Dick Nichols was the member of the family who had the foresight to advise the permanent closure of the gates of their ranching dynasty. James Davlin, Dick's maternal great-grandfather, founded the ranch in 1867. It later became known as the Nichols Brothers Ranch. In 1918 Harold Nichols, Dick's father, became manager of the ranch, and his uncle Cyril "Sid" Nichols became manager of the Brockway Store in 1922. (The store was part of the ranch.)

Richard "Dick" Nichols was born on April 5, 1929, in Brockway, Oregon. He is the son of Harold and Viola Nichols, who are deceased. His only sibling is his sister, Beverly Nichols Merchep, who is two years older than he. Dick's parents recognized a special visionary talent in Dick while he was still young. He attended the old Brockway Elementary School and graduated from Roseburg High School in 1947. After graduation he attended Oregon State University and graduated in 1951 with a B.S. Degree in Business with a minor in Farm Crops. Upon his return from college, Dick's father passed the reins of the ranch management to him. He immediately saw the ranch was not profitable and that it had been operating at a mere subsistence level. He was convinced that the family had to change their ranching practices if the ranch was to achieve profitability. His innovative ideas were first met with some resistance, but eventually he convinced the family to allow him to put them to the test. His first act was to sell off all the dairy cattle. He argued that

Courtesy of Leif Photography

they were labor intensive and unprofitable. He then concentrated on raising cattle for the beef market.

Dick's innovation paid off, and within a few years Nichols brand beef was sought throughout the state. In 1963 the ranch and the Brockway Store were incorporated as the Nichols Brothers Ranch, Inc. His uncle "Sid" was elected president, his dad elected vice president and Dick was made an executive member. With calculated expansions and consolidations the business grew to be one of the largest cattle ranches in Douglas County and the state of Oregon. Dick became an icon in the cattle ranching business and was highly respected by his peers. In the mid 1960s he was elected president of the Western Oregon Livestock Association. He was also elected vice president of the Cattlemen's Association. In 1972 Governor Tom McCall appointed him to the Oregon Beef Council to represent Western Oregon. He was a member of the Douglas County Livestock Association and served as president for several years. In 1975 he was selected to meet with President Gerald Ford as a representative of the cattle industry for the state of Oregon. In the 1980s the family made the decision to sell the Brockway Store, which they had operated for over 90 years because it just wasn't profitable. Instead, they concentrated only on raising cattle for the beef market. Dick increased the cattle stock, leased a few grazing pastures, introduced a new state-of-the-art method of cattle feeding and raised hay to sell to other ranchers. Between 1990 and 1993 the beef market was quite lucrative, and, as a result, the Nichols Brothers Ranch, Inc. business soared to profitable heights never before witnessed by the corporation. However, the 1994 slump in the beef market affected the corporation's profits. As the economic slump lingered, Dick gradually reduced their cattle stock, and by 1996, with no sign of an upswing in the beef market, he advised the family to withdraw from the cattle business.

In February 1955 Dick married Anita Young. The couple had no children of their own, but Dick adopted Anita's son Rod. They chose to live in Roseburg since Anita was working there in her father's insurance agency. Dick then commuted to the ranch each day to work. The marriage ended in divorce in 1987. Dick later married Muriel "Mo" Jorgenson.

While he lived in Roseburg, Dick became quite involved in many community and civic activities. He was a member and director of the Umpqua Lions Club and member of the Elks Club. He was a member and chairman of the Douglas County Extension Advisory Council. He was one of the three appointees on the Douglas County Budget Committee. He served on that committee for several years. Dick has a passion for development of community parks. He sees them as an important component in creating healthy community. He became a member of the Roseburg Park Commission and was highly influential in the launching of the popular summer concerts at Stewart Park, "Music on the Half Shell," in 1991. In August 2001 both he and his wife Mo were honored when the Music on the Half Shell Committee renamed the venue "The Nichols Band Shell." Those successful festivities did not come without a fight. Both Dick and Mo had several debates with the Roseburg Park Commission and lobbied the Roseburg City Council before permission was granted. In 1997 the couple launched a similar summer concert series at Riverbend Park in Winston called "Riverbend Live." For the past 13 years Riverbend Live has been a smashing success! The summer concerts draw spectators from as far south as Medford and as far north as Eugene. Dick lives many moments of his life for those events. Riverbend Live ends in August, and he begins to plan in September for the next year.

Dick appears to have both the vision and the muscle-power to bring community projects to their fruition. He is a co-founder of the Winston Area Community Partnership – WACP, a local non-profit organization whose objective is to infuse togetherness between the community of Winston and the greater Winston area. He was one of the leading fund-raisers for WACP in raising $4.7 million to construct a multi-purpose Community Center in Winston in 2008. He has been a member of the Winston Park Board since 1996. He is a member of the Winston-Dillard Area Chamber of Commerce and the Fourth of July Celebrations Committee. He was one of the driving forces behind the fund-raising campaign to build the Winston Skate Board Park at Riverbend Park. He and his family donated 10 acres of land for a park along the South Umpqua River southeast of the Lookingglass Creek Bridge to the city of Winston. On the evening of February 25, 2008, when Dick was celebrated with the award of First Male Citizen of Winston for 2007, the news came as no surprise to the majority of the guests present at the Winston-Dillard Area Chamber of Commerce 30th Annual First Citizen Banquet.

Again, Dick Nichols was born with a special talent and has altruistically used that gift to raise the social quality of his community. History will no doubt emboss his name in the archives of Winston-Dillard and the greater Winston community.

References:
The News Review, The *Umpqua Trapper*, Winston-Dillard Area Chamber of Commerce bio of Dick Nichols. Winston Park Board Minutes. Photo: Courtesy of Leif Photography

THE OSBORNE FAMILY

Webster's New World Dictionary explains the word altruism as "unselfish concern for the welfare of others." Virgle and Marie Osborne manifested that quality in their lives in Winston and other Douglas County communities. Virgle was 21 years of age and Marie was 15 when they got married. They lived a very active and satisfying life together for 56 years before Marie succumbed to death in 2002 and Virgle in 2009.

Virgle LeeRoy Osborne, Sr. was born in Rupert, Arkansas on December 10, 1924, and Esther Marie Bixler was born on October 23, 1930, in Scotland, Arkansas. They were attracted to each other from childhood. They had eight children, five biological and three adopted. Their biological children are: Amos Roy and Hilah Jane, deceased, Jimmie Lee, Reca Mae and Rita Marie. The adopted children are: Virgle Jr., Virginia Lynn and Anthony Gene. Virgle and Marie also cared for foster children in their home.

Photo: Courtesy of Family

Virgle did not finish high school, but his training in the military gave him a good foundation for his career pursuits after leaving the service. He was a decorated soldier for combat in World War II. He took part in the famous Normandy Invasion and survived the Battle of the Bulge. (19,000 Americans died and 47,500 were wounded in that battle.) Marie also did not finish high school, but was very good at anything she did. Soon after their marriage Virgle began working as a farmhand in Arkansas and moved the family to Oregon in 1950. They moved four times within the state before settling in Winston in 1957. They bought about a half acre of land on the corner of Civil Bend Ave. and Lookingglass Rd. and built a house at #14145 NW Lookingglass Rd. where they lived out the rest of their lives.

The Osborne family was very hospitable to everyone irrespective of race, economic background or religious affiliation. On several occasions, when the South Umpqua flooded Dillard and Winston, they welcomed stranded families into their home. They were especially accommodating to people of color and foreigners. There was always a pot of coffee brewing on the stove in the event a friend came by to visit. Every day and night of the week was devoted to parenting except on Tuesday nights when they played Pinochle with friends for three hours. Both Virgle and Marie worked to provide for the family. They were able to schedule their working hours so that one of them could be with the kids at all times. Finally, Marie worked nights and Virgle worked days. Eventually, Virgle found a job with the City of Winston as an equipment operator from which he retired. As Marie became older she stayed home with the kids. Hunting and fishing were more than a love to the family; they were a passion. Each year, during hunting season, they would take the kids camping so they all could hunt and fish.

Tragedy hit the family in September of 1967. They were told by the United States Marine Corps that their son, Amos, had been killed in combat in Vietnam. The family was devastated and grieved for a long time. Like his Dad and Mom, Amos was good at anything. He was especially good at wrestling and baseball. He met President Eisenhower when he was one of the few Boy Scouts chosen from Winston to go to the National Jamboree in Colorado. In his honor, the VFW Post #9745 in Winston is named after him

Snapshots Along the Umpqua   173

and so is the Babe Ruth baseball field at Riverbend Park in Winston. The dedication of the field was conducted by a group of Marines from Eugene. Virgle Sr. was a charter member of the Amos R. Osborne VFW post #9745 in Winston and on three occasions was the post commander: 1967-1968, 1968-1969 and 1972-1973. The family transformed their adversity and grief into love and altruism, of a magnitude never seen or expected in either Winston or Douglas County at that time in history. They adopted three Black children. It was 1968. The country was gripped in the jaws of racial prejudice and discrimination. Jim Crow laws were in effect throughout the country. Black people were marching for equal rights and desegregation of schools and other public places. Virgle and Marie, with the aid of an attorney, adopted a child of mixed race in Roseburg, Oregon. In August of 1968, Virgle Jr. was one day old when he became part of the Osborne family. The

VFW Amos R. Osborne Post # 9745

family went on to adopt two more Black children. Again, with the aid of an attorney, Marie went to Florida to pick up Virginia Lynn who was ten days old in October of 1971. Four years later, in 1975, Anthony Gene was one year old when he joined the family from the state of Georgia.

Education was very important to the Osborne family. Virgle and Marie were vigilant in their efforts to make sure that their kids got to school each day. They were involved with each of the kid's activities in school. As a result, all the kids attended and graduated from Douglas High School. As soon as Jimmie, known as Jim, graduated in 1970, he immediately enlisted into the Navy. In high school, Reca made the family quite proud. She was involved in many of the school activities and was selected to go to Japan as an exchange student for a term. Reca graduated in 1971. Rita kept the family quite busy during her last year in high school. She was a fast runner in track and competed in several baton contests throughout the state. She graduated in 1975. Rita later on went on to college and got an associate degree in general studies with a minor in early childhood education in 1986. Virgle Jr. adopted many of the skillful traits of his dad. He was a baseball and basketball star throughout his academic career. He graduated in 1986 and continued his tertiary education at Umpqua Community College. Jennie was very involved in most of her school's activities in both junior and high school. After graduation in 1989, she went to Western Oregon State College and later to Oregon State University and earned a BS in Microbiology. Four years later, Jennie earned a degree in Pharmacology at Portland State University. Anthony, known as Andy was a star in baseball, basketball and football. In his senior year in high school he received an academic scholarship from the College of the Redwoods to play football for the college. Unfortunately, Andy had to give up his scholarship due to an injury.

Amos R. Osborne Baseball Field dedicated in 1982 at Riverbend Park

When each of their adopted children reached the age of 18, Marie set out on a quest to find their biological parents. She located both parents of Virgle Jr. His father is African American, and his mother is of European descent. Virgle Jr. eventually met both parents. Jennie's biological parents are in the Bahamas. Marie made contact with the mother via correspondence. She was unsuccessful in locating either of Andy's biological parents.

When Marie and Virgle passed on they left behind six children, eleven grandsons, sixteen great grandchildren and an unprecedented legacy as "Lovers of Mankind."

References:
The News-Review, Information Re: family from daughter Rita, Records of Winston-Dillard VFW, City of Winston Park Board Minutes. Photo of family donated by family, the others by author.

THOMAS PARKINSON

When he rose to address his fellow senators, Senator Thomas Parkinson of Winston, and senator representative of the Fourth Congressional District from Douglas County, always commanded the respect of his fellow members for his intelligence, honesty and diligence. For the ten years he served in the senate he was known for his intransigent support for education. That came as no surprise to the residents of Winston and Dillard. Mr. Parkinson was a teacher at the Dillard Elementary School from 1920 to 1925 and was a good one too.

Thomas Parkinson was born on March 25, 1897, in Lewistown, Illinois and grew up on a farm. After graduating from high school he attended teacher training college for a year. He served in the US Army in World War I. After being discharged from the military, he married his sweetheart Sula Sala. They had a daughter, Mary Jo. They moved to Douglas County, Oregon in 1920 and began homesteading on about 49 acres of property in the Winston Section Valley. Their property, which is now owned by Ben Byrd, 44.84 acres, borders Parkway Subdivision to the southwest and overlooks the South Umpqua River. He began teaching at Dillard Elementary School in 1920 but resigned after five years to open a grocery business in

Photo: Courtesy of Douglas County Museum

Roseburg. In 1951 the family sold the farm to Mr. and Mrs. Ben Fromdahl and moved from the Winston Section Road to Roseburg.

The store was located on 619 SE Cass Ave., between SE Stephens and SE Pine St. The store also delivered groceries to customers' houses when called upon to do so. In 1955 they sold the grocery business but still maintained ownership of the building. It housed the Robertson's School of Business on the upper floor and Bradley's Market on the ground floor. During that memorable August 7, 1959, "Blast" in Roseburg, the building sustained considerable damages to the interior.

Thomas Parkinson was a Republican and was very active in many civic organizations. He was president of the Kiwanis Club of Roseburg and served for many years as Lieutenant Governor for Clubs in several counties in southwest Oregon. He was involved in the 4H club and for many years provided the club with an annual school scholarship. He was a member of the Roseburg Chamber of Commerce. He was also on the Board of Directors for the Oregon Retail Distributors Institute. He was an active member and vestryman for the local Episcopal Church in Roseburg and was a member of the American Legion.

However, Thomas Parkinson was best known for his accomplishments for education and the environment in the senate 1942 - 1952. He was chairman of the Education Committee in the senate. Of the 69 bills on education his committee reviewed, 61 of those bills passed when they were brought before the senate. He was highly influential in securing the passage of the junior college bill in the 1949 session in the senate. He was very active as a senator. He was vice chairman of the Game Committee and served on the committees for forestry and public buildings, resolutions and state affairs. He was the author of the bills that led to the removal of commercial fishing for game fish on the Umpqua River. The long sessions in the senate gnawed away at his health, and in 1952 he declined to run. Attorney Geddes of Roseburg was elected to the position.

At age 70, he and his wife moved to the community of Woodburn, Oregon. After his wife's passing in 1977, he moved to Scottsdale, Arizona to be closer to his daughter, Mary Jo, her husband, John Killip, and two grandchildren. Senator Thomas

Parkinson passed away on April 28, 1987, in Arizona. He was 90 years of age. He is buried at Roseburg Memorial Gardens.

References:
The News-Review, Douglas County Museum, *The Oregon Blue Book: 1951-1952*

MARTIN SUKSDORF

There was an obvious characteristic about the persona of Martin Suksdorf as he passed middle age. His upper torso was bending, and it bounced severely as he walked. That deformity developed as a result of polio he contracted as a child at the age of ten. The year, 1909, was very traumatic for some children and their parents. Infantile paralysis (polio) swept across the country from the Pacific to the Atlantic. Martin became very ill. His parents noticed that his spine was curving, so they took him to a doctor in Spangle, Washington. The doctor advised the parents to put Martin in a half-body cast in order to straighten the back. When the doctor removed the cast several months later, it had not straightened the spine but made it worse and caused the ribs to collapse. The parents were devastated. Martin's father took him to a sanitarium for crippled children in St. Louis. The hospital was using a therapy developed by Sister Elizabeth Kenny of Australia. On their way there, they both became very ill with ptomaine poisoning after eating fish at a restaurant. After spending about five months at the hospital receiving therapy, Martin's spine straightened by more than 50%, he regained strength in his muscles and his rib cage was normal. But as if the trauma of the polio and ptomaine poisoning weren't enough, during his stay in the hospital, an earthquake hit St. Louis and caused severe damage to the hospital while terrifying patients, visitors and staff.

Many of the people of Winston who remembered Martin described him as a short, hunchbacked old man who owned most of the land on the east side of

Photo: From Irma Gourley

Winston. He was born in Spangle, Washington, a German speaking community, on July 14, 1899. His parents were Adolph Fredrick and Anna Jons Suksdorf. He had an older brother, Adolph Detlef, and two younger sisters, Frieda and Irma. The family bought 660 acres of land in Wilsall, Montana and moved there to farm wheat and hay. At the age of 23, he moved to Winston (then called Coos Junction) with his parents and two sisters. His older brother Adolph had married and left home. In 1922 his parents traded their farm in Wilsall, Montana, plus $20,000, for 80 acres of developed fruit orchard on the east side of Winston. A few years later they bought another 34 acres from Harry Winston. The fruit orchard came with horses, cows, pigs, turkeys, chickens, plus barns and a two-story, four-bedroom, relatively new house. The house address today is 111 SE Suksdorf St.

Martin's dad suffered from severe arthritis; it became worse as he grew older and he was always in pain. He took care of the grafting of certain fruit trees, the roadside fruit stand and all financial transactions. Martin took care of the entire orchard and helped with the livestock. Martin hired helpers when necessary. He began working before sunrise and finished after the sun set. He developed the ability to repair and operate all the equipment and pruned and sprayed all the fruit trees. During harvest time he transported prunes, peaches, apples and pears to the canneries in Roseburg and Eugene. Whenever his mother made apple cider he would drive his father to the coast to sell the product. Martin never complained and was always kind to the orchard helpers. His sister Frieda left home in 1926 and Irma in 1934 as they both got married and moved away from Coos Junction.

When Martin moved to Coos Junction, the area was sparsely populated. About 30 people lived there. The only business there was a blacksmith shop owned by Charlie McGinnis. The people who lived in Coos Junction at the time shopped in Roseburg, Dillard, Brockway or Green. By the 1930s, during the Great Depression, the fruit industry tumbled. Some of the farmers in the area defaulted on their loans and, as a result, lost their farms. But Martin's family, with a diversified orchard, was able to make payments on their debts each month. By the 1940s, the price of prunes fell so low the farmers were losing money by harvesting their crop. During that slump in price, prune trees from Glendale to the Willamette Valley developed a disease, and most of the trees died. Again, Martin's parents survived the demise.

At the end of World War II there was a timber boom in Oregon. Douglas County led the state in the production of timber and timber revenues. Migrant workers from California, Texas, Arkansas, Kentucky, Oklahoma and Missouri came to Douglas County in search of work in the timber industry. Coos Junction began to grow rapidly. The influx of that many people created a shortage of housing. By 1947 Martin, with the full support of his parents, began to capitalize on the housing shortage. He got out of the fruit business and began subdividing the orchard into house lots with appropriate roads. He also started building two-bedroom houses and renting them on a higher purchase basis. He held the mortgage on the houses. He was fair, honest and extremely generous. Through his good business and ethical practices Martin became quite respected in the community. Suksdorf St., named for the family, divides the north from the south on the east side of Winston. The streets of Darrell and Gregory were named for his nephews.

In the late 1940s and early 1950s leaking septic tanks and outhouses became a nuisance for some communities across the State of Oregon. The State Sanitary Department started a campaign to get communities with that problem to form a sewer sanitary district. Martin was approached by Douglas County Health Department to organize the formation of such a district. In 1950 he was elected chairman of the Winston Sanitary District Committee. By 1952 the Winston Chamber of Commerce, of which Martin was a member, began a door-to-door campaign for signatures to petition the county for incorporation. Again, Martin was one of the leaders promoting the incorporation of the community. After the city was incorporated in June of 1953, he ran for the first City Council and was elected with 100 votes on August 25, 1953. He served two terms as City Councilor and one term as Planning Commissioner.

Before Martin came to Coos Junction he attended a business college in Eugene in 1921. His training gave him an insight into this new venture. Between 1950 and 1960 he was doing very well. He built the Suksdorf building with apartments above, otherwise known as the "Old West Building" on Main St. This building was leased to Howard Hardware Store. The business moved when it lost parking due to the widening of the highway by the Highway Department in 1975. He owned and sold the Cottage Court. That business was located where the 7-11 Store is presently located. He bought Schaeffer's Motel on Main St. He operated and lived at the motel for several years. Safari Inn is now located on that very same site and "The Old West Building" is still operating on Main St.

Martin was very self-conscious about his physical appearance and never seemed to take a serious interest in dating girls. In high school he had a few dates but never pursued them. He was frugal, never spent much on himself and had no friends. His life was devoted to work and the care of his parents. When his parents learned of his secret marriage to Margret Jameson, a young girl 42 years his junior, they were devastated. Gossiping about the marriage flew across the community. His father passed away in December of 1962, and 50% of the estate was given to Martin with the understanding that Martin would take care of his mother until her death. The remaining 50% was divided among the other siblings. He did not live with Margret when they first got married, but he supported her. He continued to live and take care of his mother until her passing in1975 at the age of 99.

Martin's health and money began to go downhill. He became financially bankrupt. The bank foreclosed on all his assets, including his parents' house that he had inherited. He divorced Margret and moved into Roseburg in 1988. He had no health insurance and lived off his Social Security monthly check. Martin William Suksdorf passed away in 1993 in Roseburg at the age of 93. His divorced wife, Margret, passed away in Alaska in 2001.

References:
Growing Up with the West by Irma Gourley, Correspondence between Irma Gourley and the Author, *The News Review,* Winston City Council Minutes. Family photo.

DR. HARRY L. VAN DERMARK

He was not the first doctor to practice medicine in Winston, Oregon, but he was the first M.D. to do so. He was a member of the American Academy of Family Practice. Dr. Harry L. Van Dermark came to Winston from Cottage Grove, Oregon where he was practicing medicine with a group of doctors. He rented an office at the junction of Main Street and Highway 42 in October 1958, which was the same office where Dr Frederick Bracker, Osteopathic Physician and Surgeon, practiced medicine in 1952. He was also on staff with Mercy Medical Hospital in Roseburg for over 20 years. In 1978 he bought the building at 470 SW Douglas Boulevard and moved his office there. It is interesting to note that Dr. Van Dermark made use of every minute of his time. He actually built some of the furniture that was used in his office and mowed his own lawn. He practiced medicine until his untimely death in 1980.

Harry Leland Van Dermark was born in Medford, Oregon on December 18, 1925. He was the son of Peter and Hazel Van Dermark. He grew up in a small house on Apple Street near the Armory. He was smart and quite active as a teenager. Unfortunately, he contracted polio when that terrible disease swept through Oregon in the late 1930s. But fortunately for him, with swift medical attention and loving parental care, he recovered from the disease without any physical impairment. After graduation from high school in 1943, Harry attended the University of Oregon studying pre-medicine. He chose to attend the University Of Oregon School of Medicine in Portland to get his medical degree.

Photo: Courtesy of Family

He earned money for school working at fruit orchards and fruit packing plants in Medford during the summer months. It was at one of the fruit packing plants he met Vada Imalee Griffin. The couple dated for a year and married in April 1952. The couple moved from Medford to Portland where their first child, Steve, was born. They had five children. They are: Steve, Karen, David, John and Mary. In 1952 he received his medical degree. The day after graduation he enlisted in the US Army and was sent to El Paso, Texas to do his internship at Beaumont General Hospital. While stationed in El Paso, their second child, Karen, was born. Dr. Van Dermark and his family were sent to Salzburg, Austria. From there he was transferred to the base at Livorno, Italy, located on the Mediterranean Sea.

In 1956 he was transferred back to the United States with his family and was soon discharged from the military. The family moved to Cottage Grove, where Dr. Van Dermark practiced medicine with a group of doctors and was on staff with the Cottage Grove Hospital for a short time. It was in Cottage Grove their third child, David, was born. Their fourth child, John, was born at Mercy Hospital in Roseburg in May 1962 and passed away in July 1962. Their fifth child, Mary, was also born at Mercy Hospital in March 1964. Before coming to Winston, Dr. Van Dermark filled a vacant position for two weeks in Drain, Oregon.

Dr. Van Dermark always had a good working relationship with his patients. Many of them still speak of his gentleness and kindness. That quality may have propelled him to run for a seat on the Winston City Council in November 1960. He won one of three available seats on the council and served for a period of four years. He was a member of the Winston Chamber of Commerce and served as secretary-treasurer of the Douglas County Medical Society. He was a member of Winston Kiwanis and was a Free Mason of Roseburg. In October 1962 Dr. Van Dermark was elected to the Board of Directors of the Episcopalian Church. That board was responsible for organizing the construction of housing for the aged in four deaneries of the Dioceses of the church. In 1964 he was elected president of Mercy Medical Staff. He was a member of the Toastmasters Club. He was quite involved with Job's Daughter's Bethel for many years and served as their associate guardian.

It is indeed admirable when children can brag about the love of a father. Dr. Harry Van Dermark was that father whose love and affection will always be remembered by her four children. He loved life and shared every spare moment of it with them. On June

29, 1980, Dr. Harry Leland Van Dermark passed away at the age of 54. He was later joined by his wife, Vada Imalee Van Dermark on September 17, 2008 and his first son Steven Van Dermark on October 25, 2012.

References:
The News Review, Family Bio. Photo of Dr. Van Dermark by Family.

LARRY WAIT

With an enthusiastic demeanor and altruistic devotion to his community, Larry L. Wait has taken volunteerism to a whole new level. He was born in Belleville, Kansas, June 11, 1936, a small community in the north of the state known for its midget auto car racing. His parents were Russell and Lucille Wait. His only sibling is Lyle Wait, five years his junior, who lives in Roseburg. Larry was about six feet tall and handsome and walked with a sway due to the braces he wore on both legs. Between the ages of four and five he came down with polio. He spent most of his childhood in and out of the Shriners Hospital in St. Louis, Missouri, receiving treatment. The disease attacked his legs, arms and hands leaving them disabled. He had several corrective surgeries to improve usability. On several occasions he had to spend as much as six months in the hospital. His treatment continued until the age of seventeen. He used braces on his legs for walking until 1976 when he was forced to use a wheelchair after shattering an upper right femur from a fall. In 1954, at the age of 18, Larry graduated from Belleville High School in Belleville, Kansas in spite of his many physical setbacks.

Courtesy of Leif Photography

That same year he and his brother moved to Roseburg with his parents.

He attended the University of Oregon for one year and then transferred to Southern Oregon College in Ashland where he earned a B.S. Degree in Education in 1960. He began graduate school at Southern Oregon College for one term but dropped out to accept a teaching position with Winston-Dillard Elementary School. He was quite popular and loved by his students. He taught third and fourth grades at Dillard Elementary School for seven years and the same grades at McGovern Elementary (the name was changed from Civil Bend in 1986) for 21 years. He volunteered for 10 years assisting with the McGovern third grade swimming program. In 1988 Larry, with an impeccable record of attendance, retired from Winston-Dillard School District 116 after 28 years of service.

During the day he was busy in the classrooms, and in the evenings he was volunteering in Winston-Dillard and Roseburg communities. In 1963 he joined the Winston-Dillard Fire Department as a volunteer fireman. He was quite versatile and held many positions such as dispatching, taking pictures of fires and auto accidents, and doing non-combatant chores. With the training he received as a first aid instructor in college, he was certified to teach both elementary and advanced first aid classes to the paid and volunteer firemen. He was also a first aid instructor for the American Red Cross for 25 years. On several occasions he operated the resuscitator when someone was having breathing difficulties. In 1969 one of the largest and longest lasting fires to break out in this area was at Permaneer Corporation on Dillard Gardens Road. The fire destroyed several buildings in the compound and spread to Roseburg Lumber log decks burning about two and a half million board feet of logs before it was brought under control. After taking more than 100 slides of the fire, Larry got into action using a one and a half inch hose line and began cooling down a portion of a warehouse for about four hours. The fire was brought under control, but not before 36 hours. Larry was forced to retire as a volunteer fireman after shattering the femur in his right leg from a fall in 1976. Larry was then, and still is, confined to a wheelchair. However, that handicap did not interfere with his passion for volunteering in his community. He accepted a position on the Winston-Dillard Fire District Budget Committee and became the chairman for the last two years of his service before being elected to the District Fire Board. He faithfully served on the board for 10 years. During that period the fire department experienced tremendous growth, especially with the addition of a full time ambulance service for the area. His devoted service with the fire department was honored on three occasions. He was named W-D Volunteer Fireman of the year in 1972 and in 1974. In 1974 he was awarded Fireman of the Year for Douglas County. Altogether, Larry has volunteered for the Winston-Dillard Fire Department for over thirty years.

Larry was a member of the Winston-Dillard Chamber of Commerce and served on its Board of Directors for four years. He was a member of the Food Pantry and served on the Board for several years. He was a charter member of the Lions Club with a perfect attendance record for 31 years. He held all the offices in the club including president three times and zone chairman for two years. He also was Deputy District Governor and was awarded the Melvin Jones Fellowship Award in 1992. He was a member and served as chairman for four years of the Special Transportation Advisory Council, an organization created to assist with transportation for the elderly and the disabled in Douglas County.

He served on the Winston City Council from 2001 to 2004 and during that period was appointed chairman of the Park Board. Since there is no wheelchair accessibility to the meeting stage in the council chamber, the city constructed a wheelchair ramp at the rear of the building behind the stage. As a councilor he was quite vocal with his opinions and articulated his ideas very well. He was one of the organizers of the Melon Festival that was started by the Lions Club. He served on its board and has assisted in every festival activity since the beginning in 1970. He takes an interest in all the city parks and is always present taking pictures whenever there is a development project. He is quite knowledgeable about the locations of all the utilities at Riverbend Park. In 1986 Larry was honored as Winston-Dillard First Citizen.

Larry is very religious and is a member of the Foursquare Gospel Church in Winston. He served on the Board of Directors for four years. Service to his community in the form of charitable donations is another attribute that makes him special. He is always ready to donate to any worthy cause in his community. He is still consumed with love and passion for volunteering, but is less actively involved due to a partial loss of hearing. The community will always remember Larry L. Wait for his love and passion to help.

References:
The News-Review, City Council Minutes, Winston Park Board Minutes, Winston-Dillard Fire Department Newsletter, Interviews with Larry. Photo: Courtesy of Leif Photography.

BRUNETTE WILSON
  Brunette Wilson left behind a floral legacy in Winston, Roseburg and several Douglas County parks when she said farewell to the communities in February of 1978. She and her husband came to Douglas County in 1955, but when they retired they returned to her birthplace, Stephenville, Texas, a small town about 70 miles southwest of Fort Worth. She was a professional landscape architect and left her mark of excellence, especially at reflection garden along the riverbank at Riverside Park in Roseburg.

Courtesy of Leif Photography

  Of the 23 years Mrs. Wilson lived in Winston, most of it was spent volunteering for several civic organizations. She was the founder of the Winston Beautification Committee. She began landscaping the Winston Community Park at the time when the park was under the ownership of Douglas County. She became a member of the Winston Community Club that was responsible for the upkeep of the park. In 1972 the county deeded the park to the City of Winston, and she was appointed to the Park Board. She was a member of the Winston-Dillard Area Chamber of Commerce and the Roseburg Women's Club. She designed the landscaping and helped with the planting around Winston City Hall, Douglas High School and Roseburg City Hall. She was director of Umpqua District No. 16 and Oregon State Federation of Garden Clubs. In July 1971 she was named director of the Landscape Study Courses and Critic's Council. She worked with professors of Oregon State University setting up courses in landscape design. She was responsible for much of the landscaping around the city of Roseburg. She was also a reporter for *The News Review* in 1958.

In 1978 the Winston-Dillard Area Chamber of Commerce began honoring outstanding citizens for their selfless contribution to the community. Mrs. Brunette Wilson was the first and only recipient for 1978 to receive the First Citizen Award of Winston. At the presentation she expressed appreciation and gratitude for the prestigious honor but announced to the more than 150 guests who attended the ceremony that she and her husband were leaving the area to return to their hometown in Texas.

She praised the Beautification Committee for making Winston a better city to live in and said: "I've seen improvements in the time I've been in Winston." She left Winston one week later.

References:
The News-Review, Winston Park Board Minutes. Photo: Courtesy - Leif Photography

WINSTON FAMILY

The Winston Family has long been a permanent fixture in the historical landscape of Douglas County. Agnes Rice Winston (better known as "Gammy"), and wife of William Chauncy Winston, is the link between the settlers of Rice Creek, Willis Creek and Rice Hill. At age one Agnes left Putnam County, Illinois with her parents, Harrison and Martha Willis Rice, crossed the Plains along the Oregon Trail, and arrived in Oregon in September 1853. The Rice family took out a Donation Land Claim along the creek southwest of Dillard, known today as Rice Creek. Her mother's family settled Willis Creek and her father's family settled Rice Hill. She was three years old when her parents' log cabin at Rice Creek was attacked by Indians during the Indian war of 1855 to 1856.

Photo: Courtesy of Douglas County Museum

Seventeen years after her birth date, May 25, 1852, Agnes married William Chauncy Winston and moved to Civil Bend District (later named Winston) to farm with her husband. They had eight children: Pearl, Eva, Ruth, Mattie, Edna, Fred, Winnie and Harry. Eva died at age sixteen. Agnes handled all the office work for their family fruit and vegetable farm and ferry business. She also served as postmaster between 1898 and 1903. "Gammy" was known as the "beloved" of Douglas County. She was one of the organizers of the Winston Merry-Go-Round Club. She was a member of the Roseburg Women's Club and the Garden Club. She spent many years as an active member of the Woman's Christian Temperance Union WCTU. Agnes Rice Winston was 85 when she passed away on May 4, 1940. She is buried at Civil Pioneer Cemetery in Winston.

Her husband, William Chauncy Winston, was born in Albany, New York, April 29, 1838. He left New York by ship in 1860 and headed for California. He found work mining there for a short while but moved to Oregon in 1862. He lived and taught school in Coles Valley until about 1867. He was an eyewitness to the

"Champagne Riot" in Coles valley and testified as a witness at the trial in Roseburg in 1867. He moved to the Civil Bend District and taught school in the Willis Creek School District. In 1869 he married Agnes Rice who was one of his students. He was 32 years of age and she was 17. The couple had eight children: Pearl, Fred, Harry, Ruth, Winnie, Eva, Mattie and Edna.

William's real trade was wagon making, but he preferred farming and gardening. In 1871 W. C. Winston, as he was commonly called, together with William McBee, purchased 320 acres of land from Richard Jenkins. It is not clear as to what happened to the partnership with McBee, but in 1876 they parted leaving W. C. Winston with 198 acres of independent farmland to farm. On his farm he planted all kinds of fruit trees especially pears, apples, prunes, cherries and peaches. He is credited with introducing broccoli to Douglas County. In 1877 he built a commercial ferryboat. He operated the ferry during high water season transporting travelers across the South Umpqua between Green and Winston. The construction of a bridge in 1887 abruptly ended the ferry business. Still, Mr. Winston built a two-story house that same year which typifies the "Classical Revival and Queen Anne" style of architecture. The house, which is a landmark in the community, is on the National Register of Historic Places. His granddaughter, Beverly Brown, lived there, until her passing in 2011, with her daughter, Cheryl Weese, who continues to live there. He was one of the founding members of Civil Bend Pioneer Cemetery in 1878. W. C. Winston passed away on April 1, 1926, and was buried at Civil Bend Pioneer Cemetery in Winston.

In 1893, when postal services came to Civil Bend District, Elijah Winston, brother of W. C. Winston, was appointed to the postmaster's position. The name of the district soon changed to Winston. Elijah held the postmaster position until 1898. Thereafter

Photo: Courtesy of The News Review

the responsibilities of the post office were taken over by Agnes Winston until 1903 when postal services were suspended.

Elijah Winston was born in Albany, New York, in 1834. He and his wife Mary Collins Winston and Daughter Alice came to Oregon in 1877. He settled and farmed lands on the west side of Roseburg along the Coos Bay Military Wagon Road. He was very successful as an orchardist and was one of the first of the pioneers to grow fruit commercially. When his wife Mary passed away in 1910, he married Fredona Moon. At age 81, he was hit by a bicycle while walking on the road near his house. Unfortunately, he never recovered from the injuries and passed away on September 11, 1915. He is buried at Roseburg Memorial gardens.

The name on the sign identifying the historic house at #350 Winston Section Rd. is Harry Winston. But Harry was born one year after the house was built by his father in 1887. However, Harry, who was the third child, took over most of the farmlands from his father and gradually bought and leased several hundred acres for the estate. He was very ambitious and expected to become wealthy through farming. He was the first farmer in Douglas County to use an aircraft to spray his orchards. He had orchards in Winston Section, Green, Lookingglass and Round Prairie while diversifying his farming techniques between fruits and vegetables, especially beans and broccoli. It seemed like it would be profitable, but when the Great Depression hit Oregon between 1929 and 1933, the price of fruit and vegetables fell to an all-time low. It cost farmers more to produce a ton of fruit than they were receiving on the open market. As a result, Harry defaulted on his loans for some of the property he was buying on contract from Douglas County Bank and lost several of his orchards.

Winston's house built in 1887

Harrison Abraham Winston, known to everyone as "Harry" was born on April 13, 1888, in Winston Section. He was tall, weighed about 190 pounds and was quite strong. He was 35 years of age when he married Ulah Renner Winston. The couple had four children: Ulah (Julie), Beverly, Virginia and Harrison. As mentioned above, Beverly Browne (deceased 2011) owned and lived in the historic house with her daughter and family, Carol Weesee. Beverly kept a diary of the family. After graduation from college she taught elementary school. She was a published poet and her work can be found at Douglas County Library. Julie was a dance instructor and owned a dance studio in the Winston Section. Harrison was an attorney and WWII Veteran. At one time Douglas County was the Turkey Capital of the World, and Harry invested in that venture. According to Harrison's memoir, he had bought 200 acres of land from Pacific Life Insurance Company for $5000.00 in 1946. The land was located on the west side of Winston Section Road between the Winston Community Park and Plum Ridge. He raised the turkeys in that area, which became known as "Turkey Hill." Harry did not make his millions but left a legacy of hard work coupled with kindness. He passed away July 26, 1952. He too was buried at Civil Bend Pioneer Cemetery in Winston.

On the other hand, his wife Ulah, who was a schoolteacher by profession before she married Harry, and a devout Christian Scientist, became wealthy after his passing. She subdivided much of the properties into lots and sold them. According to their son, Harrison, she grossed over $250,000. After paying off the estate's minimal debts, she gave the rest of the money to her children and the church in Roseburg. She donated five acres of "Turkey Hill" and an unknown sum of money to Douglas County for Winston Community Park. The picnic pavilion was dedicated in honor of her husband Harry A. Winston. The pavilion is still at the park in the picnic area. The plaque honoring her husband is a witness of Ulah's thoughtfulness and simplicity of life.

References:
The News Review, Douglas County Museum Records, *The Roseburg Ensign.* Photo of Mrs. Winston Courtesy of Douglas County Museum. *The News Review*, Photo of the Winston family and Winston House by the author.

HARRISON RENNER WINSTON

He had a bird's eye view of Nagasaki and Hiroshima before the atomic bomb was dropped on both cities in Japan while flying war correspondents and photographers over those cities and also Tokyo. Two days after the two cities were destroyed, Lt. Winston had a magnified view of the damages when he flew his B-24 bomber at low altitude over both Hiroshima and Nagasaki to see whether the Japanese had surrendered. The damages were horrific with more than 240,000 casualties.

Harrison Renner Winston was born on June 19, 1916, in the Winston Section Valley. He was the son of Harry and Ulah Winston. The City of Winston is named after his grandfather, William Chauncey Winston, and Rice Creek and Rice Hill are named after his Grandmother Agnes Rice's family. He was the only son of four children. His sisters are: Ulah (Julie), Beverly and Virginia. He was 5'-3" and "skinny" as a teenager and played very good tennis. He had a fighting instinct to win. His uncle Fred nicknamed him "Bill" after the great American tennis star William "Bill" Tilden. (William Tilden dominated the sport of tennis during the 1920s. He won seven US national titles and five Wimbledon titles.) Harrison never lost a match in his early career and was Roseburg's tennis champion from 1934 to 1936. When he was in college at Willamette University in Salem he played varsity tennis and was the number one player on the team. He and his doubles partner, Talbot Bennett, won the northwest doubles championship in 1935. By then he was 6'-2 1/2" tall and weighed 145 pounds. At age 17 he graduated from Roseburg High School at the top of the class of 1933.

It was the middle of the Great Depression. Farm products prices had fallen to an all time low. His father lost several orchards to the bank in Roseburg since he had defaulted on the payments. This devastated the family. However, his mother was determined to send him to college whether they had the money or not. He was

Snapshots Along the Umpqua 193

very fond of his father and developed quite a bond with him. In his memoir, written in 1988, he expressed that he wished he had developed the kind of human qualities his father had before his passing in 1952; and he wanted to be buried next to him upon his passing.

With $50.00 from his parents to pay for tuition and books, Harrison enrolled at the University of Willamette in Salem, Oregon, in 1933. A friend of the family gave him free boarding and lodging in exchange for work at his cannery plant in Salem. He also worked at a school for the blind transcribing Braille for fifty cents an hour. During the summers while at college, he earned money loading boxes of fruit on freight trains in Green. Two years later, in 1935, he transferred to the University of Oregon Law School and graduated with a law degree in 1938. He was a member of Delta Tau Delta Fraternity and was a Rhodes Scholar. He was a member of the Oregon State Bar Association and was licensed to practice law in Federal Court. After graduation, he married his childhood sweetheart, Dorothy Frear, in June of 1939. (She was the daughter of a prominent pioneer family, Floyd and Hazel Frear.) They had a son, Renner H. Winston, who now lives in Lake Oswego. Harrison and Dorothy divorced in 1954. After passing the Lawyer's bar examination in July, 1938, he went to work for Guy Cordon Law Firm in Corvallis Oregon. (Senator Guy Cordon is remembered for getting the Federal Government to give back a portion of the money earned from O&C timber sales to Oregon's Counties.)

He joined the US Air Force in 1943, during World War II, and received his basic pilot training at Tempe, Arizona. From there he went on to Albuquerque, New Mexico to learn to fly B-24 bomber aircrafts. During his pilot training, his wife Dorothy moved to Glendale, California and worked as a legal secretary. Lt. Winston was a decorated soldier, achieving the rank of second lieutenant before he was discharged in January 1946. He was stationed in the

Philippines and flew a B-24 liberator bomber. He flew combat missions over a wide area of the southwestern Pacific region. Of the 20 combat missions flown, he received recognition for four battles. He was awarded the Asiatic-Pacific ribbon with one silver and four bronze stars, the Air Medal with an oak leaf cluster, the Philippines Liberation Medal, and the American Theater Ribbon. On one of his combat missions, he and his crew had to crash land their B-24 aircraft. Their aircraft was hit during the raid, and upon their return they lost power in #2 and #3 engines. No one was killed in the crash, but they spent seven weeks in the hospital recovering from their injuries. It is interesting to note that Lt. Winston was petrified of snakes and chose the Air Force in order to avoid contact with such creatures. But on the air base in the Philippines, there were snakes everywhere. He encountered them in his camp, in his sleeping bag, in the outhouses, etc. When Lt. Winston was not flying, he was practicing law in the Service. He successfully defended many soldiers in the Army's general courts. But his claim to fame was when he defended a soldier who was charged with murder, and Winston was able to secure an acquittal. He was involved with flying out British and American prisoners of war from Okinawa to Clark Field in the Philippines. He was sent to Guam for treatment suffering from hepatitis and spent two months in the hospital. At the end of the war he piloted a B-24 bomber from Okinawa to Mather Field, California. He was discharged from the Air Force at Portland Air Base in January 1946.

Upon Harrison's return to Winston he opened a law office in Roseburg in the Pacific Building in January 1946. He practiced law in Roseburg, many cities in Oregon, and the state of Utah. When the City of Winston was seeking incorporation in 1953, he was hired by the Winston Chamber of Commerce as the attorney to file the court's papers on the community's behalf. He became Winston's first City Attorney in June 1953 and served until March 1956. He was involved with many civic organizations. He was a member of the Elks Club. He served on the Roseburg City Council from 1947 to 1952. He was president of the Roseburg Community Chest. He served as a VFW post commander for four years. He was always engaged, giving inspirational and informational talks to such organizations as Roseburg Chamber of Commerce, the Kiwanis Club, the Moose Club, the Rotary, to name a few. In

February 1953, he suffered a broken shoulder blade when his vehicle went over a 20 foot embankment near Canyonville. The vehicle he was driving was completely destroyed.

Before he owned his aircraft he joined the Umpqua Flying Club. However, in 1962, he bought his own Mark 21 Mooney four-seat aircraft that was faster and bigger than the aircrafts at the club. Harrison loved flying and felt safer flying than driving. He made multiple trips across the United States and Mexico. In 1952 he and his wife Dorothy, together with Paul B. Hult and his wife, flew to Havana, Cuba. The trip was a "Good Will" mission that was comprised of about 120 airplanes from across the United States. All the planes left Key West Florida at the same time for Cuba.

According to his memoir written in 1988, Harrison admitted to being an inveterate smoker, drinker and gambler. The smoking began when he was quite young on the farm in Winston, unknowing to his parents, but the drinking and gambling started in the military. He gambled on dogs, dice, horses and cards, especially poker. His insatiable appetite for poker gambling developed when he won $13,000.00 in a poker game that lasted for two days. He began the game with only $75.00, but his wallet was filled with papers to give the appearance that he had a lot of money. He did, in his memoir, make it quite clear that neither of his parents ever smoked, drank or gambled. His gambling threw his first marriage to Dorothy Frear into a tailspin that ended in divorce in 1954. By 1955, he remarried to Elsie Ruth. That marriage gave him three sons, Harold Henry Winston, James Robin Winston and Wade William Winston. However, that second marriage, even though it lasted longer than his first, suffered the same fate, and by 1973 he was again divorced. His third marriage was to Mary Elaine Elam in Reno in April 1973, and it also soon slipped into divorce.

Towards the end of Harrison's life there were obvious signs of erosion of his behavior that deviated from his parental up-bringing. By conjecture and mere speculation, and according to US Military Psychiatry evaluation of World War II Veterans, he might have been suffering from Post Traumatic Stress Disorder-PTSD. He ran into several legal problems with the law and was put on probation. However, he violated probation and was put in jail from December 1, 1988 to January 5, 1989. He used that time in jail to write his memoir. According to *The News Review,* "he was summoned before a disciplinary board of the Oregon Bar Association, which found he had not violated laws involving turpitude and was not subject to disciplinary action." Harrison Renner Winston passed away on December 18, 1989, at the age of 73. He was buried next to his father at Civil Bend Pioneer Cemetery in Winston.

References:
The News Review, Info from family, Memoirs of Harrison Winston. Pictures donated by family.

MIKE WINTERS

He is personable, community minded, and always articulates his thoughts in a captivating manner. He is a Republican and voices his concerns on political issues, especially those on small businesses and private property rights. Those were two of his mandates when he ran for County Commissioner in November 1994.

Mike Winters was born in Rochester, New York, on April 18, 1947. At the age of nine he moved to Butte Falls, Oregon, with his parents. After graduation from high school he moved to Douglas County. In September 1965 he was drafted into the US Marine Corps. At the completion of basic training he was sent to Viet Nam. After four years of service in the Marine Corps, he was given an honorable discharge with the rank of CPL E-4. While he was in the military he married his lovely wife, Mary Anntoinette Young in 1966. She is known as Mary Ann. They have five children: Jill, Michelle, Christina, John and Timothy.

Photo: Courtesy of Leif Photography

Mike is a family man and a loving father.

In 1969, soon after his discharge from the Marine Corps, ambitious Mike went back to school at Umpqua Community College. He majored in Forest Technology and Forest Recreation earning an AA Degree with distinction in 1971. While he was in school he worked for Roseburg BLM having responsibilities for timber cruising and right-of-way surveying. After graduation, between November 1971 and March 1973, Mike worked for Oregon State University as a research technician under H. J. Andreas in Blue River, Oregon. However, having his own business was a big priority in his life. In 1973 he started the family business "Wintergreen Nursery and Landscaping" in Dillard. This company is still in operation. He is also a licensed and bonded landscape and irrigation contractor.

Mike and his family live on the outskirts of Winston, but it is in Winston he invests his time, expertise and resources in making the community better. In 1991 he contributed to the development of Civic Wayside Park. His landscaping company, Wintergreen Nursery and Landscaping, constructed the irrigation system at the park. But history will remember him for the vital role he played in spearheading the project for building the Veterans Memorial Gardens at the Winston Community Park. All the plants in the garden were donated by Wintergreen Nursery. Three flags are flown continuously honoring all veterans. Both he and his wife Mary Ann donated many of the trees at Riverbend Park.

There was joy and celebration at the Beef & Brew in Roseburg on Tuesday night, November 8, 1994. The results of the election for the race for the seat on the Douglas County Commission showed that Mike Winters, Republican, defeated Bob Allen, Democrat by a margin of 67 per cent to 33 per cent. Mike was able to breathe a sigh of relief. It was a long campaign, and he was glad to get away from the barrage of insults and name-calling. He took the oath of office in January 1995. He served as commissioner tirelessly and passionately, but returned to the family business after eight years of service.

Mike is very civic minded and spends much of his time serving various organizations. He was a member of the Douglas County Park Board for several years. He served on the Umpqua Community College Horticulture Advisory Board and the Winston-Dillard School Board. He is a member of the Winston-Dillard Area Chamber of Commerce and served as vice president and president for several years. He was master of ceremonies for the Chambers' First Citizens Banquet for several years. In 1991 he was honored as the male First Citizen of the community. He is also a member of the Roseburg Chamber of Commerce and a member of the Douglas County Planning Commission. He served on the board of Umpqua Community College Small Business Development Center. In 2007 he was appointed to the board of Douglas County Advisory Committee. He also served on the board for American Legion Baseball.

Mike also takes his volunteerism beyond the county's borders and loves it. If one hears him say "que pasa" with a Douglas County accent that is the way he speaks Spanish in Guatemala. He volunteers with his church "Redeemer Fellowship" in Roseburg. Once a year the church sponsors a group of Christian professionals to go to the northwest part of Guatemala and assist the villages with various social and economic projects. The group sets up medical, dental and eye clinics. It installs water filtration systems, latrines, chicken coops and schools. At the same time the group gets to share its Christian teachings with the villagers. Mike gets a humanistic satisfaction when he is serving his fellowman in that manner.

References:
The News Review, Interview with his family. Photo by Leif Photography.

CHAPTER SIX

HISTORICAL TIDBITS 1820 - 1966

1820s: The Umpqua Indians lived in the Umpqua Valley long before the pioneers settled the area. They lived in areas like Lookingglass, Olalla and Camas Valley. They spoke an Athabaskan Language. After the Indian War of 1855-1856, the Umpqua Indians were removed and taken to the Reservations of Grand Ronde and Yachats.

1846: The Lookingglass Valley was first discovered by Hoy Flournoy, and he gave it its name. Mr. Flournoy claimed that the green grass reflected the light of the sun almost as a looking glass.

October 1847: Jesse and his wife Jane Roberts, for whom Roberts Mountain on the I-5 corridor in Douglas County is named, settled their Donation Land Claim southeast of Green District. His neighbors took shelter in his stockade during the Indian War of 1855-1856.

1848: According to Welcome Martindale Combs and Sharon Combs Ross, Camas Valley was first settled in 1848. The valley is seven miles long and three miles wide. Abraham Patterson was the first pioneer to take out a Donation Land Claim.

1848: The first church service in Camas Valley was held in a log cabin home. However, the first organized Christian Congregation Church was ministered by Reverend William Allen in the middle 1880s. The congregation was reorganized in 1899 in the Methodist Episcopal Church (now United Methodist). The church was destroyed by fire in 1913.

1850: Rev. Abbot James Todd started the first school in Lookingglass. The Reverend started with 60 students in a one-room building.

January 1852: Douglas County was created from a portion of Umpqua County on January 7, 1852. The County was named after Senator Stephen A. Douglas of Illinois. He was a candidate for the presidency in 1860.

January 1852: Jeptha Green came to Douglas County and settled on a Donation Land Claim four miles south of Roseburg. The area he settled is called Green. He donated land for the first school built in Green. He passed away on June 12, 1911, leaving over 3000 acres of land in his estate.

1852: Rev. John Dillard bought 640 acres of land in what became known as Dillard from John Slooper for $800.00. Mr. Slooper was the owner under the Squatter's Rights Act. The valley was named Dillard in 1882 by the Oregon and California Railroad when the company established a depot and railroad station there.

1852: The Lookingglass Store, which is one of the first merchandise establishments in Douglas County, began in 1852. The store is located at the intersection of Lookingglass Road and Coos Bay Wagon Road.

1853: Robert M. Gurney was the first pioneer to settle the valley of Reston. He passed away in 1878 at the age of sixty. The Gurney's ten-room house, built in 1872, is a landmark of the valley.

November 1853: Postal services were established at Round Prairie on November 22, 1853, with James D. Burnett as the postmaster. The service was discontinued from July 1, 1862, to April 3, 1877. However, service resumed again for about six years. On December 27, 1909, the post office was again re-established and operated until April 18, 1919.

January 1854: Tenmile organized its School District No. 7 making it one of five school districts in Douglas County at that time.

June 1854: Lewis Dozer Kent won the election for Sheriff of Douglas County by default. Judge C. M. Deadly of Deer Creek (renamed Roseburg) ruled the victory of the election in his favor, since his opponent James P. Day was living in Josephine County at the time of the election.

August 1854: Willis School District #14 was established in August 1854. The first school building was set on fire in 1855 during the Indian War of 1855-1856. The district consolidated with Dillard School District #116 on 1941.

1854: William P. Day built the first store in Camas Valley and established a post office in his log cabin home. However, on July 5, 1875, Mathew Reeves was appointed the first postmaster of the valley.

August 1855: Brockway School District #16 (then called Civil Bend District) was established in August 1855. The district consolidated with Dillard District #116 June 15, 1948.

October 1855: During the Indian War of 1855-1856, a company of 40 volunteers, during the predawn hours of the morning, attacked a camp of about 20 Umpqua Indians - men, women and children - in the Lookingglass Valley. The Umpqua Tribe had already surrendered to the settlers in the valley. The event became known as the "Lookingglass Massacre."

January 1857: Lewis Dozier Kent drowned when he attempted to ford the flooded South Umpqua River near Dillard. Both he and his horse were swept away by the river on January 22, 1857.

July 1857: Samuel C. Miller was born July 24, 1857 near Eugene, Oregon. In January 1890 he married Jennie Dillard, Rev. John Dillard's granddaughter. In 1893 he bought John Dillard's 1000-acre estate. The house he built in 1870 on Highway 99 is now registered with Douglas County Historic Places.

1857: The Willis Creek Cemetery was established in 1857.

1858: The Methodist Church in Tenmile was first organized in the schoolhouse in Porter Creek. In 1869 a church was built and dedicated. The Tenmile Methodist Church and Cemetery are now landmarks of the rich history of that valley.

February 1859: By an act of Congress and by proclamation of President Buchanan, Oregon became a State of the United States of America on February 14, 1859.

April 1860: The Tenmile Cemetery was established when Thomas and Caroline Coats buried their 13-year-old daughter Charlotte on a knoll on their Donation Land Claim. The family later donated two acres of land around their daughter's grave to the community. The land then was deeded to the Methodist Church.

1860: Flournoy School District #56 was established. The district consolidated with Lookingglass in 1930.

1860: Reston School District #42 was established but later joined Tenmile District #7.

1869: By an act of Congress in 1869, the Coos Bay Wagon Road was completed in 1872. The scenic 62-mile-long road, that is still passable, connects Roseburg to Coos Bay passing through the Lookingglass Valley and Reston.

July 1869: Roberts Creek began holding school with an average attendance of 15 students that increased to 18 by February 1871. By 1873 a one-room schoolhouse was built. In 1956 Roberts Creek School consolidated with Roseburg School District.

1870: Green's first school was built in 1870. In 1952 Green School District consolidated with the Roseburg School District after rejecting an offer to join Dillard District #116.

June 1870: Ten Mile Post Office was established on June 13, 1870. William Irwin was the first postmaster. The name of the post office and community was changed to Tenmile in 1918.

August 1870: District #21 was the first school district established at Camas Valley according to "Chronology of Oregon Schools

1834-1958." In 1892 a second school district #72 was established. In 1927 both district #21 and #72 were consolidated.

January 1871: The Lookingglass Post Office was established on January 9, 1871, with Albert S. Costen as the postmaster. Postal services were discontinued on October 31, 1942.

1871: The Lookingglass Cemetery was established in 1871.

1872: The Coos Bay Wagon Road, completed in 1872, passes through the community of Lookingglass from Roseburg. It was the main link between Douglas County and Coos County for about 41 years.

1873: The Great Panic of 1873, as it was commonly referred to, was triggered by a severe economic depression throughout Europe and spread to America. The depression severely affected the U.S. when the largest banking establishment of Jay Cooke & Company of Wall Street in New York declared bankruptcy. Angry customers stormed the company's establishment demanding their money. That episode of unrest ricocheted across the country as other banks went into bankruptcy. Between 1873 and 1874 over ten thousand banks and businesses went broke, affecting the lives of thousands of American families. The depression lasted for six years. During the recovery of the economy, President James A. Garfield was assassinated on July 2, 1881.

February 1874: The Davlin Cemetery, located on the north side of Douglas High School, on a knoll off Brockway Road, was established about February 1874. Pioneer James Davlin donated the land to be used by his family, neighbors and friends. Cora Bolsinger, daughter of Bernhard and Margaret Bolsinger, was the first person to be buried there.

1874: William Rose of Civil Bend District (renamed Winston in 1893), brother to Aaron Rose of Deer Creek (renamed Roseburg), was a commercial fisherman on the Umpqua River at the confluence of the north and south fork. He sold his salmon in the Portland market. He also operated a ferry on the South Umpqua

River in Roseburg. He was buried at Civil Bend Pioneer Cemetery in Winston.

May 1877: The Civil Bend Pioneer Cemetery was registered on May 12, 1877. Prior to its registration, it was called "Pleasant View Cemetery". A group comprised of B. C. Agee, I. C. Kent, W. C. Winston and Beman B. Brockway, formed the association. The land was purchased from Mr. Brockway.

1877: William Bremner, known as "Willi," bought a 360-acre parcel of land in the northwest section of Civil Bend District (name changed to Winston in 1893). Today, Bremner Hills Co-op and Adair Bridge on Lookingglass Road near Abraham Ave. are part of the original parcel. Bremner passed away in 1913 and willed the land to his daughter, Margret Bremner Adair, who was 18 at the time of his death.

1878: Winston School District #48 was started on a knoll opposite present day Sherry Street. However, in May 1940, the district consolidated with Dillard District #116.

October 1879: The community of Lookingglass bragged of having two merchandize stores, two saloons, a hotel and a school.

1879: Olalla School District #49 was established. But, by 1945, the district joined with Tenmile District #7.

1880: James M. Dillard opened the first store in Dillard. The area was then called Civil Bend District.

September 1881: The first post office at Brockway was called Civil Bend District with James Dillard as the postmaster. Service was suspended in October 1888. It reopened in November 1889 under the name of Brockway with Samuel S. Bolsinger as the postmaster. I. B. Nichols became the postmaster in 1893, and Sid Nichols took over the position in 1940 until May 1956 when postal services were discontinued.

1882: Rev. John Dillard gave permission to Oregon and California Railroad Co. to lay railroad tracks across his property. The company compensated him by naming the area and station "Dillard". The depot became known as one of the county's major shipping centers for agricultural products. The Dillard Station was taken out of service in 1936. Paul B. Hult owned the depot until 1972 when his widowed wife Dorothy sold the property to Roseburg Lumber Company. Kenneth Ford used the depot as a lunch room until 1982, when he donated it to the Douglas County Museum.

May 1883: The first train stopped at the station in Dillard on Sunday, May 17, 1883, at 10:45 AM. It was an historic occasion for the community. A large crowd of people was there to welcome the historic moment. However, regular train service between San Francisco and Portland didn't begin until 1897.

1883: Camas Valley built its first church in the summer of 1883; it was non-denominational. In May of 1899, members of the Methodist Church purchased the building and remodeled it. Reverend Carter, who lived in Tenmile, was pastor of both churches.

June 1884: The community of Dillard received postal services on June 16, 1884, with James Dillard being the first postmaster. The post office is located on Highway 99 in Dillard.

1887: Southern Pacific Railroad Co. bought out Oregon and California Railroad Co.

March 1887: The historic home built by Mr. and Mrs. William Chauncey Winston is located at 350 Winston Section Road. The home is still owned and occupied by their descendants, currently Cheryl Weesee, their great granddaughter. Beverly Brown, Cheryl's mother, lived with her there until her passing in 2011. The house was once used as the center of operations for the first post office in Winston, the ferry terminal office, and their farm operation activities.

June 1887: The first post office in Camas valley was established on June 1, 1887. Harmon Davis was the postmaster.

1889: A road between Camas Valley and Myrtle Point was constructed, and the Roseburg to Myrtle Point Stage Line started in the early 1900s.

1890: The Brockway Store, a historical landmark at the intersection of Highway 42 and Brockway Road, began operation. I. B. Nichols, grandfather to Dick Nichols, started the store. In 1986 the Nichols family discontinued operation of the store. The Brockway Store building is still in sound structural condition.

August 1890: The post office of Reston was established in August 25, 1890, with Edward E. Weekly as the postmaster. The service was discontinued on February 28, 1934. The residents of Reston received their mail at Lookingglass.

1891: Rice Creek School District was established in 1891 but was consolidated with Dillard District #116 in 1945.

June 1893: Winston Postal Services started in the house of William Chauncey Winston with Elijah Winston, brother to William, as the postmaster. The service was discontinued in July 1903 and moved to Roseburg. In July 1948 a Coos Junction Committee requested the return of the service. Marion Jackson became the postmistress.

June 1893: The first Methodist Church service in Dillard was held in a hop dryer building. The service was conducted by Reverend W. A. Kemp. In 1897 the church congregation dissolved, and the Baptist Church was established. However, in June 1920 the Methodist Church was reestablished.

February 1894: Upper Olalla School District #107 was established. The district later joined Tenmile District #7 in 1950.

1897: The Baptist Church of Dillard was established by Reverend G. W. Miller, father of Samuel C. Miller.

February 1897: Burban Brockway was ordered and adjudged by Douglas County Court to pay a fine of $50.00 and $10.00 court fees after he was found guilty of assault. On September 18, 1896, Mr. Brockway was arrested and charged with assault in the beating of Charles H. Fisher with a cane. Burban Brockway was the brother of the distinguished Beman B. Brockway of Civil Bend District, now called Winston.

1897: Dillard School District #116 was organized. Prior to its formation, children in the Dillard area attended Brockway School District #16. They had to cross the South Umpqua River in row boats or ford the river whenever it was low.

January 1899: Col. J. G. Day, a well known capitalist and gold miner, invested $50,000.00 in one of the placer mines in Olalla.

April 1900: Prior to 1900, crossing the South Umpqua River from Dillard to Rice Creek, Willis Creek, Kent Creek and Brockway was done by means of fording and row boats. In April 1900 a 412-foot footbridge was constructed 30 feet above the river. This bridge was washed out during the 1903 winter flood. Another footbridge was built, longer and higher, but that too was destroyed by flood waters.

June 1902: Leonard S. Coon of Dillard was the first farmer of that community to ship produce to Portland. He passed away in December of 1912. His wife Ollie Peters Coon passed away in 1955.

May 1903: The Roseburg-Myrtle Point Stage Line was held up by two masked robbers around Hoover Hill Road. The bandits stole mail pouches, registered mail, and $160.00 from the passengers. That was the fifth time the stage coach line was held up at Hover Hill within eight months.

November 1904: In July 1904 James Inman of Lookingglass, Oregon, announced his candidacy for the President of the United States. He chose a woman as his running mate. When the votes were tallied, Theodore Roosevelt won the presidency and James Inman got one vote. Since women did not have the right to vote, his wife could not have voted for him.

June 1907: The post office at Flournoy was established on June 20, 1907. James Masters was the postmaster. The service was discontinued in January 1908.

September 1907: A railroad train wrecked in Dillard, Oregon, killing five Japanese and injuring eight others on September 12, 1907. The Japanese were migrant workers working for Southern Pacific Railroad Company. They were housed in two railroad cars on the siding of the track. Three of the bodies were incinerated.

October 1907: A Roseburg-Myrtle Point Stage Coach fell over an embankment on October 25, 1907 at 7:00 PM six miles west of Camas Valley killing one passenger, and injuring three others. Three of the horses died from the fall while the fourth was badly injured. The injured horse was instantly shot.

March 1911: The Evergreen Grange in Green, which was established on March 22, 1911, became a pillar of stability and activity, especially during the Great Depression of 1929. It was organized by Susan Landers Winston. Susan was also Secretary/Treasurer for Civil Bend Pioneer Cemetery Association in Winston for 25 years. She was the daughter of Henry and Nancy Landers, pioneers of Green District in 1865.

December 1913: In 1912 farmers and other progressive community members of Rice Creek, Willis Creek and Kent Creek petitioned Douglas County to build a vehicular bridge to replace the footbridge over the South Umpqua River between Dillard and said communities. On December 20, 1913, the first vehicular bridge was opened for traffic.

August 1920: Women in the United States were given the right to vote after a constitutional amendment was adopted on August 26, 1920.

1920: Lookingglass School began holding classes for high school students. However, in 1941 Lookingglass students began attending high school in Roseburg.

1920: Highway 99 between Portland, Oregon and California was opened for traffic.

1922: The intersection of Highway 42 and Pacific Highway (now Highway 99 or Main Street) was constructed. It had a gravel surface.

November 1922: A covered bridge was constructed over Lookingglass Creek on Highway 42 about a half mile west of the junction of Pacific Highway and Highway 42. After the bridge was damaged by the floods of 1950, a more modern bridge was built to replace the covered bridge.

August 1924: Fire wreaked havoc on the community of Green when it destroyed four beautiful homes, two garages, two sheds and outbuildings, and threatened supplies at the Green Train Station before it was brought under control Saturday evening, August 23, 1924.

1925: Fred Beul, owner of Dillard Merchandize Store on Highway 99, was the first merchant in the area to sell gasoline to vehicles.

May 1927: The Tenmile Store was built in 1927 and had extensive renovations in 1948. The store carried all sorts of merchandise. In September 1974 Mr. and Mrs. Jerry Redenius purchased the store from Mr. and Mrs. T. M. Benedict.

May 1927: California-Oregon Pacific Company began supplying electrical power to the community of Dillard.

1934: The Winston Bridge (commonly called the Green Bridge) between Green and Winston was built in 1934 by Oregon State Engineer, Conde B. McCullough. Another concrete bridge was constructed on the north side in 1974 in order to accommodate the increased volume of traffic.

1935: The sweet Moyer prune was developed by Clarence C. Moyer of Dillard, Oregon. His place, now known as Wildwood Nursery, in Dillard, is registered with Douglas County Historic Places

1937: Roberts Creek Water District was incorporated in 1937. In the beginning the district got its water from Cooper Spring. But by 1948, when it annexed Green to the district, it began pumping water from the South Umpqua River. Cooper Spring did not have the volume to handle the increased population. The district sold water to Winston-Dillard Water District from 1951 to 1958.

January 1942: The Big Oaks Tavern in Coos Junction (later renamed Winston), formerly known as the Wigwam, closed its doors after the owner J. S. Baker passed away while visiting in California. He was 72 years of age.

June 1942: Harold Warren Rose, age 29, of Roseburg, lost his life in a traffic accident on the covered bridge over Lookingglass Creek on Highway 42.

September 1942: Thomas Parkinson of Winston Section Road taught at Dillard Elementary School from 1920 to 1925. He served in the Oregon State Senate for ten years between 1942 and 1952, representing the Fourth Congressional District. Thomas Parkinson passed away on April 26, 1987 at the age of 90.

1946: Kenneth Ford moved his sawmill from Diamond Lake Blvd. in Roseburg to Dillard. He built the mill, "Roseburg Forest Products," on a portion of Robert Phipps' Donation Land Claim along the Southern Pacific Railroad Tracks.

January 1948: Nolan D. Wilson, 24 years of age, of Upper Olalla, drowned as he was attempting to ford the floodwaters of the Olalla Creek with his horse. The horse also drowned and was found several hundred yards downstream.

January 1948: One of the bridge piers of the Pacific Highway Bridge over the South Umpqua River, about four miles south of

Dillard, loosened, causing the bridge to collapse from the force of floodwaters. A temporary bridge, an "Army Bailey" type, was put in place while the damaged bridge was being repaired.

July 1948: Postal services were reestablished in Winston on July 21, 1948.

October 1948: Winston-Dillard Water District was incorporated on October 5, 1948. The district bought water from Roberts Creek Water District until a treatment plant was built in April 1958.

October 1948: Community pressure was brought to bear on Dillard School District #116 to close the school due to the epidemic of polio that affected one of the students.

October 1948: Bud Allen, 25, was working for B & C Logging Co. when he was hit and killed instantly by a falling tree limb at 10:00 AM October 26, 1948.

June 1949: Daylight Savings Time was introduced to the Pacific Northwest.

August 1949: The Winston Community Club built the first Community Center. The 3600-square-foot structure was built by local carpenters, concerned community members and children. Materials were donated by the local sawmills and hardware stores. In 1952 community youth from Winston and Dillard raised $3,000 to install a hardwood floor for roller-skating.

.October 1949: The Melody Inn of Winston, a Las Vegas style nightclub, located at the top of the hill on Highway 99 near Sherry Street, opened for business on October 31, 1949. The nightclub was destroyed by fire on February 13, 1956, at 3:45 AM.

January 1950: The Foursquare Gospel Church was the first Christian group to hold religious services in Winston. The Winston Christian Church soon followed in April 1950.

February 1950: Model Market opened for business. The current name in 2010 is J & M Market and Deli.

1950s: An area newspaper called *The Enterprise,* serving Winston, Dillard, Camas Valley, Tenmile and Green, published a weekly issue between the early 1950s and the middle 1960s.

June 1950: Edward Nienow, age 34, was killed while logging in an area a few miles west of Cams Valley. He and his wife Loma had lived in Camas Valley since January 1939.

June 1950: The Benetta Theater in Winston, located on Main Street, opened for business on June 18, 1950. The building was a Quonset-hut structure. The building was destroyed by fire in November 1998.

September 1950: Camas Valley established its first fire department.

October 1950: Sunday, October 29, 1950, about 85 men, women and children were marooned by floodwaters in the Dillard Valley. Old-timers claimed that was the worst flood to hit Dillard since the flood of 1861.

December 1950: The new concrete bridge on Highway 99 over the South Umpqua River between Winston and Dillard was opened to traffic on December 11, 1950. The structure cost $229,329. It replaced the old wooden bridge built in 1927.

May 1951: Roberts Creek Water District began supplying water to the Winston-Dillard Water District.

May 1951: Ronald H. Barney, 52, resident of Tenmile and Camas Valley, sailed from Long Beach, California to Tahiti alone on a 26-foot sailboat, a distance of 3900 miles.

July 1951: Pacific Telephone Company completed the installation of the dial system in Coos Junction Community (what is Winston today).

Snapshots Along the Umpqua

November 1951: Fire destroyed the house built by Beman B. Brockway in 1866. The mansion was located on a knoll north of Lookingglass Rd. between Cary St. and Civil Bend Ave. in Winston.

December 1951: The first grocery store in Coos Junction (Winston) opened on December 6, 1951, owned by Frank O. True of Coquille, Oregon. Mr. True was also one of the first city councilors of Winston.

September 1951: The owner of Olalla Logging Company was killed when struck by a tree pushed over by a bulldozer.

May 1952: Oscar W. Simpson, Jr. of Winston was crushed between two logs while loading a truck on Camas Mountain. He died four days later, May 15, 1952, at Mercy Hospital of internal injuries. Oscar was 35 years of age.

June 1952: Fire destroyed one of the historic homes built in 1894 in Rice Creek belonging to John Roberts at the time of the fire. The house was built by O. J. Rand and family.

June 1952: Winston Dillard Rural Fire Protection District was incorporated June 6, 1952.

June 1952: Dr. Frederick A. Bracker, Osteopathic Physician and Surgeon, opened Winston Emergency Hospital and Clinic at the junction of Highway 99 and Highway 42. He sold his practice to Doctor Fletcher in 1954. In November 1956 Dr. Fletcher moved the hospital to 871 S.W. Main St., today known as Riverside Center.

October 1952: Douglas High School District was formed on October 22, 1952, by consolidating Dillard, Winston, Lookingglass, and Tenmile schools. William Bromley was the first superintendent, and David Potter was the first principal.

October 1952: Roseburg Lumber Company closed its operation at the Roseburg plant and concentrated its entire milling operation in Dillard.

October 1952: The Douglas County Circuit Court ordered the closure of the Tenmile Dance Hall, owned by T. M. Benedict. The action was taken by Judge Carl Hill and Commissioner Lynn Beckley after three violent murders had occurred within three months involving persons who had attended the dance.

June 1953: The City of Winston was incorporated on June 21, 1953.

August 1953: Paul Caskey of Roseburg died when a sewer trench in which he was working caved in on him at 12:30 PM, on August 18, 1953, at Douglas High School. Mr. Caskey was 56 years of age at the time of the tragedy.

September 1953: The first meeting of the Winston City Council was held on September 21, 1953, at Councilman Frank True's place of business on Highway 99. A lighted lantern was placed outside the building to notify the community of the public meeting taking place.

September 1953: Winston Emergency Hospital, operated by Dr. Frederick Bracker, bought a fully equipped ambulance for use in connection with the facility.

September 1953: The City of Winston hired Harrison Winston as its first city attorney.

October 1953: The City of Winston hired Dean Guyer as the first city recorder.

March 1954: A group from the Winston-Dillard community organized a Kiwanis Club. It was the second Kiwanis Club in Douglas County.

March 1954: The City of Winston accepted the streets of Hart, Ford and Peach in South Slopes Subdivision. The 44 homes in the subdivision were financed by Kenneth Ford for his supervisors and foremen.

May 1954: Avery Morgan of Lookingglass and Frank Collins of Dillard were swept off a rock by a "sneaker wave" at Sunset Bay and drowned. The boys were part of a class from Douglas High School on a biology field trip.

June 1954: Ramona Mendenhall, a two-and-a-half-year-old of Tenmile, fell into the Tenmile Creek and drowned. She had wandered off from the care of Berlan Richardson. The child's mother, Mrs. William Mendenhall, was in Roseburg shopping and visiting an infant at Mercy Hospital.

June 1954: George Alfred Murphy, age 45, of Dillard, died of self-inflicted gunshot wounds while engaging in a gun battle with 10 officers. Mr. Murphy was diagnosed as mentally unstable.

Mach 1955: Winston Baptist Church was incorporated in March 1955. The church was organized in January 1953. The church is now located on Cary St. in Winston.

August 1955: The City of Winston hired its first Chief of Police, Ben Scheele of Lebanon.

August 1955: Voters in the City of Winston voted on the first City Charter. On August 16, 1955, 117 voted yes and 6 voted no. That Charter spelled out the name change from Coos Junction to Winston.

September 1955: The City of Winston hired its first municipal judge, Lee Altendorf.

September 1955: Green Sanitary District was incorporated on September 7, 1955. However, three elections were held to dissolve the district, all of which failed, before a sewer system was finally built.

November 1955: The City of Winston adopted Ordinance No. 21 calling for a curfew for minors under 18 in the city.

December 1955: Even though the flood waters in Winston and Dillard Valley on Christmas morning 1955 were not as high as during the flood of 1950, the disaster lasted longer and did considerably more damage to both communities

January 1956: The City of Winston purchased three acres of land to construct the sewer treatment plant and public works office on Thompson Street. The city paid $2,700 to I. B. Thompson for the land. In July 1970 they purchased another nine acres for extension of the sewer plant. This area is now Riverbend Park. The skateboard and bicycle ramp arena is on the site of the above-mentioned sewer treatment plant.

April 1956: A chapter of the National Honor Society was installed at Douglas High School in a ceremony conducted by society members from Glide and Riddle High Schools.

April 1956: With a population of 2,456, Winston became the fourth largest city in Douglas County in 1956. At the time the city was incorporated in June of 1953, the population was 1,960.

April 1956: Roseburg School District #14 agreed to accept Roberts Creek high school students.

May 1956: Douglas High School's first graduating class had a total of 49 students. Keith Dale Ryder, a student of the graduating class, was one of 56 Oregonian high school seniors to pass the National Merit Scholarship Exam. Out of more than 50,000 students nationwide who took the exam, representing 10,000 high schools, 5,078 students passed.

May 1956: The three murals decorating Douglas High School Campus won national recognition. They were selected in a nationwide contest from which 147 high schools submitted designs.

Snapshots Along the Umpqua

June 1956: The Winston Missionary Baptist Church was organized in June of 1956, and a building was constructed in August of the same year. A parsonage was added in 1966. The Church is located on Cary Street.

July 1956: Albert R. Mow of Brockway published his book: *Man Save Thyself.* The book was printed by Vantage Press of New York City.

August 1956: Sylvester Jones of Sutherlin was killed in a sewer trench in Winston after a sidewall of a nine-foot trench caved in on him. He died from suffocation after being pinned by the wall of clay for one hour thirty-four minutes. Sylvester was only 41 years of age at the time of the accident.

November 1956: Dr. M. L. Fletcher, Osteopathic Physician and Surgeon, moved his emergency hospital from the junction of Highway 99 and Highway 42 to 671 Main St.

December 1956: Giles Cherrick of Dillard, a fifth grader of Dillard Elementary School, unearthed evidence of a horse that lived 40,000 years ago. Dr. James C. Stovall of the University of Oregon confirmed that the tooth found was from a Pleistocene horse that lived during the ice age.

January 1957: The City of Winston hired Marvin White as the first city employee for streets and sewer.

April 1957: Dr. Charles W. Claridge opened his dental clinic at 671 SW Main St. that was the office of Dr. Fletcher. The area is now known as Riverside Center.

1957: Sherley Clayton of Dillard, Oregon, wrote and published *A Story of Early Settlers*, *Memories of Long Ago*, *The Rice Family and the Kent Family*.

1958: The City of Winston Sewer Treatment Plant was constructed in April of 1958 with a capacity to serve 3500 persons. It was a trickling-filter plant with anaerobic digestion of waste solids. The plant was located on the northwest corner of what is now Riverbend Park.

October 1958: Dr. Harry Van Dermark, physician and surgeon, opened a medical office at 40 Main St. and later moved his practice to 470 Douglas Boulevard. He was the first M.D. to practice medicine in Winston. He passed away on June 29, 1980.

January 1959: Residents of Camas Valley again turned down an offer to consolidate with Dillard School District #116.

January 1959: Governor Robert D. Holmes appointed Paul B. Hult to the State Board of Forestry. Mr. Hult started Hult Lumber Co. in 1945.

July 1959: Roberts Creek School District consolidated with Roseburg School District on July1, 1959. That merger ended 39 years of operation for the one-room schoolhouse.

September 1959: Civil Bend Elementary School on Cary Street was completed to house 350 seventh and eighth graders. The school was constructed for $340,000.

December 1959: Edwin Cardwell of Napa, California drowned in Olalla Creek while rafting. He suffered an epileptic seizure and fell off his raft into the water.

December 1959: On December 7, 1959, the Winston City Council agreed to purchase the property on the corner of Highway 42 and Glenhart Street from Fred Albertus for $5,000.00 to build a city hall.

January 1960: The City of Winston organized its first police reserve under the leadership of Police Chief Ray Oliver and City Councilman Russell Turner.

February 1960: The well-known Paul H. Helweg passed away at the age of 57. He owned the largest fruit orchards in the county. They were in Sutherlin, Winston and Garden Valley.

Snapshots Along the Umpqua 219

April 1960: The Winston-Dillard Methodist Church in Dillard was dedicated on Sunday April 3, 1960.

May 1960: Bert Laurance of Winston Section Rd. was elected County Treasurer. Mr. Laurance had held the position since 1956.

June 1960: The Winston-Dillard branch of the First National Bank of Roseburg opened for business at the northwest corner of Main St. and Douglas Boulevard.

August 1960: The first set of streets lights in the City of Winston was at the intersection of Lookingglass and Cary Streets, Morgan and Sherry Streets, Highway 99 and Highway 42, Jorgen and Darrell Streets and Grape and Thompson Streets.

October 1960: Burks Fruit Stand in Dillard celebrated its 30th anniversary as a roadside fruit and vegetable stand business. Fred Burks first started the roadside stand two miles west of Winston on Highway 42 in 1930 and later moved it to Dillard

July 1961: James "Doc" Parret of Winston won the world championship trophy for power saw bucking in Hayward, Wisconsin. He sawed a 21-inch log in half in eight seconds to set a new world record. His prize was $500 cash and a 33-inch trophy.

August 1961: Douglas High School was burglarized, and a sum of $749.03 was taken from the safe on Tuesday night about 11:30 PM That was the school's second burglary in the month. Winston's police said the thief was a professional.

December 1961: The new Winston Post Office on Rose St. was dedicated on Saturday, December 2, 1961. About 100 spectators attended the ceremony that was sponsored by the Winston Area Chamber of Commerce.

June 1962: The Tenmile Volunteer Fire District, which includes Tenmile, Olalla, Reston, Porter Creek, and Suicide Creek, was formed.

September 1962: The community of Green welcomed its long-awaited Rural Fire Protection substation from Roseburg Fire Department.

October 1962: The Columbus Day Storm has been documented as one of the ten top natural disasters to hit Douglas County. On October 12, 1962, a section of a typhoon in the Pacific Ocean broke away from its main body and headed eastward to the mainland. The storm did considerable damage to the coastal towns from Crescent City to Reedsport and farther north. It also affected many areas in the South Umpqua Valley.

December 1962: Rex and Bea Stevens, owners of R & B Grocery, purchased the Model Market on Main St. in Winston. Today the market is called J & M Market and Deli. The Stevens are now retired and live in Dillard.

January 1963: Green Sanitary Sewer System went into operation on January 28, 1963, after eight years of persevering amidst strong opposition.

June 1963: Dr. Aaron M. Novick opened a dental clinic in Winston. The office was located in the old post office building on Main Street.

July 1963: The Board of the Winston-Dillard Methodist Church and its members brought pressure on the county to pave Fourth, Fifth and Reston Streets in Dillard. The streets were paved in the fall of 1963.

July 1963: The Junction Tavern and Cafe, now Willee's, in Winston, changed ownership from Mr. and Mrs. Clarence Bowker to Mr. and Mrs. Jim Lewis of Myrtle Creek. Steven Fisher is now the owner of Willee's.

November 1963: Residents of Winston and surrounding areas went into shock and mourning on learning of the assassination of President John F. Kennedy on November 22, 1963.

December 1963: Camas Valley Hornets defeated Eagle Valley 31–0 for the State "B" Eight-man Football Team Championship. The Hornets became the first high school west of the Cascades to win the title since it was established in 1959. It was also the first state championship ever won by Camas Valley High School.

February 1964: A 128-foot section of the Dillard Bridge over the South Umpqua River between Dillard and Brockway collapsed when 51 year-old A. J. Bartley of Camas Valley was crossing it with his truck fully loaded with logs. Mr. Bartley escaped the incident without any injury. The bridge was constructed in 1913.

April 1964: The Winston Chamber of Commerce changed its name to Winston Area Chamber of Commerce. The change was made to accommodate the participation of surrounding and outlying areas.

July 1964: The first supermarket to open in Winston was Byrd's Market managed by Lloyd Stutsman. The market has changed hands many times.

July 1964: The City of Winston hired Marvin White as superintendent of streets and drainage. Mr. White was the city's first employee to work in that position.

September 1964: The Winston-Dillard Kiwanis Club was responsible for opening up a branch of the Douglas County Library in Winston. The library was located in what was once a building supply store at the junction of Highway 42 and Highway 99. It was then moved to the northeast wing of City Hall in 1965. In 1976 it was relocated to the building once used by the post office on Rose St. In January 2008 the Library found a permanent home in the new community center in Winston. It is called the Paul and Dorothy Hult Library.

October 1964: The dedication of the new City Hall in Winston took place in the presence of an enthusiastic crowd of 75 people on October 31, 1964. The guest speaker for the occasion was Congressman Robert Duncan.

October 1964: Winston-Dillard Fire Protection District was listed as the second lowest in percentage of fire losses in the state.

December 1964: According to old-timers, the flood of 1964 in Douglas County was the worst since that of 1861.

January 1965: A fire in Lookingglass destroyed Elbert Ching's barn. It housed 500 hogs at the time of the fire. All the hogs died in the fire.

February 1965: Fire destroyed the landmark "Old McCulloch place" built about 1856. The house was located on the Tenmile Road to Olalla and owned by the Nichols Family of Brockway.

March 1965: Several citizens of the city attended the Winston City Council meeting on March 1, 1965, to protest the placing of "Winston Asphalt Plant" on Thompson Avenue between Highway 99 and Gregory Avenue. The above-mentioned asphalt plant belonged to Ralph Fisher. By September 1970, the State Environmental Control Board brought pressure on the plant to install air emission controls.

June 1965: Grandway Shopping Center on Highway 42 and Glenhart Ave. was a development of McKay Investment Co. of Eugene. Rex and Bea Stevens were the first proprietors of the market.

October 1965: Cpl. Bruce Jameson of Winston was the only survivor when his helicopter was shot down by the Viet Cong. Cpl. Jameson was in command of 12 marines at the time the helicopter was hit.

November 1965: Fifty-year-old Sherman William Davis killed himself at his home on Baker Street about 2:30 PM on November 21, 1965, when he shot himself in the neck with a .300 Savage rifle. His grandchildren were in the house at the time of the shooting.

February 1966: Tom E. Schiermeister of Dillard and student of Douglas High School lost his life when the vehicle he was driving went over an embankment on Rice Creek Road. Tom was only 17 at the time of the accident.

March 1966: Delores Sue Hockersmith of Winston lost her life when the station wagon she was driving overturned while travelling on Happy Valley Road at 1:40 AM. March 2, 1966. Ms. Hockersmith was 24 years of age at the time of the accident.

September 1966: Sherley Clayton of Dillard, the late icon on the history of early pioneers in the South Umpqua Valley, was honored for his work on early pioneer stories by the Douglas County Historical Society. Sherley Clayton passed away on December 27, 1971.

October 1966: *The Winston Wire*, an area newspaper serving Winston, Dillard, Camas Valley, Tenmile and Green, began publication in November 1966 and terminated in January 1968. Ray Milton was the editor of the newspaper.

1966: The State of Oregon lowered the state's voting age from 21 to 18.

References:

The News Review, The Winston Wire, The Umpqua Trapper, Winston City Council Minutes. *The History of Dillard* by Shirley Clayton, *God Made A Valley* by Martindale Combs and Sharon Combs Ross, *Roseburg Ensign*, The *Plaindealer, Roseburg Evening News, Land of the Umpqua* by Stephen Dow Beckham, *Portraits and Biographical Records of Western Oregon, Winston-Dillard School District No. 116* by Larry Moulton, Douglas County Museum Records.

HISTORICAL TIDBITS 1967-2012

September 1967: Cpl. Amos Roy Osborne of Winston, Oregon, was killed in combat in the Vietnam War on September 18, 1967. He was the son of Virgle and Esther Osborne.

September 1968: The Winston-Dillard Melon Festival was organized by the Winston-Dillard Lions Club. Beginning in 1969, on the third weekend in September, it became an annual event.

December 1969: Al Hooten was appointed the first city administrator of Winston. He resigned from the position in October 1972 to accept a managerial position with World Wildlife Safari. Al was a member of the Winston City Council from April 1967 to November 1969. He resigned from the council to accept the position of city administrator.

July 1971: Charles Louis Bierod of Winston was only 19 years of age when he died in a fire at his home on 381 SE Darrell Ave. The teenager was alone and asleep when the house caught on fire.

July 1971: The City of Winston honored Douglas High School student Mike Palmer with a trophy for his achievement of winning nine wrestling matches in Japan. The city named July 26, 1971, "Mike Palmer Day." Mike was a member of the Oregon Cultural Exchange wrestling team.

July 1971: The voting age for both men and women in the United States was lowered from twenty-one to eighteen on July 1, 1971.

August 1971: The Winston City Council named the community park Winston Community Park instead of Harry A. Winston Park.

September 1971: A Holstein heifer gave birth to three calves on Larry Chrisenbery's dairy farm in Lookingglass on September 4, 1971. Mr. Chrisenbery told *The News Review* that this type of birth takes place only once in every 100,000 births.

Snapshots Along the Umpqua

October 1971: At a special public hearing on October 18, 1971, regarding the City of Winston's proposed withdrawal from the Winston-Dillard Water District, citizens from Winston and the Winston-Dillard Water District opposed the proposal and brought pressure on the city to remain in the district.

December 1971: Sherley Clayton of Dillard, the author of several books and newspaper articles on the history of the pioneers and the community of Dillard, passed away on December 27, 1971. He was buried at Civil Bend Pioneer Cemetery in Winston.

May 1972: Governor Tom McCall of Oregon reappointed Dick Nichols of Brockway to serve on the Oregon Beef Council. That was his second term on the Council.

1972: A Winston newspaper *The Herald* published one issue of the paper.

September 1972: Wildlife Safari, a 600-acre drive-through park near Winston, began construction about September 1972 and opened to the public in the spring of 1973.

January 1973: Jim Herbison, 35, was hired as city administrator of Winston. He replaced Al Hooten who had resigned to accept a position with World Wildlife Safari near Winston.

February 1973: The Winston City Council, by an Act of Resolution, changed the name of Highway 42 to Douglas Blvd.

July 1973: The Winston Community Club signed over the deed to the community center to the City of Winston. That action took place at a city council meeting on July 16, 1973.

September 1973: Joanne Riley was the first woman to serve on the Winston City Council, and in November 1981 Betty Fortino was the first woman to be elected as mayor.

September 1973: Henry Dale Thompson, a Douglas High School student, died after he was hit by a car driven by Kathlene Ann

Woods of Lookingglass. The accident took place on Highway 42 at 11:10 a.m. in front of Douglas High School.

October 1973: The gasoline shortage started when members of the Organization of Arab Petroleum Exporting Countries or OAPEC declared an oil embargo in response to the United States support for Israel during the Yom Kippur War. The embargo ended in March 1974 when former President Nixon lifted the rationing on gasoline sales. The crisis created hardship, panic and long lines of frustrated customers nationwide.

January 1974: The flood of 1974 created a hardship for many families in the Winston and Dillard communities. Families in the Winston Section, Helwig and Barnes Road, and Brantley Drive areas had to be evacuated due to high water from the South Umpqua River.

March 1974: An unknown amount of sewerage flowed into the South Umpqua River for about seven hours due to a mechanical failure at the Winston-Green Treatment Plant.

August 1974: Dale A. Ennor, 32, was appointed city administrator of Winston. He replaced Jim Herbison who resigned to move to Canada.

January 1975: George Jacobs resigned from his position as Winston Police Chief to become the Douglas County Sheriff. Harold Forney, a lieutenant and nine-year veteran, was promoted to the position of Winston Chief of Police that same month.

May 1975: According to Oregon travel statistics, Wildlife Safari Park was the No.1 tourist attraction in Oregon.

June 1975: The Chamber of Commerce designed and sold medallions honoring the 25th anniversary of the organization. The medallions were designed by Ms. Vandella Darling of Winston. They depicted the State of Oregon on one side and the Melon Festival and Wildlife Safari on the other.

September 1975: Governor Bob Straub appointed Dorothy Hult of Dillard to serve on the Oregon State Fair Commission. Mrs. Hult served as the Fourth Congressional District member on the commission.

December 1975: A masked robber held up the Junction Tavern with a knife at 2:30 AM. December 2, 1975. The robber took $538.00 in cash. Marjorie Snyder was the barmaid at the tavern the morning of the robbery.

August 1976: Dr. M. L. Fletcher, Osteopathic Physician and Surgeon, well-known to the community of Winston, closed his office at 671 SW Main Street in Winston after 22 years of medical practice. In 2010 the building and property, now referred to as Riverside Center, became the center of controversy between the City of Winston and the Riverside Board of Directors.

November 1976: Fred Schroeder, 23, an unregistered voter, won a seat on the Winston City Council on November 2, 1976. He beat the incumbent Walter Lindner to win one of three vacant seats on the council. After the election, Mr. Schroeder was nick-named the "Political Mystery Man" since he could not be found.

May 1977: Dennis Boyd, a Douglas High School graduate, was drafted from Oregon State University by the NFL's Seattle Seahawks. He played for the team as both a defensive and offensive lineman from 1977 to 1982. Dennis received a scholarship to play football for OSU in 1973. He majored in chemical engineering. He also obtained a Masters Degree in Chemical Engineering from Washington State University.

May 1977: Khayam, the cheetah at Wildlife Safari near Winston, was a guest on The Johnny Carson Show. Also, ABC TV network filmed a special of Khayam in Africa in her hunting habitat.

July 1977: Mia Hansen, a Douglas High School student, was one of 500 young persons who joined "Up with People" in Tucson, Arizona. "Up with People" is an educational program which helps people understand cultures other than their own by visiting many communities and observing how people live in other parts of the United States or in other nations. Mia was multi-talented and was able to contribute much to the organization.

September 1977: Fifteen-year-old Gail Palmer of Lookingglass was crowned Winston-Dillard Melon Festival Queen.

September 1977: The Winston police pistol shooting team won the Oregon Police Officers Associates annual pistol shooting match held near Salem on Saturday, September 17, 1977. The four-man team also won 13 individual trophies. About 200 police officers, representing police departments throughout the state, took part in the event.

December 1977: Voters in the City of Winston approved the revision of the charter by a vote of 109 to 23. That revision gave the voters the right to directly elect the mayor of the city.

December 1977: The groundbreaking ceremony for the construction of the LDS Church in Winston, located on the corner of Glenhart Avenue and Lookingglass Road, took place on Monday, December 26, 1977. The construction was completed 1978.

January 1978: Burnette Wilson was presented with the First Citizen Award by the Winston-Dillard Area Chamber of Commerce. She was the first and only recipient to receive that prestigious award at a banquet held on January 31, 1978. Since then the award has been given to a female and a male each year in the month of February.

March 1978: Winston's population jumped from 1800 in 1970 to 3120 in 1977. The city became the third fastest growing city in Douglas County.

May 1978: Winston and the Greater Winston Area mourned the passing of Charley Stanton on May 17, 1978. Mr. Stanton was Editor Emeritus of *The News-Review* for 36 years. Douglas County named Stanton Park in his memory.

November 1979: After the city's charter was amended to allow for direct election of the mayor, Harley Means was the first to be elected. Prior to 1979, all mayors were appointed by the city council.

November 1979: Mike Parker, owner of Map Engineering, was the first superintendant of public works for the City of Winston.

June 1980: The Community of Winston moaned the passing of its doctor and friend, Harry Van Dermark, on June 29, 1980. A few months later, the family and friends joined together in honoring his life with a plaque and a drinking fountain in front of Winston City Hall.

May 1980: Ben Erving Reservoir, located in Olalla, Oregon, was completed about May 1980. The reservoir was so named in memory of the late Benjamin Barton Irving. He served Douglas County as a surveyor and engineer from 1945 to 1966. He was a flood control advocate. He was credited with the location of many dam sites in the county, the establishment of a flood warning system and the development of precipitation and stream gages. He passed away in December of 1967.

November 1980: The City of Winston elected Betty Fortino as mayor of the city. Mrs. Fortino was the first woman to be elected to that office.

February 1982: Mr. and Mrs. Justis of Winston operated a foster home from 1982 to 2001. During those 19 years they fostered over 300 children. The Justis family also raised three of their own children and one adopted.

August 1982: The City of Winston appointed Mike Parker as City Administrator pro-tem, but he resigned from the position to pursue his engineering career.

October 1982: The City of Winston hired Dave Waffle as city administrator. He replaced Dale Ennor who resigned from the position in June 1982.

December 1982: A 57-year-old woman from Los Angeles and her passenger were killed when her car collided with a log truck on Highway 42 near Hoover Hill Road about three miles west of Winston on December 27, 1982. The log truck was driven by Don Bloss of Roseburg.

March 1984: The Winston City Council, by Resolution No. 166, mutually adopted Tokoroa of New Zealand as its international sister community under the "People-to-People" program inaugurated by President Dwight D. Eisenhower in 1956.

May 1985: The City of Winston began using the DOS System of computers.

November 1985: William Zuver was the youngest person to be elected as mayor of the City of Winston on November 5, 1985. He served as mayor for two years.

January 1986: Winston and the entire nation were paralyzed with shock and sadness on learning of the tragedy the crew of the space shuttle Challenger suffered when their spaceship burst into flames killing all seven astronauts aboard.

January 1986: Darryl Johnson resigned as the municipal judge for the City of Winston.

1986: The book *Land of the Umpqua* was written by Stephen Dow Beckham Ph.D. It is a history of Douglas County that gives an account of: "common people, their labors, accomplishments and at times short-comings." The book was commissioned by the Douglas County Commissioners and paid for by a grant through the C. Giles Hunt Charitable Foundation.

March 1986: Mr. R. McElmurry of Tokay Street in Winston suffered a heart attack at the city council meeting on March 3, 1986. Mr. McElmurry was addressing the council during a public hearing on the proposed Tokay Street area annexation. He died on the way to the hospital.

June 1986: Dillard School District #116 honored Vince McGovern by renaming Civil Bend Elementary School in Winston McGovern Elementary School for his 34 years of service to the district. Mr. McGovern retired as principal of Civil Bend Elementary School in June 1986.

November 1986: Khayam, the celebrity cheetah, died on November 26, 1986, of kidney failure. The Winston community honored the cheetah by making a bronze statue of Khayam and placing it in the center of the town on May 2, 1987.

January 1987: Dave Waffle resigned his position as Winston City Administrator. Mr. Waffle accepted a position with the city of Platteville, Wisconsin.

March 1987: The City of Winston hired Ron Schofield as the City Administrator.

April 1987: Attorney Bill Wolke resigned as the attorney for the City of Winston.

April 1987: The City of Winston hired attorney Bruce Coalwell as the city's attorney. Mr. Coalwell still represents the city.

April 1987: The City of Winston hired Gloria McGinnis as the city's municipal judge.

April 1987: James McClendon retired as the Public Works Superintendent of the City of Winston.

April 1987: The City of Winston hired Eric Wilson as the Superintendent of Public Works. Mr. Wilson was the first Afro-West Indian to be hired in that position and retired in April 2005.

May 1987: The City of Winston switched from a General Fund Tax Levy to a Law Enforcement Tax Levy under Resolution #240. All property taxes paid to the city go to support the Police Department.

December 1987: At a ceremony in Phoenix, Arizona, Larry Swanger, a special education graduate of Douglas High School, was honored by the National Athlete Congress as the Outstanding Disabled Athlete of the Year 1987. Larry is legally blind, but his athletic accomplishments were phenomenal. In 1980 he completed the 26-mile Portland Marathon in three hours, twenty-seven minutes. In 1983 he competed in the International Special Olympics Summer Games at Baton Rouge, Louisiana. In April of 1987 he completed the Boston Marathon.

June 1988: Bremner Hills Co-op, west of Winston, rejected the City of Winston's invitation for annexation. The community is still outside of the city limits but lies within the urban growth boundaries. The city treats the co-op's sewer under a special agreement.

November 1988: Bruce Justis was appointed to the position of Chief of Police in the City of Winston. George Jacobs, the previous Chief, passed away.

1989: In an effort to stop Roseburg Forest Products Co. from reducing the workers' wages by $1.00 an hour, about 4,300 workers in all 15 plants in Oregon and California went on strike for about four months. The strikers manned picket lines for 24 hours. The strike ended with the workers agreeing to accept a 60-cent per hour wage cut.

November 1989: Mayor Ken Hull was the only mayor of the City of Winston to be recalled. He was replaced by Jim McClellan. An attempt to recall Mayor Rex Stevens in November 2003 failed.

November 1989: Gus Jennings was the only City of Winston Councilor to be recalled.

January 1990: Ron Schofield, Winston City Administrator, was asked to resign without prior notice. He was replaced by Jim McClellan as pro-tem city administrator. Bruce Kelly was hired as the city administrator in July 1990.

March 1990: Kathy Holcomb was appointed to the position of planning coordinator for the City of Winston. In June of 2003 the city eliminated the position due to a budget shortfall. In a highly charged public meeting regarding the proposed budget and the subsequent dismissal of the planning coordinator's position, many irate citizens accused the city of alleged retaliation against Kathy for joining the Union - International Association of Machinist and Aerospace Workers (IAMAW).

October 1990: The City of Winston adopted an RUOK program for the elderly. The program no longer exists.

November 1990: On November 6, 1990, voters in the Umpqua Basin and throughout the State of Oregon voted in favor of Ballot Measure 5. That contentious measure was an amendment to the Oregon Constitution that established limits on Oregon's property taxes on real estate. Its passage became a benchmark in Oregon's voting history.

January 1991: Theresa Aulman, a graduate of Douglas High School in 1990, served in the Gulf War as a Navy Corpsman for three months.

June 1992: Senate Bill No. 66 mandated cities with a population of 4000 or greater to have a recycling program. Winston began its recycling program in June of 1992.

November 1992: The Dial-A-Ride program was set up through the Police Department in Winston and is currently operating. The program received recognition from the League of Oregon Cities. The drivers in the program are all volunteers.

May 1993: Anna Marie Powell, 17, died at Portland's Oregon Health Science University as a result of injuries suffered from a head-on collision with a delivery truck on the "Schattenkerk Curve" on Highway 42. Miss Powell was a senior at Douglas High School.

February 1995: The City of Winston, by Resolution No. 530, adopted the City of Elgin, Oregon, on February 6, 1995, as its sister city.

1995: Ron Poland, a Douglas High School graduate, won the gold medal in the Special Olympics marathon in New Haven, Connecticut.

June 1996: The community of Brockway lost a dear friend and an icon of knowledge of Douglas County. Cyril "Sid" Nichols passed away on May 28, 1996 at the age of 91. Sid was the postmaster of Brockway Post Office from 1940 to 1956. The family operated the post office from the store since 1890.

December 1996: Gloria McGinnis resigned her position as municipal judge for the City of Winston.

July 1997: Riverbend Live kicked off its free outdoor concerts at Riverbend Park in Winston on July 4, 1997, from 7:00 PM to 9:00 PM. The outdoor concerts have taken place every Friday in July for the past 15 years. Dick and Mo Nichols spearhead the committee that puts on the concerts.

August 1997: Bobbie Jo Dwight was only 19 when she died from head injuries sustained from a car crash on Highway 42 not far from Douglas High School. The three teenagers, Brady Duke, 14, Terry Creach, 19, and Carrie Ross, who were traveling with her, sustained minor injuries. Bobbie Jo was the sister of Anna Marie Powell who died in a car accident on Highway 42 in 1993.

September 1997: Mayor Jim McClellan received the "Home Town Leaders Award" from the National Center of Small Communities - NCSC.

January 1998: Author Paula D. Riggs of Dillard, Oregon, published the 32nd book of her career. The romance novel is called *Taming the Night*.

January 1999: Troy Polamalu, all-state football player for Douglas High School, accepted a scholarship at the University of Southern California to play football. He accepted USC from a roster of colleges who offered him scholarships.

February 1999: At the 21st annual First Citizens Banquet sponsored by the Winston- Dillard Area Chamber of Commerce, Gary Vess, then city councilor, and his wife Lucille Vess, then fulltime volunteer, were honored with the title of First Citizen for 1999. The ceremony was held at the Middle School in Winston on February 22, 1999. The Winston-Dillard Food Pantry was awarded the 1999 Civic Award for its service to the community.

April 1999: Dillon Exceen, a four-month-old baby boy, burned to death in a mobile home at 198 Frisk Lane in Green. Dillon was sleeping when the home caught on fire. His grandfather Terry Exceen was seriously burned when he attempted to rescue his grandson. Terry was flown by helicopter to Portland to the Oregon Burn Center.

April 1999: The communities of Winston and Dillard mourned the death of Kyle Matsen, 14 years old, after he accidentally shot himself while playing with a .38 caliber revolver on Sunday, April 11, 1999. Kyle was hanging out with his friends at the time of the accident.

May 1999: Ethel Stutzman, age 72, of Winston was found dead in the snow near South Umpqua Falls at 9:35 AM after she had been missing for three days. After their motor home had become stuck in the snow, she left her older sister in the vehicle and went for help.

June 1999: Matthew Little and Zachary Wilson, students of Douglas High School, were honored for their outstanding achievements in mathematics by the Oregon Council of Teachers of Mathematics and the Oregon Department of Education.

August 1999: Winston Abacela Winery was incorporated in June 1994. The 500-acre vineyard began marketing its wine in 1999.

December 1999: The Winston-Green Regional Treatment Plant spilled over 10,000 gallons of anaerobic digester sludge into the South Umpqua River.

February 2000: Joe Rosjak, former president of Riverside Center, requested the City of Winston to co-sponsor a Community Block Grant for $600,000. The City Council unanimously agreed to do so.

April 2000: Kevin Parker and Ryan Beauchamp of Winston, 19 and 17 respectively, lost their lives at Sunset Bay, Coos Bay. The boys were swept off a rock they were climbing by a "sneaker wave" and drowned. Kevin and Ryan were part of a hiking team of five youth.

April 2000: Winston Area Community Partnership WACP, better known as "Wake-up," received its 501 c (3) nonprofit status in the spring of 2000. WACP's manifesto expresses bringing "Quality and Unity to our Community."

May 2000: At the State 1A Track and Field Championship Games held at Western Oregon University on May 20, 2000, Candace Weaver, a junior from Camas Valley High School, out-heaved her opponents in the discus competition winning the gold medal for the second straight year. She threw the discus for 119 feet 8 inches, beating her closest competitor by 11 feet. She also captured the gold medal in the shot put competition with a throw of 35 feet 10 inches.

June 2000: Douglas High School honored retiring Dan Withers by naming its baseball field "Dan Withers Field". Mr. Withers graduated from Douglas High in 1965, and in 1985 he returned to teach and coach for 15 years. Mr. Withers was vice principal and head of the athletic program at the time of retiring.

June 2000: Winston Area Youth & Family Resource Center, an extension of the Roseburg YMCA opened its facility on June 10, 2000 at 153 Douglas Blvd. in Winston near Priceless Foods. The Center closed its doors in 2001 for lack of funds.

June 2000: 53-year old Victoria Spragg of Roseburg died in an accident on Highway 42 at mile post 70, when the 1998 Chevrolet passenger car she was driving was hit by a 1996 Ford pick-up truck driven by Stacy Levin of Winston. It appeared that Ms. Spragg attempted a U-turn on the highway when she was hit. No citations were issued according to Trooper Kirk Freeman.

October 2000: Whatever happened to Hazel Chamblen on the night of October 20, 2000? That is the question her family and the Community of Tenmile want to know. The eighty-six-year-old volunteer for the Winston Seniors was last seen dropping her great-grandson off at Douglas High School on Friday evening at 7:00 PM. Two weeks later her red Toyota station wagon was found in the hills in the vicinity of Loon Lake.

November 2000: Rex Stevens, a former city council member, defeated the incumbent, Jim McClellan, for the position of mayor of the City of Winston. When the votes were canvassed, Rex finished with 907 votes to Jim's 667. Jim served as mayor for 11 years.

February 2001: Fire destroyed the 123-year-old Brockway Schoolhouse at 8:30 AM on 2002 Brockway Road. The school was built in 1878 and closed its doors in 1945.

August 2001: The Music on the Half Shell Committee of Roseburg renamed the band shell facility at Stewart Park the "Nichols Band Shell" in honor of Dick and Mo Nichols of Winston.

October 2001: Eugene Fisher of Tenmile lost his life in an accident on Reston Road. The 1976 Chevrolet pickup truck he was driving went over an embankment.

December 2001: Lindsey White of Winston, who was 83 years of age, was found dead in a ravine near a BLM road 15 miles northeast of Coquille. Mr. White had been missing for seven days.

January 2002: Sgt. Jaime Greer of the Winston Police Department was exonerated from all charges of ethics violations by the State Ethics Board with regards to soliciting business while on duty.

January 2002: Valynn Currie of Green was named Realtor of the Year for 2002 by the Douglas County Board of Realtors. She is the owner of Currieco Real Estate Inc. in Winston, Myrtle Creek and Green and sister of Winston's Mayor, Rex Stevens.

February 2002: Rescuers from the Tenmile-Olalla and Camas Valley Fire District extricated Frances Allene Forty from wreckage on Highway 42 near Bear Creek. Frances was pronounced dead on the scene. Her two dogs and cat that were in the vehicle with her were taken to the Douglas County Animal Shelter.

February 2002: Viola Witt was 76 years of age and her friend Ralph Hanley was 80 when they were killed in a car accident on Highway 42 a few miles west of Tenmile. They were from Lookingglass.

February 2002: Nine members of the City of Winston administration and public works employees joined the International Association of Machinists and Aerospace Workers (IAMAW). In *The News Review* section "Public Forum" dated June 10, 2003, three employees: Dawn Flippence, Ted Johnson and Kathy Holcomb explained: "in order to protect their jobs and receive management respect, these three employees searched for a group to represent them, as management was not taking care of their responsibilities to the employees."

May 2002: Winston Veterans Memorial Gardens was dedicated at the Winston Community Park on Memorial Day, May 27, 2002. The monuments and gardens were designed by Roseburg architect Paul Bentley.

August 2002: The Riverside Center expansion was completed in August 10, 2002. The center, located at 671 SW Main Street, was an adolescent day treatment program for children and adolescents. The 54,000-square-foot addition cost $980,000. The funds to build the new structure came from grants from the Ford Family Foundation, the C. Giles Hunt Charitable Trust, a US Government Grant and private contributions.

January 2003: Ethan Scott Yocham of Winston was the first baby to be born in Douglas County for the year 2003. His parents, Adrienne Fairchild and Carlos Yocham, welcomed him at 4:21 AM at Mercy Medical Center Family Birth Place.

January 2003: The 21st Century and state-of-the-art Brockway Elementary School was constructed at a cost of $7 million. The 57,000-square-foot building is located at 2520 NW Brockway Road near Lookingglass Road. Paul Bentley of Roseburg was the architect, and Harmon Construction Co. of Coos Bay was the builder. The construction was made possible through the passage of a bond issue for $9.5 million.

February 2003: Dentist Ron Tribble of Winston successfully performed a root-canal on a 350-pound female lion at Wildlife Safari in Winston on Friday, February 21, 2003. Safari's veterinarian Modesto McClean assisted the dentist with the two-hour procedure.

February 2003: At the 25th annual Winston-Dillard Area Chamber of Commerce First Citizens Banquet, held at the Winston Middle School on February 24, 2003, Dave Quanbeck, Scout Master of Troop #118 in Winston and Sandy Lipphardt, owner of Sandy's Corner Book Nook, also in Winston, were honored with the area's First Citizen for 2003. More than 150 guests were present to witness the ceremony. The guest speaker was Josh Bidwell, a Douglas High School graduate and NFL punter for the Green Bay Packers.

April 2003: Winston Chief of Police, Bruce Justis, retired from the police department on April 31, 2003. Bruce served the police department for 28 years and as chief for 15 years.

June 2003: *Winston Area News*, a newspaper serving the greater Winston, Dillard, Tenmile, Camas Valley, Lookingglass and Green areas, began publication in June of 2003 and ended in June of 2006. Rose Mary Smith was the editor and publisher.

June 2003: At an emotionally charged budget meeting on June 4, 2003, Winston-Dillard School District approved a four-day school week. The decision was reached due to a shortfall in the budget for fiscal year 2003-2004.

June 2003: Janet Morse, manager of Premier West Bank Branch in Winston, was promoted to Vice-President of the Premier West Banking Establishment on June 23, 2003. Janet is a member of WACP and was one of the leading figures in the building of the new Winston Community Center in 2008.

June 2003: Ronald P. Harwood, 45, Dillard, was found after being lost for six days in the woods in the Calf Creek Area. He disappeared on Monday, June 9, 2003, while on a camping trip with his family at Twin Lakes. Douglas County Search and Rescue Team found him on Saturday evening, June 15, 2003. He was taken to Mercy Hospital suffering from dehydration.

December 2003: The 57-year-old Porter Creek Store (also known as C & M Market) changed ownership. Dave Wellbrenner and Shawn Henshaw are the new owners of the store.

December 2003: Beverly Winston Browne of Winston published a book of poems called *Young Love And Other Poems*. Mrs. Browne passed away in June 2011.

January 2004: Douglas County Board of Commissioners approved a loan of $400,000 to Wildlife Safari. The drive-through animal park had been experiencing financial difficulties since the 9/11 terrorist attack, and, as a result, visitors to the park had fallen by six percent. That was the second time the county helped bail out the then struggling park. In 1984 the county, through its industrial board, loaned the park $400,000.

February 2004: The side of the mountain upon which Sundance Rock Inc. was mining for construction rock in Dillard came thundering down at 4:00 PM Monday, February 2, 2004. The landslide brought millions of cubic yards of dirt, burying a section of Southern Pacific Railroad tracks and covering a huge portion of a 40-acre farm belonging to Jim Lee.

April 2004: Tampa Bay Buccaneers, the professional NFL team, signed Josh Bidwell as a punter to fill the position Tom Tupa left when he signed to play for the Washington Redskins. Josh was a graduate of Douglas High School and a former punter for the Green Bay Packers drafted out of the University of Oregon.

April 2004: A large crowd from Winston, Dillard and the surrounding areas gathered on the grounds of the proposed new fire station building and medical clinic in Winston to witness the groundbreaking ceremony.

May 2004: The City of Winston hired David Van Dermark as city administrator. He replaced Bruce Kelly who decided to take an early retirement. Mr. Kelly served as city administrator for 14 years.

June 2004: Joe LaFountaine, former principal of Winston Middle School, published his first book. The name of the book is *Colastic Moon Temple.*

July 2004: Scott Gugel, Senior Patrol Officer was appointed to the post of Chief of Police for the City of Winston. He replaced Bruce Justis who retired after 29 years of service.

April 2005: Army Spc. Ricky William Rockholt, Jr. 28, of Winston was killed when a homemade bomb detonated near his vehicle in northern Iraq.

April 2005: The City of Winston hired Jennifer Sikes as the superintendent of public works. Mrs. Sikes was the first woman to work in that position and still works in that capacity. She replaced Eric Wilson who retired after 18 years in that position.

October 2005: Steve and Mariza Perry of 91 NE Ronald St. in Winston won a court judgment against the City of Winston regarding the expression of free speech. The city ordered the family to remove a controversial sign in their yard since it violated a city sign ordinance. The family refused and took the city to court.

November 2005: Norman Johnson of Winston was struck and killed on the South Umpqua Bridge between Winston and Dillard about 9:20 PM.

November 2005: Troy Polamalu, a Douglas High School graduate in 1999, was featured on the cover of *Sports Illustrated* for the November 15, 2005, issue as "Steelers' Harding-hitting Safety." He was a two-time All American Safety for the University of Southern California, USC. In 2002 he was drafted from USC as a safety to play in the NFL for the Pittsburg Steelers. He was selected to play in the Pro-Bowl in 2004 and 2005.

January 2006: Al Hooten of Winston, an intarsia design artist, created and sculptured the City of Roseburg's logo. The artwork now hangs in the chamber of the Roseburg City Council.

February 2006: Jeannette Jeannings and her seven-month-old son Timoteo of Winston died in a car accident on Highway 99 near the Winston-Dillard Bridge. The car Ms. Jeannings was driving hit the abutment on the Dillard side of the bridge killing her instantly. Her son, Timoteo Jeannings died at a Portland hospital.

February 2006: For the first time in pro football history, two professional football players from the same 3A Level high school played in the Pro Bowl in Hawaii on February 16, 2006. The players were: Troy Polamalu #43 of the Pittsburgh Steelers and Josh Bidwell #9 of the Tampa Bay Buccaneers. The men are graduates of Douglas High School in Winston, Oregon.

February 2006: Sandi Koberstein is the first female patrol officer to be hired on the Winston Police Department.

February 2006: At the Winston-Dillard Area Chamber of Commerce 28th Annual First Citizens Banquet, Mayor Rex Stevens and his sister, Valynn Currie, were honored with the distinction of First Citizens for the year 2006. The ceremony was held at the Winston Middle School on Monday, February 27, 2006, before a crowd of 100 people.

May 2006: Justin Smithhisler, a junior at Umpqua Valley Christian School, won the State Junior Golf Championship at Trysting Tree Golf Course. It was Umpqua Valley Christian School's first state title since 2002 when the school won the 2A/1A baseball championship.

June 2006: Max Montano, a Douglas High School graduate of 1996, was awarded a Ph.D. Degree in Chemistry from the University of California, Berkeley. Max graduated magna cum laude from Pacific University, Oregon with a Bachelor's Degree in Physical Chemistry in 2000.

June 2006: About 130 residents of Winston and the Greater Winston area attended the groundbreaking ceremony for the proposed new Winston Community Center and Library.

November 2006: Joe Laurence of Dillard defeated Dan Hern by a margin of 3000 votes to win the seat for Douglas County Commissioner Position 2, formerly held by Dan Van Slyke.

March 2007: *Winston Reporter,* a weekly newspaper, published its first edition on March 8, 2007, with Monte Muirhead as the editor. Unfortunately, the paper stopped its publication in November 2007.

March 2007: The YMCA of Downtown Pittsburg, PA., named Troy Polamalu, a Douglas High School graduate, who plays football for the Pittsburg Steelers, their Person of the Year for 2007.

June 2007: Halle Brown Ford, former wife of Kenneth Ford and cofounder of Roseburg Lumber Co. and Ford Family Foundation, passed away on June 5, 2007. She left behind a legacy of philanthropic accolades.

July 2007: Pittsburgh Steelers safety Troy Polamalu, a Douglas High School graduate in 1999, signed a four-year contract extension on Monday, July 23, 2007, worth $30.19 million. That contract made Troy the highest-paid player in the team's history and one of the highest paid defensive backs in the NFL.

July 2007: Areta Bass Stelle of Winston, author of children books, published another children's book, *The Amazing Mr. Frog*.

July 2007: Eric Wilson, retired superintendent of public works for Winston, published a book of poems called *Contemporary Spice*.

July 2007: Mark Stephen Wafford, 35, of Winston, died in Green in an accident at the corner of Ingram Drive and Speedway Road at about 10:00 p.m. on July 1, 2007. Mr. Wafford was driving a 1999 BMW when the crash occurred.

August 2007: Frank Hart of Winston, Wildlife Safari founder and conservationist, passed away on August 3, 2007, at the age of 84.

September 2007: Robert Benedict lost his life in a traffic accident in Green when he attempted to save his wife from getting hit by a speeding van. Robert managed to push his wife out of the path of the speeding vehicle but got hit in the act of doing so. The accident occurred at the crosswalk on Pacific Highway and Chadwick Lane in Green at 2:35 PM.

December 2007: Gov. Ted Kulongoski congratulated Special Olympian Ron Poland at an awards dinner in Portland. Ron won a bronze medal in the 5000 meters at the Special Olympics World Games held in Shanghai, China in October 2007. Ron graduated from Douglas High School in 1988.

January 2008: The new Winston Community Center and Library was dedicated on January 26, 2008. The 18,000-square-foot building was constructed at a cost of $4.7 million.

March 2008: The cover story of the March issue of the *Smithsonian Magazine* discussed cheetahs and "A plan for their survival." The article pointed to Laurie Marker, Ph.D., as their savior. Laurie Marker worked as a trainee with cheetahs at Wildlife Safari in Winston between 1972 and 1986. She was referred to as the "mother" of Khayam. In 2002 she earned a Ph.D. from Oxford University. Her dissertation was on the "Aspects of Cheetah Biology, Ecology and Conservation Strategies on Namibian Farmlands." Dr. Marker now lives in Namibia, Kenya and is executive director of the Cheetah Conservation Fund, a million-dollar-a-year non-profit foundation.

April 2009: Lookingglass Grange, No 927, celebrated its 60th anniversary as a Grange in Douglas County. The organization was first established on April 20, 1949, by the local community of the valley. Granges in Douglas County have been and still continue to be social pillars of the communities.

March 2010: Josh Bidwell, a Douglas High School graduate, signed as a football punter to play for the Washington Redskins. He spent six years playing for the Tampa Buccaneers. He was drafted out of the University of Oregon to play for the Green Bay Packers. He played for the Green Bay Packers from 1999 to 2003.

May 2010: Douglas High School Symphonic Band won the state 4A division championship trophy at the Oregon School Activities Association State Band Championships. That victory was the school's second time in a row after winning the 2009 championship trophy.

October 2010: Winston's Baptist Minister, Steven Schenewerk, Pastor of Winston Community Baptist Church, was named Outstanding Adult Volunteer of the Year at the Governor's Volunteer Awards Luncheon in Salem.

November 2010: Sharron Harrison of Harrison Hardware defeated incumbent Rex Stevens for the mayor's position for the City of Winston on November 2, 2010. When the votes were canvassed,

Sharon got 1096 votes and Rex got 547. Rex served as mayor of the city for 10 years.

November 2010: Bruce Cronk of Green District ran for the U.S. Senate challenging Ron Wyden, the incumbent, and Republican nominee Jim Huffman. Mr. Cronk ran as the nominee of the "Working Families Party". Ron Wyden was victorious in that race.

November 2010: The City of Winston voters amended the City Charter, changing the title of City Administrator to City Manager. The amendment will allow a city employee to fill in for the City Manager when he/she is out of the office instead of the mayor having to take on that role.

November 2010: David Wiggins, age 53, was struck and killed by a 1998 Chevrolet van at the intersection of Main St. and Highway 42 in Winston about 5:00 PM on Wednesday, November 17, 2010. The van was driven by Alan Sabin of Camas Valley. Allan was also 53 years of age.

May 2010: The City of Winston filed a lawsuit against Riverside Center regarding ownership of the 3.75 acre-property and buildings at 671 SW Main Street. In the lawsuit, the city accused the center's board of directors of violating the terms of the deed. The Riverside Center closed the Adolescent Day Treatment Program for lack of funding and now houses ADAPT Alcohol and Drug Prevention and Treatment. As a point of historical interest, in 1993 when the property was purchased, Riverside Center and the Ford Family Foundation paid $235,000. The City of Winston paid for the construction of the 5500-square-foot annex to the largest building through a $600,000 US Government grant. The intent of the wording of the deed which states that: "Ownership of the 3.75-acre-property and buildings reverts to the city if the center stops operating" needed arbitration interpretation.

November 2010: The Douglas Trojans football team defeated Estacada 8-0 in Class 4A semifinals to play for the state championship. Unfortunately, the Trojans were defeated by the Baker Bulldogs 34-20 for the state title on December 4, 2010 in

Hillsboro. It was Douglas's first state football championship game since 1992.

November 2010: The Camas Valley Hornets football team defeated the Cove Leopards in the Class 1A OSAA semifinals by a score of 30-14. Disappointedly, the Hornets lost the championship game against St. Paul's Buckaroos 22-8 for the state title on December 4, 2010, in Hillsboro.

December 2010: Troy Polamalu, Pittsburg Steelers Safety, was awarded the Associated Press 2010 NFL Defensive Player Award. Troy is a Douglas High School graduate of 1999.

May 2011: On Monday, May 2, 2011, under a new mayoral leadership, the Winston City Council voted 4-1 in favor of the agreement reached during a 10-hour mediation session held between representatives of the city and that of Riverside Center. Both parties resolved the two-year dispute regarding ownership of the 3.75 acre property and buildings at 671 SW Main Street. The city agreed to withdraw its lawsuit against the center and allow the non-profit group to use the property and buildings. In exchange, the Riverside Center would make a $20,000 contribution to the Winston Community Center.

June 2011: Friday, June 24, 2011, at 3:00 PM, the Winston-Dillard Area Chamber of Commerce awarded Jim and Bernice McClellan a Lifetime Achievement Award for the years of service given to the community. The chamber punctuated the honor by naming all such future awards given to anyone "The McClellan Award".

February 2012: South River Community Health Center, located at 671 SW Main Street, began operating a medical facility on February 27, 2012.

March 2012: Voters in the Winston Fire District voted by an overwhelming majority to recall three board members on March 8, 2012. When the votes were canvassed, 79 percent voted yes and 21 percent voted no to recall Dale Stutzman, the board's chairman. 80

percent voted yes while 20 percent voted no to recall Stan Keeler, and Lyle Jeffries was recalled with 78 percent voting yes while 22 percent voted no. (*The News Review* issue of March 9, 2012 carried the story.)

June 20, 2012: An excited crowd of 60 people attended the ground breaking ceremony for a boat ramp at the Harold & Sid Nichols Park in Winston. The park is located at the confluence of Lookingglass Creek and the South Umpqua River near Highway 42. The boat ramp and park were made possible through a donation of eight acres of land from the Nichols Family, a grant of $395,000 from state boater fees and the Federal Sport Fish Restoration Fund and a donation of $12,000 from the Cow Creek Band of Umpqua Tribe of Indians. Four months later, on October 25, 2012, the recreational park was dedicated and declared open to the public.

References:

The News Review 1967 – 2012, The *Umpqua Trapper*, Winston City Council Minutes 1967 - 2012, Winston Dillard School District#116 Records, *Sports Illustrated* September 2005, The *Coos Bay World*, *The Smithsonian Magazine* - March 2008, *Winston Reporter*, *Winston Area News*, Douglas County Elections and Boundaries Records.

CHAPTER SEVEN

History Stories

THE CHAMPAGNE RIOT OF 1866
Just about every newspaper in the State of Oregon carried the trial of John Fitzhugh and John Hannan for the murder of Robert Forbes and D. F. Barringer at the "Champagne Riot" as that tragic affair later became known. Even though Oregon was not a part of the Mason-Dixon Divide, Oregonians were quite passionate about the Civil War and its outcome. That passion did not end on the steps of Appomattox Courthouse in Virginia when Gen. Robert E. Lee surrendered to Gen. Ulysses S. Grant on April 9, 1865. Once again, tempers would soar, guns would fire and men would die in Coles Valley of Douglas County, Oregon, on December 25, 1866.

Coles Valley, today sparsely populated, located six miles west of Sutherlin and nine miles north of Melrose as the crow flies, was the "hot spot" in Douglas County at the time Oregon became a state. The fertile valley attracted early settlers seeking donation land claims. On Christmas Eve night, 1866, John Fitzhugh, with a group of his southern buddies, attended a Christmas dance at Goode's Mill. On the other side of the valley, in the French Canadian Settlement, Joseph Champagne was also having a Christmas dance that was attended mostly by northerners with a few southern girls who preferred the lively music the Canadians provided.

It was about one hour before midnight, with the brightly shining moon in mid-sky. John Fitzhugh, his nephew Solomon Culver, Abram Crow, John Hannan and Robert Forbes left Goode's Mill for their homes feeling the good cheer of holiday drinking and dancing. As they were crossing the creek, a few of them stopped to wash the sleep and alcohol from their faces. From that vantage point they saw lights and heard music coming from Champagne's party. Culver knew that George Bennett, whom he hated, was going to that dance. He also knew that George had invited two southern girls to go along with him. He suggested to his traveling companions that they come along with him to Champagne's dance and watch him whip that ugly Bennett's butt. Fitzhugh was eager to go along to make sure his nephew Solomon had a fair fight. Fitzhugh was quite outspoken about his hatred for northerners. He never liked to be reminded of how the North kicked the South's "ass," a common expression used by northerners to intimidate southerners.

At Joseph Champagne's house, the party was heating up with joy and laughter. The older folks, dressed in fancy gowns and split-tail coats, were chatting on the side chairs, while the young were swaying their hips from side to side to the rhythm of Ashford Clayton's fiddling. The children were already in bed and fast asleep. It was not unusual for the party to end at dawn, just in time to get home to milk the cows and feed the other animals.

D. F. Barringer was about 36 years of age. He was tall, husky, soft spoken, and weighed about 280 pounds. He worked as a farm hand for Champagne's family, and that night he was the manager of the Christmas dance. Fitzhugh, on the other hand, was 31 years old, of medium stature, weighed 210 pounds and worked as a land surveyor for the county. His father was Solomon Fitzhugh, a distant relative of Gen. Robert E. Lee, and had been elected Probate Judge in Douglas County in 1852. He served one term as State Senator in 1863. Several months before, Barringer and Fitzhugh had had an argument about a girl they both liked, and Barringer challenged Fitzhugh to a fistfight. Fitzhugh declined, and instead challenged Barringer to a pistol shootout. When Barringer declined, the disagreement was put to rest.

Fitzhugh and his four southern companions suddenly burst into Champagne's dance wearing hats and long black winter coats. It was the custom to wear a holster with a pistol, and sometimes a knife for protection. When Barringer saw the men, he tried to stop them before they climbed the stairs. He knew they came for trouble. As they pushed their way past him, he cautioned them not to make any fuss or disturbance at the party. Ignoring Barringer, Abram Crow was rudely bumping into the dancers to intimidate them. Solomon Culver wasted no time once he found Bennett. He began by banging him on the head with his revolver and kicking him as he fell to the floor, using insulting words mixed with profanity. At that point all hell broke loose, and the disturbance grew into a riot. Pandemonium replaced the cheerful holiday spirit. The women were screaming and scrambling for cover. The weapons used were knuckles, chairs, broken-bottles, oakwood clubs, knives and guns. At the trial, William Chauncey Winston (for whose family the City of Winston was named), who was living and teaching school at the time in Coles Valley, thought that the riot lasted for about five minutes and that he heard six gun shots. Thomas Thompson and Cy Smith were able to get Fitzhugh to surrender his gun to them. One of two shots allegedly fired from Fitzhugh's gun hit Ashford Clayton in the head. However long the riot lasted, Robert Forbes and Barringer died from gunshot wounds. John Hannan and Ashford Clayton, the fiddler, were seriously wounded. Three men held Fitzhugh at gunpoint in a side barn while another rode into Roseburg to get the sheriff and the doctor. The annual Champagne Christmas party was over, leaving much trauma in its wake. Of the five southern intruders, Fitzhugh was in custody, John Hannan was seriously wounded and couldn't be brought to jail, Abram Crow and Solomon Culver were indicted for assault with intent to kill, and Robert Forbes was dead.

John Fitzhugh was very apologetic and worried he would not live to see daylight. He felt lucky and happy to see the sheriff, as he knew a group of the northerners were planning a necktie party. Lynching was against the law, but the men at the Champagne's dance felt they needed quick justice since Barringer was a very popular and respected man in the valley. The memory of that tragic and inhumane act, about 1860, was still fresh in the minds of the people of Deer Creek (the area known today as Roseburg), when an angry mob hanged McPherson, an Irishman, from Deer Creek Bridge for killing Bradford Robinson, a popular hotel manager.

The trial was a very long and interesting one. It began in January of 1867 and ended in May of that year. It brought back memories of the passion that caused disunity in the county during the Civil War. As a result, it was very difficult to find jurors who had no definite sympathy towards either side of the conflict. The court examined 67 jurors before seven were impaneled for the Grand Jury.

They were: B. Brockway, Samuel Handsaker, John McCulloch, D. C. Underwood (Foreman of the Jury), Ralph Cockeran, N. Imbler and H. Barnett.

John Fitzhugh's father, Solomon Fitzhugh, an attorney by profession, did not have to look hard for southern attorneys to defend his son and his companions. The law firm of Mosher & Lane was his first choice. Mosher was a leader of Knights of the Golden Circle, a southern fraternity whose purpose was to disrupt the influence of the Union League. And, of course, Gen. Joseph Lane, whose son was a graduate of West Point, and had served in the Confederate Army and was a partner of Lafayette Mosher.

The courtroom was filled with jurors, witnesses, reporters and spectators. Among the spectators was Gen. Joseph Lane, father of Lafayette Lane and father-in-law of Lafayette Mosher. Attorneys for the state J. F. Watson (Prosecuting Attorney), J. F. Gazley, W. R.Willis and Binger Herman quietly walked in and took their seats. When the attorneys for the defense came in, they were dressed alike, stepping with pomp and pageantry as they took their seats. They were former Gov. Gibbs, S. F. Chadwick, Mosher and Lane. There was even applause on one side of the aisle. The last to enter was Hon. Judge A. A. Skinner, clothed in a beautiful violet robe with a red sash over his left shoulder. Deputy Williams asked everyone to rise. John Fitzhugh, John Hannan, Solomon Culver, and Abram Crow, the bailed defendants, sat in the prisoner's box staring into the packed courtroom anticipating the outcome of their fate.

Between the preliminary hearings and the verdict in the Circuit Court, about 55 witnesses were examined. Thirty individuals of the county, both men and women, were subpoenaed to testify to the character of the accused. The attorneys for the state and the defendants were given four hours each in which to make their closing arguments. On Saturday, May 18, 1867, after three hours of deliberating on the evidence in the Champagne Riot, D. C. Underwood, foreman of the jury, returned a verdict of manslaughter against John Fitzhugh and John Hannan. The jury was polled, and all seven members answered, 'Guilty.' Also attached and signed by each juror was a recommendation to the

court of clemency towards the prisoners. Abram Crow and Solomon Culver were found not guilty of any of the charges. There were mixed feelings of joy and outrage in the courtroom. The following Monday, the attorneys for the defense filed a motion to set aside the verdict on the grounds that:
1. The jury was never given the opportunity to examine the pistols or the bullets.
2. The jury had access to law books during its deliberation which influenced its decision to the detriment of the defendants.
3. The jury's decision was also influenced by a preacher who was conducting a religious service on the Sabbath in the adjacent room of the courthouse while the jury was deliberating. The preacher was speaking at the top of his voice rebuking and calling the defendants murderers.

That motion was argued and overruled. John Fitzhugh was then sentenced to five years in the state prison and John Hannan to one year. Both men were released on bail pending an appeal to the Oregon Supreme Court. Fitzhugh's bail was $6,000 and Hannan's $2,000.

The September session of the Supreme Court examined the case of the Champagne Riot and upheld the Lower Court's decision. John Hannan served his short sentence. John Fitzhugh, on the other hand, was pardoned by Governor George L. Woods, in October of 1869. It appeared that the pardoning of Fitzhugh sent political ripples of outrage across the state. The Democratic Press in Salem published an editorial accusing Gov. Woods of corruption and implied he had received sums of money in payment for signing the pardon of John Fitzhugh. Two weeks later Solomon Fitzhugh, upset with the rumors of bribery and corruption, sent a letter to the *Roseburg Ensign* (which was the official paper of Douglas, Coos and Curry Counties) in which he categorically denied ever paying a cent to Gov. Woods for the pardoning of his son or for anything else.

References:
Roseburg Ensign 1866 - 1869, *The Plaindealer* 1866 - 1869, Douglas County Museum Records. Photo of Douglas County Court House.

WHO KILLED ALEXANDER MCNABB

Who killed Alexander McNabb on or about June 14, 1911, was the concern that echoed throughout the tiny communities of Brockway, Dillard and Olalla. It seemed that that year was a very rough and unforgettable period in the history of Douglas County. In that same month there were two train robberies of registered mail valued at several thousand dollars of cash and jewelry. One occurred on the Shasta Limited between Drain and Yoncalla, and the other on the California Express in Cow Creek Canyon outside Glendale. But McNabb's death was the tragedy and mystery that disturbed the entire county. Sheriff George Quinn abandoned his involvement in the search for the mail bandits and returned to Roseburg in order to give his full attention to the search for and arrest of the murderers of Mr. McNabb. Both newspapers, *The Roseburg Review* and the *Roseburg Evening News* carried the story for a week. McNabb's family printed several hundred fliers offering a $200 reward for information leading to the arrest and conviction of the murderer or murderers. His remains were buried in the I.O.O.F Cemetery of Roseburg, Oregon.

Since 1894 Alexander D. McNabb, known in his neighborhood as "Alec," lived alone on a ranch about four miles from Brockway off the Olalla Road. He was attracted to that valley because of its beauty, its seclusion and the swift running creek, known today as "McNabb Creek." He was born in Michigan and, with his two brothers Peter and George, was raised on their parents' farm in Brockway. Alec loved farming and chose to remain in the area. His big dream was to own the entire valley on both sides of the creek. Alec was a "loner," perhaps because he was hard of hearing, but was liked and highly respected in the area. At the time of his death he was 34 years of age, tall, and walked with a limp as a result of an injury he sustained from a fall off his horse when he was seventeen. He was blonde, muscular, had large and sinewy hands and wore a shabby beard. He was an inveterate smoker and developed certain facial expressions that gave him the persona of a very strong rancher. No one had ever beaten him in the arm wrestling contest at the annual county fair.

But Alec was kind and gentle and was always ready to help a stranger in need. His best and closest friend was Cuthbert Multimore, who was three years his junior, and lived about two miles from him on the Olalla Road near Hoover Hill. Alec called him "Multi", because he was a handyman and could do and fix anything. They first met at a meeting of the Independent Order of Odd Fellows in Roseburg. They both shared the same kind of passion for the land and, of course, politics. They were Republicans and were saddened by the schism that divided the Party at that time because of the rift between President Taft and Theodore Roosevelt. They visited each other's place quite often to chat or to help with some sort of project. Alec never got married but did date a young lady from the community of Dillard about two years before he was murdered.

It was a very hot and windy day on Friday, June 16, 1911. It had not rained since April. The ground was dry and dusty and crops were withering in the fields from the heat. Multi was on his way home from Dillard and decided to stop in to see Alec. His horse was sweating profusely and seemed to be quite tired under the weight of the buggy and its contents. When he approached the steep driveway off the Olalla road that today is designated as "McNabb Creek Rd.", he had a "gut-feeling" that something was wrong. Between the clouds of dust in the air he could see vultures hovering in the sky over Alec's ranch. He yelled to his horse to go faster, but the dust was so dense the animal was having trouble seeing the road. Multi dismounted the buggy and began to run as fast as he could, calling out to Alec at the top of his voice.

Multi came upon a mosaic of burnt rubble of what was left of Alec's cabin. He was still calling Alec with tears pouring from his eyes. In spite of the heat and the dryness, the fire did not spread outside the confines of the house lot. He found Alec's charred remains lying on the spring frame of the bed. His knees buckled from under him as he fell to the ground in grief, a grief that developed into moans ricocheting off the fir trees throughout the gulch. For quite some time Multi was lost in his sorrows.

Multi was very religious and attended church services at the Baptist Church in Dillard. He was sure Alec did not kill himself, but thought it could have been an accident since Alec had the habit of smoking in bed. He knew Alec had just secured the title to his 160 acres of land under the "Homestead Act" in February of 1910 and had bought another 10 acres from his brothers Peter and George about that same time. With tears still running down his cheeks, he bade his best friend, Alexander D. McNabb, a last goodbye. He jumped on his buggy and drove off into the dusty wind to the Brockway Store to report the incident to the Sheriff in Roseburg.

The gusting winds had calmed down, and the sun had already set when two officers from the Sheriff's Department, coroner N.T. Jewett, and Dr. R.F. Smick, arrived on the scene to investigate the cause of the death of Alexander McNabb. There were already several members of the Brockway and Olalla communities at the scene waiting for the sheriff to arrive. The coroner and the doctor examined the charred remains of the victim, and within a few minutes they were able to determine, from the fractures in the skull, that Mr. McNabb had sustained two massive blows to the head. Either one of the blows was enough to kill him, the coroner reported.

The officers, with the aid of a few of the neighbors, discovered that McNabb's 22-caliber rifle, a pistol and a wrist watch were missing. They also observed that McNabb was preparing to go to Roseburg because his horse was still hitched to the buggy and there was a sack of feed and a bundle of hay in the buggy for the trip. He had a doctor's appointment in Roseburg that day where he was being treated for an ear infection in his deaf ear. Darkness had fallen upon the investigations now, and the search for more clues continued under two lighted lanterns. They thoroughly combed the site for clues. At the end of the search, they observed that all of McNabb's valuables were missing. Murder! Robbery! Were the angry cries that were raised by his friend Multi and echoed by the other neighbors. Coroner Jewett, in consultation with Dr. Smick and the officers, called for an inquest to be held on the following Monday, June 19, 1911, at 10:00 a.m. at the Brockway School.

McNabb's brothers and their wives visited the scene on Saturday searching for clues and information that would lead them to the cause of their brother's death. They questioned many of the neighbors in the area as to their brother's state of mind prior to his death. Alec was last seen on Monday of that week at the Brockway Store en route to his ranch coming from Roseburg. He was seen displaying a handful of silver to his fellow ranchers and drinking two bottles of beer. He departed for his ranch early that afternoon. He also mentioned in conversation that he had a doctor's appointment in Roseburg on Wednesday of that week. A few of the neighbors informed his brothers that they had seen three strangers on his ranch the day before his death. They were not sure about the identity of these strangers. One neighbor thought they looked like Greeks. Ever since the "Greek Riot" in Glenbrook in 1905, where fifty Greek men were arrested, stereotyping of Greeks was quite common in Douglas County. Others thought the strangers were Indians. Peter and George were determined to find out the true identity of the strangers.

The tiny Brockway School, scene of the inquest, sheltered beneath a grove of huge oak trees, sat on a knoll overlooking Lookingglass Creek. Its location was off Brockway Road, just northwest of present-day Douglas High School. The meeting room was packed with people. Some came from as far away as Camas Valley. Pandemonium and anxiety were in the air, mixed with the ambient heat of the morning. It was hot, and people were using any kind of flat objects they could find to fan themselves.

A jury of twenty members of the community was selected. District Attorney George Brown and Coroner N. T. Jewett conducted the inquest. They explained to the jury that from the evidence gathered from the scene they concluded Mr. McNabb was brutally murdered with a motive of robbery. His body had been placed on the bed and his cabin set on fire to destroy the evidence. After deliberating for a few minutes, the jury's verdict read:

"He, Alexander McNabb, died by means of violence in his cabin on his homestead on Wednesday morning, June 14, 1911. We believe that he was unlawfully and feloniously killed by some person or persons whose names are to the coroner's jury unknown."

The verdict was signed by S. L. Dillard, W. D. Bell, W. M. Buxton, R. Donaldson, Chas. A. Lotz and I. C. Kent. The verdict cast an aura of fear mixed with curiosity and anger in the room, satisfied yet vengeful. As the crowd left the room, with their heads hung in disbelief, they were plagued with the thought of who committed that brutal crime. Peter, who lived in Portland, was determined to remain in the county to hunt for those criminals and bring them to justice.

Photo: Courtesy of Douglas County Museum

Sheriff George Quinn took the first train out of Yoncalla to Roseburg the moment he heard the news of the jury's verdict. He was determined to catch the murderer or murderers of McNabb. He had to restore his reputation as an outstanding sheriff, one who was capable of solving just about any crime. But, with the public's knowledge that two sets of train bandits were still at large, the loss of the county's penitentiary bloodhound that had been in his care, and this new murder of a respectable homesteader, he feared his career might be dragged through the political quagmire in the county.

Quinn headed directly to the district attorney's office to pick up the warrant which gave him the right to search for and arrest the criminals. He then went to the scene to look for any new clues left behind by the alleged strangers. At the corner of the fence, not far from the burned cabin, he and his officers found a wagon canvas, upon which was found a tobacco sack and loose tobacco. When the neighbors were questioned, they claimed that the deceased never owned such a wagon canvas, and they believed the same must have been brought there by the person or persons responsible for the crime. Sheriff Quinn and his officers retraced the footsteps of these suspected strangers from Grant Clayton's residence near Dillard, where they were seen on the Tuesday before the murder, over the hill to the deceased's fence where the wagon canvas and the tobacco sack were found. Sheriff Quinn was able to visualize exactly how two of the alleged strangers overpowered the victim, murdered him, robbed the premises and then set the cabin on fire, while the third person kept watch at the corner of the fence. Unfortunately, there were no known eyewitnesses to the murder or the fire.

Sheriff Quinn continued to track the suspects' movements and got word that they had headed to Coos County. They were seen at a saloon in Coquille where they tried to pawn a wristwatch, and they later secured jobs at a logging camp near Bandon. Sheriff Quinn telephoned Sheriff Gage of Coos County and informed him of the crime and movements of the three suspects. Peter, the brother of the deceased, was already in Marshfield in an effort to assist the sheriff and his officers in identifying the suspected strangers. One of the suspects received a telegram from his sister in San Jose, California, informing him that their mother was very ill in the hospital, and he was asked to come home. He was lucky to find a ship leaving for San Francisco the very next day. The other two quit their jobs and headed north to Portland by boat. Two days later Sheriff Gage, two of his officers, and Peter arrived at the very camp in Bandon, only to be told the men no longer worked there. While in Portland, a misunderstanding that led to a scuffle had developed between two of the suspects as to who should carry what was assumed to be McNabb's pistol. They broke friendship, and one of them headed south to California, while the other remained in Portland.

Officer Wade of the Portland Police Department was on a routine patrol in the areas of Third and Couch Streets around noon about two weeks after the murder of McNabb. That area was known to be rough and dangerous and needed routine police surveillance quite often during the day. The Portland Police Department had not yet been informed of McNabb's murder in Douglas County, and so Officer Wade was not aware of such a crime being committed. He came upon a Mexican by the name of Julius Alverazo, about 30 years of age. Alverazo was drunk and troubled, and was obviously disturbing the peace with his loud and abusive language to a companion. Officer Wade was forced to arrest him for being under the influence of alcohol and disturbing the peace. He put him in hand-cuffs and placed him in custody. His companion told Officer Wade that Alverazo had killed a rancher near Roseburg about two weeks before. Alverazo was so drunk he was unaware of what his companion had told the police. Officer Wade took Alverazo to jail and left his companion without even asking him his name. No sooner had the officer left with the prisoner for jail, than Alverazo's companion disappeared and later took a train to Seattle, Washington. Officer Wade was not aware of Alverazo's arrest record, but at the jail, the booking officer was. He knew Alverazo was homeless and wanted a hot meal and a bed to sleep on. As soon as Alverazo became sober and calm, the department released him from jail.

Sheriff Quinn was furious when he heard that Julius Alverazo was released from jail. He thought the Portland Police Department had been incredibly lax and incompetent for releasing the prisoner without first notifying the Douglas County Sheriff Department after such a reported confession about Alverazo from the companion. He called the department and asked to speak to the chief. At the end of their conversation, Sheriff Quinn was very apologetic for his behavior. He assumed the Portland Police Department knew about the case, since it was so well publicized through the press in Roseburg, Myrtle Creek, and Yoncalla. He informed the chief that Alverazo and his companion were suspects in the murder of Alexander McNabb a few weeks before near Brockway. He then begged for the Department's assistance in tracking down and arresting the suspects if they were still in the city. Curiously, Peter McNabb checked out the identification, arrest and release history of Julius Alverazo and assumed him to be innocent and not one of the three suspects being sought. Peter did get assurance from the Portland Police Department that they would extend their search within the city for Alverazo's companion.

One year later, June 14, 1912, the Sheriff's Department had no clue as to the whereabouts of the three murder suspects. The department was very busy with the campaigns of the presidential and county elections. The bandits who had held up and robbed the Shasta Limited Train around Yoncalla were caught. However, the neighbors in the Brockway and Olalla communities were still on the lookout for strangers who looked like Greeks, Indians or Mexicans. Multi got married to a lady from Sutherlin, sold his fifty acre ranch, and moved into the community of Roseburg.

Alexander McNabb had been a generous contributor to the lodge of the Odd Fellows. At one of their monthly meetings the Lodge Grand Noble asked the members to all stand and bow their heads in silence. He asked that they reflect on the kind and gentle character of their departed brother Alexander McNabb. He also asked them to reflect on the principles that embodied the mission of the Odd Fellows. Even though the room was filled with members, it was a silence broken only by pigeons playing and mating on the rooftop. But that silence was soon shattered by the sound of Multi's anger when he yelled, "who and where are the bastards who killed our brother Alexander McNabb?"

I.O.O.F:
Independent Order of Odd Fellows is an altruistic fraternal organization founded in Roseburg in 1859. Rebekah is the female counterpart organization.

Peter McNabb's wife was Mattie Winston McNabb, one of William Chauncey Winston's six daughters. The town of Winston, Oregon was named in honor of that family who pioneered to the area in the 1870s.

Sheriff George K. Quinn served two terms as sheriff for the County from 1911 to 1919. From 1923 to 1935 he served as County Commissioner for Douglas County.

The Brockway Store, built in 1890, closed its doors for business in 1987.

The Brockway School was built in 1855 and was incorporated with Dillard in 1948. The old school building was burnt in 2001.

References:
The Roseburg Review, Roseburg Evening News, Genealogical Society of Douglas County, Douglas County Records, Photo: of Sheriff George Quinn - courtesy of Douglas County Museum and illustrations by Charles Nemitz

TRAIN WRECK IN DILLARD 1907

There was an unusual serenity about the weather in the Dillard Valley on the evening of September 12, 1907. A steady wind was blowing from the southwest disseminating the fragrances from the blooming roses. The sky was clear except for a thin blanket of clouds drifting across the mid sky. Calvin W. Davis, a longtime foreman for Southern Pacific Railroad, was responsible for a crew of 15 Japanese workers. He had started work for the railroad in 1872 when it was called Oregon and California Railroad. He lived with his wife and three children in a cabin on Kent Creek Road, while his crew lived in three freight cars on the siding about two miles south of Dillard's train depot. Two of the cars were used for sleeping while a third was used for cooking and dining. The crew had completed a paving project in Green and returned to their quarters earlier than usual. Foreman Davis was on his way home and had just crossed the footbridge over the South Umpqua River when he heard a loud bang around him, with sounds ricocheting off Mt. O'Bette. That big bang was the sound of a collision of an oncoming freight train with the emigrant cars housing the 15 Japanese workers. Foreman Davis looked at his pocket watch. It was exactly 6:45 PM. The sound cut through the stillness in the valley and was heard by people living as far away as Rice Creek. The wreck was recorded as the most disastrous train accident to occur in Douglas County for the decade.

A mushroom of black smoke mixed with steam now filled the area over the siding where the accident occurred. That escaping steam from the locomotive could be heard all through the evening and into the night. Pandemonium replaced the serenity. People and horse and buggy traffic raced to the scene of the accident. Railroad officials quickly informed its dispatch office in Roseburg of the severity of the accident and requested immediate medical assistance. Within an hour the dispatch office in Roseburg had Dr. Shearer, Dr. Seely and two nurses on a train to Dillard.

By the time foreman Davis got to the scene, several of the freight cars were engulfed in flames, including the locomotive, but the Japanese cars were the inferno. He closed his eyes and made the sign of the cross on his forehead. The fire started after the impact reduced the dining car and a sleeper to splinters. The kerosene lamp and cooking stove quickly ignited the kindling. Five men were already in the dining car eating and were trapped by the blaze. The ambient temperature was unbearable, and as a result the rescuers were having a difficult time untangling and retrieving the trapped men in the fire. However, even with their little or no experience in firefighting, they were able to rescue 12 of the 15 emigrants while three were completely incinerated. Two of the rescued men died soon after, one immediately, while the other died at the hospital in Roseburg from internal injuries. With the spread of the fire to a fourth car, railroad authorities became quite nervous, since the sixth car was filled with black powder. The fire getting to that car would cause an explosion making the catastrophe even worse. They concentrated all their meager resources on preventing the fire from reaching that car. There was debris all over the track from broken freight cars, which impeded their movement. Part of the debris consisted of several broken sacks of brown sugar.

When the doctors and their staff arrived, they were quickly put to work treating the rescued workers and some of the rescuers. They worked until 11:00 PM that night trying to make the victims comfortable. They were commended and praised for their professional skills used to alleviate the suffering of those caught in that unfortunate accident.

Foreman Davis was sad, but, at the same time, furious. He wanted to know how and why the collision occurred. He was told that a southbound freight train #221 had orders to take the siding in order to permit passage of a northbound freight train. The southbound train was quite long and therefore shoved the emigrant cars forward through the switch and onto the main track. Shortly afterward, the northbound freight train came along at a reasonable speed, conducted by Roy Dixon, Engineer Patrick Sharp and Fireman David Vinson, expecting clearance for its passage through, and crashed into the emigrant cars. Conductor Dixon explained that at the speed he was traveling he had enough time to stop the train, but the air brakes failed, and, as a result, he crashed into the emigrant cars. All three men were slightly injured when they jumped from the cab of the locomotive before impact with the emigrant cars. The railroad officials accepted Engineer Sharp's explanations, but the County Sheriff called for an investigation to determine the reasons for the alleged defect in the braking system.

The railroad workers and helpers were so focused on protecting the car with the black powder from igniting, they did not see when the fire jumped the track and caught the adjacent field on fire. The families living in the area were quickly evacuated and taken to George B. Laurence's farm. With the South Umpqua River not very far from the railroad, a bucket brigade started and the fire was kept from spreading. However, a large section of a hay field was burned.

Coroner Carl Mammitte called for an inquest at his office in Roseburg Saturday, September 14, 1907 at 9:00 AM. A jury was selected and 10 witnesses to the accident were examined. Engineer Sharp was the first to take the stand. He explained that he saw the danger in plenty of time but was powerless to avert the collision since the air brake failed to work. His statement was collaborated by the fireman who stayed with the locomotive just before impact. A number of other witnesses were examined including the conductor, two brake men, the section supervisor and Foreman Calvin Davis. All the testimony heard demonstrated that the collision was purely accidental. The five men jurors deliberated for a while and returned with a verdict exonerating the railroad company from all blame, calling the wreck an unavoidable accident.

The 10 rescued Japanese remained working for the railroad company, but were transferred to another community, while the two dead bodies were taken to Portland for burial. Calvin Davis remained depressed and never recovered from the trauma of the accident.

Reference: *The News-Review* 1907 and 1908.

HOUSEWIVES FOR HIGHWAY 42

Photo: Courtesy of The News Review

When 72 women from Coos and Douglas Counties called upon Governor Robert Holmes at his office in Salem in November of 1957, without an invitation, demanding improvements and re-pairs to Highway 42 between Winston and Coquille, it was not the first time that women in Oregon exhibited such tenacity and togetherness. In September of 1859, seven months after Oregon received its statehood, women demanded their equal rights with men forcing the legislature to pass the "Married Women's Separate Property Act." Back to the 1957 delegation, Governor Holmes was overwhelmed and impressed and told the women that they were the "largest delegation ever to storm the state capitol." The women were housewives from Coquille, Myrtle Point, Remote, Camas Valley, Tenmile, Olalla, Brockway, Winston, Dillard and intermediate points along the way. They came with a litany of complaints and requests.

Speaking on behalf of the group of housewives, Mrs. Jean Nichols of Brockway told the Governor that Highway 42 was the most crooked and dangerous stretch of roadway in Oregon with a very high volume of traffic using it, especially logging trucks. She said that mothers living in the area were concerned for the safety of their children in the six school districts on that route riding the buses to and from school each day. During the winter months when the weather was bad, she said that driving conditions were frightening with the raging Coquille River jumping its

Mrs. Jean Nichols Family picture

banks at low areas and possible landslides from the loose embankments. She spelled out a list of requests for improvement that would make driving conditions easier in the near and distant future. Mrs. Nichols said the group would like the roadway straightened and widened wherever possible and a systematic program each year of road base repairs and removal of tree encroachments.

The Governor was very receptive. He thanked and assured the group of his support for their cause. Before leaving Salem, the group stopped in to visit with the State Highway Engineer W. C. (Dutch) Williams to give him the same list of their demands. Mr. Williams thanked and encouraged the women to show more organized support for the highway project. With a small measure of encouragement in their purses, the women set their focus on confronting the State Highway Commission and lobbying the area's state representatives. They began a campaign to recruit as many housewives as possible between Coos Bay and Roseburg who were sympathetic to their cause.

After visiting with Governor Holmes, 19 housewives, representing the communities of Myrtle Point, Camas Valley, Brockway, Winston and Roseburg, marched into Judge V. T. Jackson's office seeking support from the Douglas County Court for their cause. Speaking on behalf of the group, Mrs. Imogene Powrie of Myrtle Point, Central Committee Chairperson, relayed the group's concerns regarding the crooked stretch of roadway between Winston and Coquille and asked the court for its wholehearted support. She told the Court that 250 housewives had signed up to attend the December session of the State Highway Commission in Portland. Douglas County Court informed the women of its commitment to the construction of Highway 225 (Sutherlin to Elkton) and the North Umpqua Highway, but agreed to support the women's cause and would send a letter to the State Highway Commission in Portland endorsing their cause and agenda.

The two-day session of the State Highway Commission's monthly meeting was held on December 6 and 7, 1957, in Portland. The Commission was besieged with delegates from all over the state. While most of the delegations came with their portfolios filled with complaints and requests, the Tillamook delegation representing Oregon Coast Association arrived with a horse and carriage. They told the Commission that the Tillamook County roadway section "hasn't been improved since the horse and buggy days." But the most impressive delegation was Housewives for Highway 42. Several chartered buses carrying 150 women descended on the meeting. They were carrying placards, wearing appropriate nametags and shouting slogans in favor of improvements to Highway 42. One of the signs read: "The longest distance from us to you is highway 42." Mrs. Imogene Powrie addressed the Commission on behalf of the 150 housewives. She elaborated on the history of the building of the highway and said that there were sections with as many as 160 curves per mile. She said school buses carrying as many as 2,000 kids each day encountered as many as 40 loaded log trucks. In closing, she told the Commission that the group was prepared to carry the fight to the legislature. The Commission was impressed, but politely turned them down contending that they did not have the money to spend on improvements to Highway 42. The women were disappointed and told the Commission that they would be back.

The group's growing popularity created controversies between itself and supporters for Highway 225 and the North Umpqua Highway in Douglas County. The controversy sparked a hearing conducted by the Legislature Highway Interim Committee at the Douglas County Courthouse in March 1958. The first group to take the stand was Housewives for Highway 42 led by Mrs. Stanford Buell of Dillard representing 25 housewives attending the hearings. She told the Committee her group would like to see immediate action in the straightening, widening, and general repairs to Highway 42. She pointed out that the highway was built in 1922, 26 years ago, with little or no change. She cited several accidents, many of them fatal, including Mrs. Veralee Lou Cunningham of Winston who lost her life on Camas Mountain in a head-on collision last December 1957. She went on to show how vital the highway was to the area with its extensive logging activities, transporting of farm produce, recreational access to the coast and most of all the extensive bus traffic transporting kids to and from school. Another group, calling itself Southern Douglas Highway Association, led by Al Flegel, endorsed immediate improvements of Highway 42 stating that the highway was vital to our national defense since it was the first crossroad north of the California border. Supporters of Highway 225 and the North Umpqua Highway told the Committee they wanted the assurance from the court that it was still committed to the completion of both highways.

Friday, May 9, 1958, was a day of joy and compensation for persistence when the State Highway Commission told the Housewives for Highway 42 that $600,000 was allotted for fixing the first section of the crooked highway. The housewives attending the meeting began a celebration of crying, hugging, kissing and clapping that sparked the Commission to call a recess of the meeting. At the resumption of the meeting, the Commission told the housewives that improving the entire highway of 70 miles between Roseburg and Coos Bay would cost about 14 million dollars and at this time they could only afford to improve about two and a half miles between Coquille and Powers junction. State Highway Engineer W. C. Williams wanted the housewives to know that the $600,000 represented nearly all the federal emergency money allotted to the State's Division 3.

The campaign for reconstructing Highway 42 picked up steam when the Coos Bay Port Commission, a very influential governmental body, which had endorsed the construction of Highway 38, then close to completion, unanimously endorsed the cause. It called upon the residents of Coos County to give the cause their full support so that a first class highway could be built as soon as possible. The campaign soon attracted agencies like the Coos County Highway Council, the Coos County Chamber of Commerce and the Coos County Civil Defense Agency. Businesses from as far as Josephine and Jackson Counties voiced their support for the cause, since the completion of a modern highway would make it easier to transport their goods to the Coos Bay port.

In September of 1958 W. C. Williams, chief of Oregon Highway Department called a meeting at the Camas Valley Grange Hall regarding the status of funds or lack thereof, for reconstructing Highway 42. It was estimated that about 100 people representing

Photo: Senator Dimick
Courtesy of Douglas County Museum

Douglas and Coos Counties attended the meeting. Among those who attended were groups like Housewives for Highway 42 identifying themselves with name tags, Coos County Chamber of Commerce, Roseburg Chamber of Commerce, Southern Douglas Highway Association, Coos County Highway Council and some of the log truck drivers. Mr. Williams told the gathering that his department recognized the need for improvements to Highway 42 between Winston and Coquille, but it would be at least two years before any work could be done on the highway. He said that the department did not have the funds then to adequately address the problems. He told the gathering that he had estimated that the project would cost the department about $10 million for the necessary improvements which would include re-routing sections of the highway to bypass critical slide areas. He went on to explain the department's benchmark that was used to rate potential projects in order of priority. He explained that 50% of a project's rating was based on need, 25% on a population basis and 25% on the basis of area. Mr. Williams also took the opportunity to address a proposal for a Winnemucca-to-the-sea route sponsored by a few Coos County groups. He said that the amount of study and planning required for such a highway certainly ruled out any consideration of a Nevada-to-Coos Bay Highway in the near future.

The outcome of the meeting was a tremendous disappointment to those who wanted immediate action on improvements to Highway 42. Housewives for Highway 42 decided to take their fight to the legislature. That idea was quickly supported by several groups in Douglas and Coos Counties. With the help of Senator Dimick of Douglas County, Senator Chapman of Coos County and a boost from Governor Mark Hatfield, supporters of Highway 42 got the issue on the agenda of the 1959 Oregon Legislature. In April 1959, the Legislature supported the measure and authorized a $4 million bond issue, but tied it to matching federal funds. The State Highway Commission accepted the mandate from the Legislature, but with reservation, and budgeted $1 million a year for reconstructing the highway. Unfortunately, the bonds were not sold, since the federal matching funds of $6 million were not available. However, the Commission did begin reconstructing two sections on the highway between Myrtle Point and Powers Junction.

Two years later, in April of 1961, the Legislature approved a similar bill permitting the bonds of $4 million to be issued without any matching federal funds. The bill was quickly sealed into law with Governor Mark Hatfield's signature. That action by the Legislature and the governor sent joy and satisfaction among the supporters for improvements to Highway 42. Housewives for Highway 42 were especially satisfied that their four years of hard work of seeking to get funds allocated to reconstruct the dangerous highway paid off. But, opponents to the bill called the move "pork belly" politics and argued that the legislature had no right to go above the heads of the State Highway Commission to issue such bonds. The three commissioners were furious with the legislature's decision and accused them of injecting politics into the highway business. They argued that the issue of bonds to build highways was too costly due to the interest on the bonds and as a result deprived the rest of the state of highways and road repairs.

Between 1958 and 1963 the State Highway Department scheduled four reconstruction projects on Highway 42. Three of those projects were in Coos County, between Coquille and Powers Junction, and one in Douglas County between Remote and Camas Valley. Again, from May of 1974 to July 1976, the communities of Green and Winston welcomed with open arms the improvements to Highway 42 between I-5 and Winston. The project included the widening of the highway from two to four lanes from the intersection at I-5 Freeway to Winston at the junction of Highway 99 and Highway 42. Included in the project was the construction of an overpass over the Southern-Pacific Railroad track southwest of I-5 and an additional bridge across the South Umpqua River down stream from the Winston Bridge. The scope of the project went south beyond the junction of Highway 42 and Highway 99 to the Dillard Bridge. The entire project cost about $7.4 million. As an added bonus, the business section of Winston was given a new face-lift with the construction of traffic lights at the intersection of Highway 42 and Highway 99.

In November of 1974, the State Highway Commission launched its six-year construction plans for the Douglas County area. The plans showed seven construction projects for the I-5 Highway and only one for Highway 42. Members of the Economic Improvement Association Board, EIA, of Coos, Curry and Douglas

Counties, were disappointed with the State Highway Commission's plans. At their first meeting in January of 1975, the Board drafted a letter expressing their disappointment with the division's six-year plans for Douglas County. The letter conveyed concerns with the State Highway Commission's "failure to plan sufficient effort to improve significantly Highway 42, the primary link between Roseburg and Coos Bay areas." The letter explained the highway's importance to the economic growth of those areas and recommended that the highway division "evaluate the adverse impacts that continue to accrue due to the continued substandard status of Highway 42." The letter concluded by calling on the State Highway Commission to significantly increase construction efforts to improve Highway 42. Four months later they followed up their letter with a lengthy report explaining the economic need to improve Highway 42 and why the commission should revise its six-year plan for Douglas County. The report specifically pointed to a section of the highway between Remote and Camas Mountain which offered the most resistance to commercial traffic flow and thereby impacted the region's economy. The report claimed that Douglas County was "a net loser of highway funds totaling $19,461,083 during the period 1963-1972." Adding that, "those dollars were monies collected by the state for vehicle license fees and other highway user-related payments. Those funds, generated in part, on the sections of Oregon 42 in Douglas County, apparently were not returned to the county for improvement of the deficient sections of the highway." The report continued by inferring that "the highway division failed to equate the importance of Oregon 42 to the region's economy, the economic trends influencing the rapid rise in commercial traffic over Oregon 42 and the responsibility to accommodate those trends by returning revenues operated in the system." The Association enclosed several letters from businesses and agencies in the region endorsing improvement to Highway 42. From Douglas County came letters from Allyn Ford, Vice Chairman of Roseburg Lumber Co. Dillard, the mayor of Roseburg, Mike Wyatt, Al Hooten, president of the Winston-Dillard Area Chamber of Commerce and the Greyhound Bus Co.

The *Coos Bay World* daily newspaper began publishing articles exposing the dangers of Highway 42, criticizing the highway commission for doing "damn little" and called on the State Legislature to take action to improve the driving conditions on the highway. For a third time the State Legislature stepped in to support improvements to Highway 42. In April of 1975, the House approved a Resolution by a unanimous vote calling upon the governor and the Oregon Department of Transportation to redirect future highway construction priorities. The Resolution 64 specifically directed the Governor and the Transportation Department, in cooperation with the Economic Development Association, EIA, "to oversee Highway Division development of new priorities as part of the state's 1977 Master Highway Construction Plan."

The highway did not take ten years to be completed as estimated by W. C. (Dutch) Williams who passed away in November of 1961, but about 45 years. Today, Highway 42 is a safe and scenic route between Winston and Coos Bay. The last sections of the highway to be improved were in Winston between Lookingglass Creek Bridge and Highway 99 and the straightening of the locally named "Schattenkerk Curve" about three miles west of Winston. The group, Housewives for Highway 42, no longer exists, but its legacy continues, a legacy that underlines the concept of "never underestimate the power of a woman." In 1980, that power was seen in Candice Lightner of Sacramento, California, after a drunk driver killed her 13-year-old daughter as she was walking along the sidewalk in her neighborhood. Candice formed the organization MADD, Mothers Against Drunk Driving. This organization has taken root in all 50 states of the United States.

References:
The News-Review 1957- 2002. Photos: *The News Review*, Nichols's Family, and Douglas County Museum.

THE TRAGEDY OF THE RUNAWAY STAGE COACH IN 1907

Within a span of six weeks, two fatal accidents rocked Douglas County, Oregon. On September 12, 1907, five Japanese were killed in a train wreck in Dillard. The next month, October 7, 1907, a salesman and four horses were killed when a coach on the Roseburg-Myrtle Point Stage Line fell over an embankment six miles west of Camas Valley.

Charles Archambeau, better known as Charlie, was a driver for Fenton Stage Coach between Roseburg and Marshfield for ten years and had worked on the Roseburg-Myrtle Point route for the last three years. He knew every inch of that road and the behavior of the horses. Unfortunately, his ten-year-old daughter was very sick, and he had to take her to the doctor. He got hold of his friend, Thomas Gurney, who was on two weeks' vacation, to make the run for him. Mr. Gurney had worked for the Fenton Stage Line for about three years on the Myrtle-Point to Marshfield route. Charlie chose Thomas because of his charming personality and because he did not drink alcohol. He was always neatly dressed for his job and conversed well with the passengers when necessary. He was of medium height and very strong. Charlie explained all the logistics for that route and the care he should take on steep slopes. He especially cautioned him about using the whip on Old Betsy, the leader of the four-horse stage team. He explained that she was highly sensitive and could get out of control if she was hit.

It was a beautiful morning Friday, October 25, 1907, even though the ground was wetter than most drivers would want it to be, since it had rained the night before. Thomas Gurney had the horses and coach ready to leave the Roseburg Station at 9:00 a.m. He examined the passenger list which was made up of: J. F. Quirk of San Francisco, C.W. Page, a lumberman from Drain, Oregon, Thos. N. Morehouse, a travelling salesman from Sacramento, and I.P. Baldwin from Reno, Nevada. In addition to the four passengers he loaded ten bags of mail onto the coach. He greeted the passengers with a gentle smile and a "good day" gesture and slowly pulled out of the station. As he expected, the entire four-horse team was laboring under the soggy road conditions. He also heard an unusual sound coming from the left rear wheel. When he got to Brockway, he drove the coach to Sam Bolsinger's

Blacksmith Shop. The three-seat deluxe stage coach had been built by Mr. Bolsinger. Within 30 minutes Sam refitted the wheel with a new set of bearings, and Thomas and his passengers were off. The coach was rolling smoothly, the sun was hot and bright and the road conditions were far better. At Camas Valley he stopped to feed and water the horses.

Thomas examined the condition of the horses and the coach before he announced the continuation of the next leg of the trip. As he travelled west through the valley, the sun was just perfect, illuminating the entire landscape, but not too hot. The oncoming traffic waved their whips and said "hello" as they passed by. His passengers appeared to be comfortable when he heard the strumming of a guitar coming from within the coach. As the coach came upon "Rocky Hill," the most dangerous section of the route, Old Betsy slowed down her pace and caused the other horses to do the same. Thomas cracked his whip and hit Old Betsy across the back. Without warning, she became fractious, which frightened the rest of the horses. She and her partner bolted at top speed down the slope dislodging the coupling between themselves and the wheel horses. The sudden jolt pulled Thomas off the coach, and he landed at the base of a madrone tree. In spite of that terrible fall, he sustained only a few scratches and a sprained wrist. Old Betsy and her partner went off the main road and tumbled over the embankment into the Coquille River below. Both horses died instantly on impact. The wheel-horses were also galloping at full speed causing the coach to overturn on its side. The overturned coach dislodged all the passengers except Thos. Morehouse who was dragged to the bottom of the embankment along with the two wheel-horses. Unfortunately, one of the horses landed on top of Mr. Morehouse's chest. He was heard calling for help, saying "a horse is on top of me."

Thomas and the more fortunate passengers, Quick, Page and Baldwin, immediately scrambled over boulders and tree stumps to get to Mr. Morehouse on the river floor. The horse that was on top of him was not dead but had sustained a broken back. Both Mr. Morehouse and the horse were in excruciating pain. Thomas quickly used his shotgun to shoot the horse in the head. Then the four men dragged the carcass off of Mr. Morehouse. As soon as Mr. Morehouse was freed, Page, the lumberman from Drain, attempted to administer CPR. He tried valiantly to save his life, but was too late. He gently closed Mr. Morehouse's eyelids. He then got up, removed his hat from his head and whispered a prayer in silence. It was not the first time C.W. Page had witnessed such a traumatic death. He looked at his pocket watch and it registered exactly 7:00 PM. He took one of the blankets from the coach and covered up the body. The other wheel-horse companion was found dead not far from the coach. Thomas decided to go to Sheep Ranch Stage Station for help which was only two miles away. With the driver off to seek help, Page and his companion passengers slowly scaled the hill to the main road above.

Thomas returned with a two-horse coach and took his passengers back to Camas Valley so they could get medical attention. He called Fenton, his boss and proprietor of the stage line, and appraised him of the accident and the death of Mr. Morehouse. Mr. Fenton immediately called Coroner Hammitte and notified him of the accident and the death of a passenger. From Fenton's description of the accident, the coroner made the decision not to go to the scene since an inquest was not necessary. After Dr. Vincil was notified, both he and Fenton left Roseburg for Camas Valley at 2:00 AM and arrived at the Stage Coach Station within a few hours. Soon after, Sheriff C.T. McClallen arrived. He took a statement from Thomas, the coach driver, as to the cause of the accident and also individually questioned the passengers. Dr. Vincil physically checked them out and found that they were more traumatized than injured. They were then transported to Sheep Ranch Station where they were put on the stagecoach returning to Marshfield so that they could get to their respective destinations.

Both Dr. Vincil and the sheriff examined Mr. Morehouse's body. The doctor observed that his chest plate was depressed but not broken and that he had a few bruises on the forehead. He then concluded that suffocation was the cause of death. In the sheriff's report he said that the three passengers he had questioned exonerated the driver of the coach and placed the cause of the accident on the horses becoming uncontrollable.

Information found in Mr. Morehouse's wallet and luggage revealed that he was 32 years of age and married with one child. He was a member of the Order of Knights of Pythias Lodge No. 50 of Ottawana, Minnesota. He carried two life insurance policies:

one for $5,000.00 with the Lodge and the other with Mutual Life Company, the amount unknown. As soon as the local lodge learned of Mr. Morehouse's membership in the Order of Knights of Pythias, they sent two of their members to the site to take possession of the body and bring it to Roseburg. The lodge wrapped the body in their ritual cloth and took it to Hammitte Undertaker to be shipped to his wife. On the coffin the lodge placed an inscription which read: "If fraternal love held all men bound, how beautiful this world would be."

References:
The Roseburg Review 1907, *Roseburg Umpqua Valley News*, *The Umpqua Trapper* 1971.

PLANE CRASH IN DILLARD 1953

Sunday, March 8, 1953, was an exceptionally gorgeous day. The scar of winter had peeled away. Evidence of leaves on many deciduous trees gave signs that spring was just a few weeks away. By midday temperatures had reached 60°F in the Dillard Valley. Richard Blair slowly rose from slumber. He had been to a dance at Lindy's the night before with his friends Forest Collins, Robert Kline and Delbert Commins. Delbert was on a week's leave from the US Navy Base in San Francisco. By that time on Sundays, Richard would have been attending services at the Roseburg First Presbyterian Church had his wife, Susan, been at home. But she was away visiting her sister in Portland for that weekend. He had just come out of the shower when the door bell rang.

It was his friend Collins who lived a block away on Fifth Street. He was president of the Winston-Dillard Rural Fire District and was highly respected in the community. Collins, too, was still half asleep, wearing shorts and a T-shirt. He was 34 years of age, 5' 10" tall and weighed 190 pounds. He had never been to the gym, but his upper body had the look of a body-builder from years of lifting chain saws, axes and logs in the woods. He was a self-employed logger and had a contract falling trees for D.R. Johnson Lumber Co. On the other hand, Richard was 22, tall and handsome with a slim body, and he worked as a lumber salesman for A & J

Lumber Co. in Roseburg. Even though they were 12 years apart, they had a unique friendship. They behaved as though they were brothers. They were both U.S. War Veterans. Richard was a pilot in the U.S. Navy in the Korean War, and Collins was an airplane mechanic in the U.S. Air Force in World War II. Richard owned a four passenger 1950 Cessna 170 airplane he had bought from the widow of a Roseburg pilot who had died in 1952. She sold the plane because she did not want to continue paying the storage fee on the aircraft. The aircraft had needed minor repairs, and Richard, with the help of Collins, was able to get it in top working condition. Collins was amazed at how well maintained the interior of the aircraft looked.

There was a look of urgency on Collins's unshaven face. He told Richard that Delbert had missed the Greyhound Bus to San Francisco and there was not another one until 9:00 AM the following day. By that time Delbert would be AWOL. Delbert had told Collins that he would be willing to pay Richard to fly him to San Francisco or any city close to San Francisco. Richard had never landed an aircraft in San Francisco, but had flown his Cessna 170 into Oakland Airport on two occasions. He agreed to take him as far as Oakland and invited Collins and Robert to come along for the ride. Robert, who also lived in Dillard, had driven up with Delbert to Richard's house in time to learn about the good news. They all agreed to go to the Dillard Steak House for lunch before leaving on the trip.

When Richard and his companions arrived at Roseburg airport, there was very little activity going on at the compound. Richard was very meticulous when it came to getting his airplane ready for flying. He began by inspecting the cockpit thoroughly. He made sure that the combined weight of his three companions plus his own was below the 700 pounds maximum weight limit his aircraft could carry when filled with fuel. He made sure that the airworthiness certificate, registration and operation limitation papers were all together in the cockpit glove compartment. Both he and Collins checked the engine, fuel and the exterior of the aircraft. Even though the weather in Roseburg was good and appeared stable, Richard called the Flight Service Station—FSS—in Oakland for a weather report between Roseburg and Oakland. When he was sure his companions were buckled up and comfortable, he started the engine, turned on the radios, and the VOR tracking device, and began taxiing to the 4600 ft. grass runway.

At the airport the wind was light and blowing the windsock in a northwest direction. Richard double-checked the gas and oil pressure, set the flaps and made sure the area was clear while revving the engine at the end of the runway. He began accelerating the aircraft, keeping the nose in line with the center-line of the runway, and with about 2500 ft. of acceleration his Cessna 170 was airborne. At an altitude of 3000 feet, he set the aircraft on a specific course to Oakland. As they were flying over Dillard, both Collins and Robert were able to identify their respective homes. To the southwest of Dillard, at the beginning of the Rice Creek Canyon, Richard identified his friend Bert Smith's house and decided to buzz it. As soon as he entered the canyon, Richard experienced a difference in the wind currents. Nevertheless, he continued with the dive but was unable to climb out of it fast enough to clear the hill behind Smith's house. Before Richard could react, the nose of the aircraft had clipped the trees on the hill near Barrett Creek.

Frank Smith and his family, who lived along Rice Creek Rd., were in their backyard enjoying the beautiful sunshine when they heard and saw a plane struggling to regain altitude. Not long after, they heard a crash and an explosion. The aircraft had burst into flames. The Smith's family quickly ran to the scene to try to rescue the pilot. They could not get close to the plane since a large area around the wreckage was engulfed in flames. The smell of gas permeated the air in the immediate area. The fire was too large and hot to attempt a rescue. George Wood, who also saw and heard the crash, quickly called the sheriff in Roseburg and the Winston-Dillard Rural Fire Department. Within 30 minutes of receiving the call, Sheriff Dalles Bennett and two officers met George Wood on Rice Creek Rd. who then took them to the scene of the wreck. Before leaving Roseburg the Sheriff also informed the County Coroner of the accident and its approximate location.

The Fire Department quickly had the fire extinguished and the wreckage cooled down. The four bodies found were severely charred. Collins wife Frances was already at the scene because she knew her husband had gone along with Richard. Coroner L.L.

Powers examined the charred remains in order to determine the identity of each body. As soon as Collins' body was identified, Frances closed her eyes, screamed, and went into shock. Her daughter, Perley Jane, and son, Frank, took her away from the immediate scene. All four bodies were removed and taken to the Chapel of the Roses in Roseburg. The remains of Richard Warner Blair and Forest Dean Collins were buried at the Civil Bend Pioneer Cemetery in Winston, and that of Robert L. Kline and Delbert Cummins were taken to Klamath Falls for burial.

The next day, Monday March 9, 1953, two men from the Civil Aeronautics Administration, one from Eugene and the other from Seattle, WA, went to the scene of the crash. They were accompanied by a deputy sheriff and Coroner L. L. Powers. They examined every square inch of the wreckage, but found not a clue as to what caused the accident. However, they concluded that, at the time of the buzzing of the house, low power to the weight ratio of the aircraft and wind variables could have contributed to the accident.

Reference:
The News-Review 1953, *How to care & maintain your airplane* by Ron Delp. *Pilot's handbook of navigation* by James C. Elliott and Gene Guerny.

CHAPTER EIGHT
Historic Scenes

Photo: Courtesy of the News Review

The Winston/Green Bridge over the South Umpqua River on Highway 99 between Green and Winston during the 1964 Flood.

Photo: By the author

Snapshots Along the Umpqua 281

The Winston/Green Bridge over the South Umpqua River between Green and Winston on Highway 99/42 in 2012. The first two-lane wooden bridge was built in 1890. The steel bridge was added when the wooden one was damaged in the flood of 1934. Another concrete bridge was built on the north side in 1974.

WINSTON CITY COUNCIL/MAYOR 1985

Photo: City of Winston Archives

The picture above shows the swearing in of the new mayor William Zuver into office by the city attorney Bill Wolke in January of 1985. Sitting from left to right are: Dennis Mills, Marjorie Vaughn, Dave Waffle (City Administrator), Erv Gubser (outgoing Mayor), Mary Lee Weinberg and Brian Otten. Mr. Zuver was the youngest mayor to serve the city of Winston in its 59 years of incorporation.

WILLIAM GEORGE 'BILL' ZUVER

This book memorializes the life of Bill Zuver for the selfless contribution he has given to Winston and the greater Winston area. He was knowledgeable but humble, eloquent yet calm. He exercised those necessary values during his governance of the city of Winston from 1985 to 1987. In 1995 he was elevated to the platform among the community's outstanding citizens when he was honored with the title of First Citizen of the Winston-Dillard Community. As noted above, he was the youngest person to serve as mayor of the city of Winston. At the very young age of 52, William George Zuver passed away on April 26, 2011. He is buried at the Civil Bend Pioneer Cemetery in Winston.

Photo: City of Winston Archives

An aerial view of Winston in May of 1993. The water tanks in the foreground belong to the Winston-Dillard Water District.

TENMILE METHODIST CHURCH 1869

The Methodist Church of Tenmile was built in 1869 and dedicated in 1870. Thomas Coats donated the land for the church and the parsonage. The first pastor of the church was Rev. J. H. Skidmore. The first trustees were: Thomas Coats, A.E. McCulloch, C. Andrews, K.B. Ireland, Thomas Beal, J.A. Richards, Thomas Newland, Thomas Ollivant and W. F. Flook.

Snapshots Along the Umpqua   283

TENMILE STORE AND POST OFFICE 1870

Photo: Taken in 2011

WINSTON CHRISTIAN CHURCH

Winston Christian Church dedicated in 1951

Winston Christian Church was not the first Christian group to hold services in Winston, but it was the first church to be built. The

Foursquare Gospel Church held services in Winston in January 1950, and the Winston Christian Church held its first service in April 1950. The Winston Christian Church was dedicated in April 29, 1951.

RIVERBEND PARK THEATER

Riverbend Park Theater built in 1994

Between 1957 and 1981 the area of Riverbend Park was used to house the city's sewer treatment plant, sewer waste disposal and indiscriminate burying of garden and household trash during spring cleanup. In 1981, by an intergovernmental agreement between the community of Green and the city of Winston, a new sewer treatment plant was constructed across the South Umpqua River in Green. The two communities are still sharing the use of the plant. Soon after, Winston-Dillard Area Festival Association began using the area as a park to hold their annual festival. In 1994 the association built the Riverbend Park Theater and donated it to the city. In addition to the theater, they built the pavilion, the rest rooms and the lighting system in the park.

WINSTON COMMUNITY CENTER

Winston Community Center and Library built in 2008

Building Quality and Unity for Our Community

Winston Area Community Partnership (WACP) - referred to as "Wake up" - has only 13 years of existence in 2012, but has already left an unprecedented legacy of community building and community sustainability. WACP is responsible for a long list of community projects and programs. Among its most significant are: the construction of a $4.7 million Winston Community Center and Library, a play area for toddlers, a skateboard and bicycle park for the older kids and a teen center.

Winston-Dillard Melon Festival

"A FUN FILLED FESTIVAL DEDICATED TO THE OREGON FAMILY!"

Snapshots Along the Umpqua 287

Melon Festival Grand Marshal 1999

Winston-Dillard Melon Festival began in 1968 under the sponsorship of the Winston-Dillard Lions Club. Its main objectives are to use the proceeds from the festival to build its community and to support the institution of the blind. In 1969 it became an annual event on the third weekend in September under the leadership of the Winston-Dillard Festival Association. This three-day annual event attracts spectators from as far south as Ashland, Oregon and as far north as Eugene, Oregon. The festival first started in the area north of City Hall and south of the Dollar Store. Between the late 1970s and the early 1980s the venue was moved to Riverbend Park. In 1994 the Winston-Dillard Area Festival Association, with the aid of Winston Public Works and hundreds of volunteers, under the leadership of Roy Harkins, built the Riverbend Park Outdoor Theater. Some of the materials were donated, and the rest were paid for by the Festival Association. The architectural design was done by Winston Public Works, and the engineering and inspection were done by engineer Dave Philippi of BTS Engineering & Surveying Inc. The entry sign was designed and donated by architect Dallas Horn of Roseburg. The event features a "Melon Queen" and a "Grand Marshall". In September of 2012 the Winston-Dillard Area Festival Association celebrated the 44th year of the Melon Festival. (Please note: The date of the Melon Festival Festivities has been changed to the second weekend in September.)

WILDLIFE SAFARI

Photo date: 2012

Much of the history of Wildlife Safari can be found under the biography of Frank Hart. But no history of the game park is complete without mentioning the cheetah, Khayam, and her accomplishments. The five and one half foot bronze statue that stands in the triangle at the intersection of Highway 99 and Highway 42 in Winston is a tribute to her memory and greatness. Of the 40 years the game park has been in operation and of the hundreds of animals that have roamed the park, no other animal can match the celebrity status of Khayam.

She was born on June 4, 1976, at Wildlife Safari Game Park. She was one of five cubs in the litter. Her personality attracted the attention of the workers at the park when she was being vaccinated.

She was relaxed, calm and playful. It was that charming personality that sparked the interest of Laurie Marker, who was then the curator for cheetahs at the park. Laurie wanted more than a breeding program for the cheetahs and decided then to hand-raise one of them. She chose the above-mentioned cub and called her Khayam, a name meaning "maker of tents" in Swahili. Laurie's dog Sheso became Khayam's surrogate mother, and Laurie and Sheso together raised Khayam. Like Sheso, Khayam slept at Laurie's bedside each night and went to work with her each day.

When Khayam was 14 months old, Laurie took her to Namibia, Africa on a hunting trip. She wanted to see whether Khayam had to be trained to hunt or whether she had that natural carnivore instinct. The trip was also used to understand whether captive-born cheetahs could be re-introduced into the wild. Laurie first had to teach her the technique of hunting by crawling on her hands and knees in the bushes. It did not take long for Khayam's natural instinct to kick in. They spent two month in Namibia, and she became proficient at hunting. Unfortunately, Khayam became ill and had to have surgery before returning to Wildlife Safari. Upon her return to the United States Khayam became a celebrity, showing off her skills on National TV shows like ABC's American Sportsman, and as a guest celebrity on a special TV show with Olivia Newton-John. She spent the rest of her life publicizing Wildlife Safari and its cheetah breeding program. She met with schools, movie stars and state governors. She was honored with the distinguished title of Ambassador to Wildlife Safari Game Park.

Photo: Courtesy of The News Review
Laurie Marker with model of Khayam

In 1986 Khayam became ill with kidney failure and died after receiving a kidney transplant. The news of her death shook up the community. People from all over Douglas County mourned the loss of her beauty, incredible power, charm and calm demeanor around people. Letters of condolences and hundreds of telephone calls conveying sympathy encouraged Wildlife Safari to establish a Khayam Memorial Fund. Upon hearing the news, the children of McGovern Elementary School were the first to contribute to the fund. The idea was quickly embraced by the community, and the Winston-Dillard Chamber of Commerce spearheaded the project to construct a bronze statue of Khayam in the middle of Winston. The Chamber hired the artist Dennis Jones of Eugene for a contract sum of $30,000 to sculpt a bronze statue of Khayam. They then set up a committee to raise the funds for the project. The Committee raised funds through donations, grant writing, a spaghetti feed and bricks sold with the name of the buyer engraved on the brick which were used as part of the foundation for the sculpture. The Khayam statue was unveiled and dedicated before a huge crowd on the annual event of Winston Safari Days, May 2, 1987. Khayam stands majestically not only as a goodwill ambassador for Wildlife Safari Game Park but as a symbol for the preservation of endangered Cheetahs.

(Laurie Marker worked for Wildlife Safari Game Park from 1974 to 1988. She has earned several international awards for her work with Cheetahs, and in the year 2000 *Time Magazine* named her as one of its "Heroes of the Planet." In 2002 she earned a Ph.D. from the University of Oxford, England. Her dissertation was "Aspects of Cheetah (Acinonyx jubatus) Biology, Ecology and Conservation Strategies on Namibian Farmlands." Dr. Marker is the founder and Executive Director of the Cheetah Conservation Fund. The Headquarters for this non-profit organization is in Namibia, Africa.)

References:
The News Review, Winston-Dillard Area Chamber of Commerce News Letters, *Smithsonian Magazine* March 2008: *Cheetahs—A Plan for Their Survival*, *Midday at Oregon's Oasis* by Steve Cohen, Jim McClellan's website: http://winstonoregon.net.

BIBLIOGRAPHY:

Beckham, Stephen Dow. *The Land of the Umpqua: A History of Douglas County*, Oregon published 1986.

Bidwell, Josh. *When it's Fourth and Long: Keeping the Faith, Overcoming the Odds, and Life in the NFL.*

Combs, Welcome Martindale and Combs, Sharon Combs Ross: *God Made A Valley.*

The Coos Bay World: 1954 & 2000

Cubic, Keith L: Director. Douglas County Planning Department Third Edition 2003: *A Place Called Douglas County*

Cubic, Keith L: Director. Douglas County Planning Department: *Dillard Urban Unincorporated Area Comprehensive Plan 1999.*

Cubic, Keith L: Director: Douglas County Planning Department: *Green Urban Unincorporated Area Comprehensive Plan 1998.*

Delp Ron: *How to care for & maintain your airplane.*

Dias, Tricia. *From Tricia's Desk: The Novice Years.*

Douglas County Historical Society: *The Umpqua Trapper.* Stories by Sherley Clayton: "*The History of Dillard*" and "*Memories of Long Ago.*"

Douglas County Library: The Vertical Files

Douglas County Museum History Records

Douglas County News

Douglas County Oregon Cemetery Records Book 3

Elliott James C. and Guerny Gene: *Pilot's handbook of navigation.*

Gourley, Irma: *Growing Up with the West: Memoirs of the Suksdorf Family.*

Historical Douglas County: Oregon 1982

Moulton, Larry. *Douglas County Schools: A History Outline.*

Douglas High School Year Book: 1970 - 1999

News Review-Roseburg: 1920 – 1949

The News Review: 1949 - 2012

The Oregon Blue Book: 1951 - 1952

The Plaindealer: 1870 - 1905

Portraits and Biographical Record: Western Oregon.

The Register Guard, Eugene: August 1984

Reminiscences of Southern Oregon Pioneers:

Roseburg Ensign: 1867 - 1869

The Roseburg Evening News: 1901-1920

Roseburg Woodsman (Special Edition)

RSVP, Retired Senior Volunteer Program: *Reflections on the Umpqua.*

Smith Lucia Rogers and Maier Margaret Rogers: *Lookingglass: Emma's Little Patch of Ground.*

Smithsonian, March 2008 Edition: *Cheetahs: A Plan for Their Survival.*

Wetzell, Ruby Laurance. *Memoirs of the Laurance Family:*

Winston, Harrison Renner. *Memoirs of the Winston Family:*

Winston Branch of the Douglas County Library: *Winston Scrap Book*

Winston City Council Minutes: 1953 to 2012.

Winston-Dillard Fire Department: *Scrap Book and News Letters.*

Winston-Dillard Water District Minutes: 1948 to 1978.

Winston Reporter. 2007

Winston Area News: 2000 - 2006

The Winston Wire: 1966 – 1967

ABOUT THE AUTHOR

Eric Wilson was born in Grenada, West Indies and moved to the United States to study civil engineering. Upon graduation, he worked for Porter, Ripa, and Associates Engineering Firm in Newark, New Jersey and Tronoff Engineering in San Francisco, California.

In 1971 he and his wife Vickie moved to Belize, Central America. In Belize he worked as a civil engineer and helped with the construction of the new capital city, Belmopan. He returned to the United States with his family, Vickie and three children, after spending fifteen years in the country.

Eric retired in 2005 after working for the City of Winston, Oregon, for eighteen years as Superintendent of Public Works. Throughout his career he found time to paint and write poetry. He became a member of the writer's group, "An Association of Writers," in Roseburg, Oregon. In 2007 he published his first book of poems, *The Contemporary Spice*. He wrote a synopsis of the early history of Winston, and it can be found in the Douglas County History Pages of the 2006/2007 Phone Book of Roseburg, Oregon. His book of poems can be found at wilsonfedor@charter.net.

Made in the USA
San Bernardino, CA
03 March 2020

65273360R00164